Repeat the Sounding Joy

MERCER UNIVERSITY PRESS

Endowed by

TOM WATSON BROWN
and
THE WATSON-BROWN FOUNDATION, INC.

Repeat the Sounding Joy

REFLECTIONS ON HYMNS BY ISAAC WATTS

David W. Music

MERCER UNIVERSITY PRESS

Macon, Georgia

2020

MUP/ H1000

© 2020 by Mercer University Press
Published by Mercer University Press
1501 Mercer University Drive
Macon, Georgia 31207
All rights reserved

25 24 23 22 21 20   5 4 3 2 1

Books published by Mercer University Press are printed on acid-free paper
that meets the requirements of the American National Standard for
Information Sciences—Permanence of Paper for Printed Library Materials.

Printed and bound in the United States.

This book is set in Adobe Caslon Pro.

Cover/jacket design by Burt&Burt.

Library of Congress Cataloging-in-Publication Data

Names: Music, David W., 1949- author.
Title: Repeat the sounding joy : reflections on hymns by Isaac Watts /
David W. Music.
Description: 1st. | Macon : Mercer University Press, 2020. | Includes
bibliographical references and index. |
Identifiers: LCCN 2020024298 | ISBN 9780881467697 (hardcover)
Subjects: LCSH: Watts, Isaac, 1674-1748. | Hymns, English--Texts.
Classification: LCC PR3763.W2 Z78 2020 | DDC 264/.23092--dc23
LC record available at https://lccn.loc.gov/2020024298

CONTENTS

Acknowledgments

Introduction   1

1. Alas! and Did My Saviour Bleed?   23

2. Am I a Soldier of the Cross   31

3. Before Jehovah's Awful Throne   41

4. Come Holy Spirit, Heavenly Dove   49

5. Come Let Us Join Our Cheerful Songs   56

6. Come Sound His Praise Abroad   61

7. Come, We That Love the Lord   69

8. From All That Dwell Below the Skies   79

9. How Beauteous Are Their Feet   85

10. I Sing th'Almighty Power of God   91

11. I'll Praise My Maker with My Breath   105

12. I'm Not Ashamed to Own My Lord   113

13. Jesus Shall Reign Where'er the Sun   119

14. Joy to the World; the Lord Is Come   129

15. My Shepherd Will Supply My Need   141

16. Our God, Our Help in Ages Past   149

17. Salvation! O the Joyful Sound!   159

18. Show Pity, Lord, O Lord Forgive   165

19. Sweet Is the Work, My God, My King   171

20. The Heavens Declare Thy Glory, Lord   181

21. There Is a Land of Pure Delight   189

22. This Is the Day the Lord Hath Made   199

23. Welcome Sweet Day of Rest   205

24. When I Can Read My Title Clear   211

25. When I Survey the Wondrous Cross   217

Bibliography   235

Index   243

To the memory of Cecil Roper,
my teacher, colleague, and friend.

ACKNOWLEDGMENTS

I am grateful to the staff of Moody Library at Baylor University for their assistance in gathering materials for this study. Appreciation is also due to Ted Brauker, a PhD student at Baylor University, for reading and commenting upon the manuscript of the book.

HYMNS
AND
Spiritual Songs.

In THREE BOOKS.

I. Collected from the Scriptures.
II. Composed on Divine Subjects.
III. Prepared for the Lord's Supper.

By *I. WATTS*, D.D.

*And they sung a new Song, saying, Thou art
worthy, &c. for thou waſt ſlain, and haſt
redeemed us, &c.* Rev. v. 9.
Soliti eſſent (i. e. *Chriſtiani*) convenire, car-
menque Chriſto quaſi Deo dicere. *Plinius
in Epiſt.*

LONDON:

Printed for W. STRAHAN, J. and F. RIVINGTON,
J. BUCKLAND, G. KEITH, L. HAWES,
W. CLARKE & B. COLLINS, T. LONGMAN,
T. FIELD, and E. and C. DILLY.

M DCC LXXV.

INTRODUCTION

Isaac Watts is universally recognized as one of the greatest English-language hymn writers of the eighteenth century, the "Golden Age of English Hymnody."[1] Matched or exceeded in both productivity and quality only by his younger contemporary, Charles Wesley, Watts was an innovator whose work changed the course of Christian congregational song and worship in English.

Watts was born into an Independent family in Southampton, England, on July 17, 1674, and attended a grammar school there under John Pinhorne.[2] In 1690, he became a student at the Nonconformist academy in Stoke Newington, a village outside London, where his tutor was Thomas Rowe. After completing his studies in 1694, he moved back to his Southampton home for two and a half years then became a tutor to the son of Sir John Hartopp in Stoke Newington (1696). He preached his first sermon on his birthday in 1698 and in that year was called as assistant pastor of the Independent chapel at Mark Lane in London, where Isaac Chauncey was the principal minister. Upon the resignation of Chauncey in 1701, Watts became the church's senior pastor (1702), but, because of his poor health, an assistant, Samuel Price, was appointed in 1703. In 1704, the congregation moved to Pinner's Hall and in 1708 to Bury Street.

During the years 1712–1716, Watts suffered a significant illness that caused him to be unable to supply his own pulpit. At the onset of the illness, Watts was invited to spend a week at the home of Sir Thomas and Lady Mary Abney but ended up living the rest of his life (thirty-six years) in the Abney household. During Watts's incapacitation, Samu-

---

[1] The eighteenth century has been nicknamed the "Golden Age of English Hymnody" because of the number of hymn writers active during that period and the high quality of many of their hymns.

[2] "Independents" were so called because they were "independent" from the Church of England. They were also called "Nonconformists" and "Dissenters."

el Price's role at the church was upgraded from assistant to co-pastor and he evidently carried out most of the ministerial duties until Watts's recovery. In 1728, the universities of Edinburgh and Aberdeen conferred upon Watts the honorary doctor of divinity degree. Watts and Price continued as co-pastors of the Bury Street congregation until the former's death on November 25, 1748.[3] The hymn writer was interred in the Dissenter's burying ground at Bunhill Fields, a bust was placed in Westminster Abbey, and a statue was erected to his memory in Southampton. Watts, who was described as no more than five feet, two inches tall, with a body that was "spare and lean, his face oval, his nose aquiline, his complexion fair and pale, his forehead low, his cheek-bones rather prominent," and a voice that "was rather too fine and slender," never married.[4]

Watts's Theological and Educational Publications

Watts was a prolific author in several fields, publishing sermons, theological and philosophical works, educational textbooks, and collections of poetry. Among his theological and philosophical works were *A Guide to Prayer* (1715), *The Christian Doctrine of the Trinity* (1722), *Death and Heaven* (1722), *(Three) Dissertations Relating to the Christian Doctrine of the Trinity* (1724, 1725), *An Humble Attempt Toward the Revival of Practical Religion among Christians* (1731), *A Short View of the Whole Scripture History* (1732), *Philosophical Essays on Various Subjects* (1733), *The Strength and Weakness of Human Reason* (1737), *The World to Come* (1739, 1745), and *The Glory of Christ as God-Man Display'd* (1746). His textbooks included *The Art of Reading and Writing English* (1722), *Logick: or, the Right Use of Reason* (1725), *The Knowledge of the Heavens and the Earth Made Easy* (1726), *Watts's Compleat Spelling-Book* (1737), and *The Improvement of the Mind* (1741).

Almost all of these books went through multiple editions and re-

---

[3] Many sources state that Watts left the leadership of the Bury Street church upon the outbreak of his 1712 illness or are ambiguous about his continuation in the pastorate of the church. Milner includes Watts as pastor until his death in 1748 (*The Life, Times, and Correspondence of the Rev. Isaac Watts, D. D.,* 722). It may very well be that both Watts and Price officially continued as the ministers of the church but that because of the former's ill health, Price carried on most of the pastoral duties.

[4] Gibbons, *Memoirs of the Rev. Isaac Watts, D. D.,* 332.

prints, and some—such as his 1725 volume on logic—became standard university texts at Oxford, Cambridge, Harvard, and Yale.[5] His theological works sparked considerable controversy, especially his writings on the Trinity because his views struck some Christians as unorthodox. Over and over again, Watts expressed his belief in both the full divinity and full humanity of Jesus, and he considered himself to be a Trinitarian who sought to explain the doctrine to those who were of a different persuasion or were uncertain about it; for example, one of his *Three Dissertations* (1724) was titled "The Arian invited to the Orthodox Faith." Unfortunately, his speculations often confused rather than clarified the issue; for example, he attempted to prove that Christ's soul existed before the incarnation by suggesting that the "Michael" mentioned in Daniel 10 (whom he also identifies with the archangel Michael in Revelation 12:7) was actually the soul of Jesus in human form.[6]

Though Watts's weighty theological books were widely criticized, he was highly respected for the hymnic works he had published early in his career. His hymns present completely orthodox positions, and, because of this, his later theologically questionable writings have generally

---

[5] According to one of his biographers, Watts "was the first man who reduced this complicated subject [logic] to intelligibility, and mixed plain sense with the science." See *The Posthumous Works of the Late Learned and Reverend Isaac Watts, D.D.*, 2:xxxiv.

[6] See Watts, *The Glory of Christ as God-Man Display'd in Three Discourses* (1746), 37: "It is also very probable that Michael is Jesus Christ." Watts later notes that "if in this or any other of my Writings I speak of the Soul of Christ as being an Angel or an Angelick Spirit, or in an Angelic State, I mean nothing else but his existing without a Body as angels do, or his being a Messenger of God the Father as they are" (153). As one early biographer observed, "Dr. Watts studied the doctrine of the Trinity, as some Indian devotees are said to have contemplated the sun, till their own sight was darkened" (*Memoirs of the Life and Writings of Isaac Watts, D. D.*, 38). One of the contemporary critics of Watts's hymns, Thomas Bradbury, perhaps hit on another reason for suspicion of Watts's Trinitarian theology when he complained that "You have shewn a thousand times more meekness to an Arian, who is the enemy of Jesus, than you have done to king David, who sung his praises" (*The Posthumous Works of the Late Learned and Reverend Isaac Watts, D.D.*, 2:204).

been either forgiven or forgotten.[7] Indeed, his hymns have been at least partially credited with helping preserve orthodoxy among Independents during the eighteenth century.[8]

Congregational Singing in
Late Seventeenth-century England

At the time of Watts's birth, congregational singing in English churches of nearly all Protestant denominations followed the principles of John Calvin in being restricted principally to metrical psalmody, the Old Testament book of Psalms rendered into English poetry to fit strophic tunes. The purpose of psalmody was—as Calvin had put it—to "be like spurs to us, to incite us to prayer and to praise God, to meditate on his works, in order to love, fear, honor, and glorify him." In Calvin's view and that of his followers, the only material worthy for Christians to sing to a holy God was what God himself had given them, "the Psalms of David, which the [H]oly Spirit has spoken and made through him."[9] To the psalms were added certain lyrical passages from the Old and New Testaments, canticles such as the second song of Moses (Deuteronomy 32) and the Benedictus, Magnificat, and Nunc dimittis from Luke 2, as well as a few nonbiblical texts.

The most popular psalter ever published in English was Thomas Sternhold and John Hopkins's *The Whole Book of Psalms*, commonly known either as "Sternhold and Hopkins" or the "Old Version," and first published in complete form in 1562.[10] More than six hundred editions or reprints of this psalter were issued, and it was still in print three hundred years after its first publication. Many other Englishmen tried their hand at versifying the psalms during the sixteenth and seventeenth centuries,

---

[7] For example, in his sermon on the death of Watts, *Reflections on the Fall of a Great Man*, Caleb Ashworth mentions many aspects of Watts's life and work but pointedly omits any mention of his writings on the Trinity.

[8] Davies, *From Watts and Wesley to Maurice, 1690–1850*, 94–95.

[9] John Calvin, "Epistle to the Reader" from *Cinquante Pseaumes en francois par Clem. Marot* (1543), in Music, *Hymnology*, 67.

[10] Though typically attributed to Sternhold and Hopkins, who published the earliest versions of the English psalter, the Old Version also contained material from the Anglo-Genevan psalters of 1556–1561, including alterations of Sternhold and Hopkins's work as well as psalms they had not versified.

but none achieved anything like the widespread use of the Old Version. The psalter that came closest to replacing the Old Version was Nahum Tate and Nicholas Brady's *A New Version of the Psalms of David*, issued in 1696, when Watts was twenty-two years of age. Tate and Brady were a little freer than Sternhold and Hopkins in rendering the biblical text, and their book was also somewhat smoother in its poetry. Though the new version never completely replaced the older psalter, it did see considerable use, particularly in city churches, and it helped prepare the way for the work of Watts by increasing the demand for more singable texts.

Watts's Poetic Publications

Watts's major poetic publications all came early in his career. His first book of any kind, *Horæ Lyricæ* (dated 1706 on the title page but in print by December 1705), was a collection of poems that introduced Watts to British readers as a literary figure of consequence and served as a "trial run" for some of his hymns and psalm versions.[11] Of the latter items, Watts says in the preface that "These are but a small part of two hundred Hymns of the same kind which are ready for Public Use if the World receive favourably what I now present."[12] *Horæ Lyricæ* contained both sacred and secular poetry (in Latin as well as English), and much of it was designed primarily for reading rather than singing, though some of its pieces reappeared in Watts's song collections (often in revised form) and others have frequently been set to music.[13]

Watts's most important congregational song publications were *Hymns and Spiritual Songs* (1707) and *The Psalms of David Imitated in the Language of the New Testament* (1719). *Hymns and Spiritual Songs* included 210 hymns and a group of doxologies (some of the latter in several

---

[11] For the evidence that the book was available in December 1705, see Hood, *Isaac Watts*, [345] (a transcription of Watts's "Memorable Affairs in my Life"), and Escott, *Isaac Watts, Hymnographer*, 35.

[12] Watts, "The Preface: The Songs Sacred to Devotion," *Horæ Lyricæ: Poems Chiefly of the Lyric Kind*, n.p.

[13] An example of the latter is the poem on the Nativity, "Shepherds Rejoice, Lift Up Your Eyes," which was frequently set in English and American tune books of the late eighteenth and early nineteenth centuries. For a psalm version that first appeared in *Horæ Lyricæ* and subsequently in the congregational song collections, see chapter 3.

stanzas) divided into three books, the first containing hymns based on specific Scriptures; the second, texts that are freely written (though Watts hoped that "the Sense and Materials will always appear Divine"[14]); and the third, hymns for the Lord's Supper. The book concluded with "A Short Essay toward the Improvement of Psalmody" that was omitted in later editions.

The Psalms of David Imitated contained versions of all but twelve of the 150 psalms, some of them in multiple renderings to provide a variety of metrical options or to emphasize different aspects of the biblical text.[15] Fourteen of the versions had appeared previously in *Hymns and Spiritual Songs*, from which they were removed in the second edition, but several of them were extensively revised for the 1719 book.[16]

Perhaps the most important feature of *The Psalms of David Imitated* is that the texts are paraphrases rather than versifications. In a psalm versification, the poet renders the passage into English rhyme and meter, keeping as much of the original thought and even the original wording as intact as possible. In a paraphrase, on the other hand, the author uses the psalm as a basis for elaborating other ideas, in the case of Watts, specifi-

---

[14] Watts, preface to *Hymns and Spiritual Songs*, xi.

[15] The twelve items that Watts left unparaphrased were Pss 28, 43, 52, 54, 59, 64, 70, 79, 88, 108, 137, and 140. He considered these psalms to be unsuitable for Christian worship, not understandable by the average congregant of his day, or to contain only material found elsewhere (Pss 28, 43, 108). Watts provided a paraphrase of Psalm 137 in *Reliquiæ Juveniles*, 73–75.

[16] The texts that appeared in both books were "Why Did the Jews Proclaim Their Rage?" (Ps 2), "Unshaken As the Sacred Hill" (Ps 125), "Firm and Unmov'd Are They" (Ps 125), "Blest Is the Man Whose Cautious Feet" (Ps 1; "Happy the Man Whose Cautious Feet"), "There's No Ambition Swells My Heart" (Ps 131; "Is There Ambition in My Heart?"), "Ye That Obey th'Immortal King" (Ps 134), "Shine, Mighty God, on Britain Shine" (Ps 67), "Lord, What a Thoughtless Wretch Was I" (Ps 73), "Lord, What a Feeble Piece" (Ps 90), "Ye Saints, How Lovely Is the Place" (Ps 84; "My Soul, How Lovely Is the Place"), "Sing to the Lord with Joyful Voice" (Ps 100), "Lo, What an Entertaining Sight" (Ps 133), "Loud Hallelujahs to the Lord" (Ps 148), and "Look, Gracious God, How Numerous They" (Ps 3; "My God, How Many Are My Fears"). Louis F. Benson pointed out that stanzas from another hymn, "In Vain the Wealthy Mortals Toyl," were altered and used in Watts's long meter version of Psalm 49, "Why Do the Proud Insult the Poor[?]"; see "The Early Editions of Watts's Hymns," 269.

cally New Testament ones. This is suggested particularly by the extended title of Watts's collection, *The Psalms of David Imitated in the Language of the New Testament*. Thus, Watts's book is not a collection of "psalms" but of "imitation psalms"; as the author himself put it, his goal was to make the psalms "always speak the common Sense and Language of a Christian."[17]

John Dryden's preface to *Ovid's Epistles, Translated by Several Hands* (1680) describes "imitation" in poetry as "an Endeavour of a later Poet to write like one who has written before him on the same Subject: that is, not to Translate his words, or to be Confin'd to his Sense, but only to set him as a Patern [*sic*], and to write, as he supposes, that Authour [*sic*] would have done, had he liv'd in our Age, and in our Country" (n.p.). This definition fits the goals and construction of Watts's psalm imitations perfectly. The methods he employed included making "substitutions, omissions, additions, contractions, transpositions, or divisions" to the original text of the psalm.[18]

A clear example of one of Watts's approaches can be seen in the initial line of his paraphrase of Psalm 72, "Jesus Shall Reign Where'er the Sun," which corresponds to v. 5 of the psalm: "They shall fear thee [the king, referred to in v. 1] as long as the sun and moon endure." Here Watts has introduced the name of Jesus into the psalm, thus "Christianizing" it.[19]

With the publication of these two books, Watts provided what Louis F. Benson called a complete "System of Praise" based on Paul's exhortations in Ephesians 5:19 and Colossians 3:16 to sing "psalms and hymns and spiritual songs," the *Hymns and Spiritual Songs* of 1707 encompassing the latter two categories and *The Psalms of David Imitated* the first one.[20] Churches that were not prepared to abandon exclusive metrical psalmody could sing from *The Psalms of David Imitated*, while those that were open to "hymns of human composure" could employ both collections. Furthermore, because of his use of paraphrase rather than versification in the 1719 volume, exclusive metrical psalm singers

---

[17] Watts, preface to *The Psalms of David Imitated in the Language of the New Testament* (1719), xvi.

[18] Bishop, "The Poetical Theories of Isaac Watts," 17.

[19] See chapter 13 for further discussion of this hymn.

[20] Benson, *The English Hymn*, 108, 120.

were—perhaps unknowingly—helped along the road toward the use of hymns. These two books were often published or bound together as the "Psalms and Hymns of Dr. Watts" and saw widespread use on both sides of the Atlantic.

Between these two specifically congregational song collections, Watts issued *Divine Songs Attempted in Easy Language for the Use of Children* (1715), generally acknowledged to be the first book of sacred song designed especially for children. Most of the lyrics in the volume are either too moralizing or too naïve to find much use as congregational songs for general worship, with one exception, "I Sing th'Almighty Power of God."[21] Hymns were also appended to some of his collections of sermons.

The hymns of Watts, especially *Hymns and Spiritual Songs* and *The Psalms of David Imitated*, revolutionized English-language congregational song. Because of their many editions and reprints during Watts's lifetime and after his death, Watts almost singlehandedly broke the monopoly of versified psalmody and brought "hymns of human composure" into the singing of the churches.[22] Indeed, in many congregations, the monopoly of psalmody now became a near-monopoly of Watts, a situation that lasted in some places well into the nineteenth century. Watts's popularity and longevity are evident in a painstakingly compiled bibliography by Selma L. Bishop, in which she lists more than 650 dated editions of Watts's *Hymns and Spiritual Songs* between the first printing of 1707 and 1881, many of them in combination with his *Psalms of David Imitated*.[23] For his work in breaking the stranglehold of exclusive psalmody, Watts is often credited as the "Father of English Hymnody."

---

[21] See chapter 10.

[22] Cyprian T. Rust observed that "It seems little short of a miracle that a young man, twenty-one years of age, fresh from college, who had not even preached his first sermon, should commence a crusade [in favor of hymns] against the whole kingdom, and all the best and wisest men in it, that he should have begun the fight and *won it too!*" See Rust, *Break of Day in the Eighteenth Century*, xviii.

[23] Bishop, *Isaac Watts's Hymns and Spiritual Songs (1707): A Publishing History and a Bibliography* (Ann Arbor, MI: Pierian Press, 1974).

8

Watts's Hymns

Watts's particular genius when it came to congregational song was in providing lyrics that were faithful to Scripture, evangelical, expressive of personal faith, ecumenical, practical for congregational singing, liturgically appropriate, and of high quality.[24] His biblical fidelity is evident in the Scripture references that head many of his *Hymns and Spiritual Songs*, the wide-ranging and frequent biblical allusions contained in his texts, and his remarkable knowledge of both the Old and New Testaments demonstrated in *The Psalms of David Imitated* (1719). Watts's thinking and language were so profoundly steeped in Scripture that "Even when one of the hymns does not remind the reader of a specific biblical passage, the poetic language and the sentiments expressed are in such close accord with scripture that the verse seems taken directly from the Bible."[25]

The evangelical nature of the hymns can be seen particularly in their emphasis on Christ, and especially on the cross.[26] For Watts, the congregational song was a primary vehicle for the expression of the gospel message of the birth, life, death, resurrection, and salvific work of Jesus. Thus the "central figure" of the hymns is

Christ, the Son, Redeemer and Conqueror, puissant and glorious. He is the risen, regnant Christ of the latter times, ruler of the heavenly host and lord of earth. All-conquering, by the very fact of his irresistible mercy and salvation, he is of magnificently heroic stature. Man's life has value and meaning only as it becomes a preparation for union with this figure.[27]

---

[24] In "Isaac Watts: Father of English Hymnody," Cook points out several other important aspects of Watts's texts: grandeur, evangelicalism, objectivity, fervour, and catholicity (universality) (34–44).

[25] Plett, "The Poetic Language of Isaac Watts's Hymns," 40.

[26] By "evangelical," Watts meant that the psalms should carry the message of the gospel, not that of the sacrificial system of the Old Testament.

[27] Stephenson, "The Heroic Hymn of Isaac Watts," 27. Stephenson also notes that the Watts hymns that "have survived the centuries are the very ones which present in essence the glorious figure [Christ] at the center of the original 'heroic' hymnody" (220).

Even in his psalm paraphrases the focus was on New Testament concepts such as the atoning work of Christ, often including specific language drawn from that portion of the Bible.

The personal nature of Watts's hymns is evident from the frequency with which first person singular pronouns are used (emphasis added): "Alas! and did *my* Savior bleed," "Am *I* a soldier of the cross," "*I* sing th'almighty power of God," "*My* shepherd will supply *my* need," "When *I* survey the wondrous cross," etc. Certainly, many Watts hymns are corporate in nature ("Come let *us* join *our* cheerful songs" and "*Our* God, *our* help in ages past," to choose only two), but significant numbers of them are essentially personal testimonies of the individual singer's faith.

Two things set Watts's individualized approach apart from later expressions using personal pronouns. First, as noted by William Eaton Stephenson, "All is seen from the viewpoint of a universal 'I', largely an observer recording his emotional reactions, an individual speaking as a representative of 'we' the congregation, never as the identifiable single figure of the author."[28] A second feature is that the personal element is "always clearly related to a historic stress on dogma."[29] Thus individual faith is linked with theological substance.

An important feature in the success of Watts's hymns is their ecumenical character. This was done deliberately; in the preface to *Hymns and Spiritual Songs*, the author claimed that he had "avoided the more obscure and controverted Points of Christianity, that we might all obey the Direction of the Word of God, and sing his Praises with Understanding."[30] Though a Calvinist whose views on the subject can be readily identified in his hymns, his goal was to exalt Christ and the church, not to promote or attack controversial points of doctrine; as Cyprian T. Rust put it, "Dr. Watts is the most unsectarian of all hymn writers."[31]

---

[28] Ibid., 27. See also Plett, "The Poetic Language of Isaac Watts's Hymns," 114.

[29] Davies, *Worship and Theology in England*, 2:100.

[30] Watts, preface to *Hymns and Spiritual Songs* (1707), viii.

[31] Rust, *Break of Day in the Eighteenth Century*, xxix. As one example of the hymn writer's nonsectarian approach, Rust notes that Watts "has one hymn for those who practise adult, two for those who practise infant baptism." Exceptions to this general nonsectarian rule are the hymn writer's occasional jabs at the "Papists."

Watts made his hymns practical in a variety of ways. He most often employed the hymnic meters that were common in contemporary psalm singing so his texts could be sung to tunes the people already knew.[32] His hymns are generally characterized by brevity, often with four to eight stanzas; longer texts, such as some of the psalm versions, are frequently broken up into several distinct hymns or have pauses inserted. Beginning with the second edition of *Hymns and Spiritual Songs*, he often indicated by brackets (he called them "Crotchets") that certain stanzas could be omitted if desired to shorten the text while preserving its coherence.[33]

Another characteristic feature is his tendency to use short, simple words and, as he put it, "Metaphors [that] are sunk to the Level of vulgar Capacities" so as not to "darken or disturb the Devotion of the plainest Souls."[34] In other words, he wrote his hymns for the common people, not the *literati*.

However, his texts also maintain a sense of dignity and an elevated tone, giving them what James Wendall Plett appropriately called "restrained sublimity, combining majestic subject matter with simple poetic language."[35] The reader or singer seldom gets the sense that the text has been "written down" to the congregation. Plett points out another feature of Watts's language that made the hymns useful for his eighteenth-century readers and singers: "As much as possible, he employed the vocabulary of scripture, a body of words familiar to his audience."[36]

Watts's practical nature also manifests itself in the structure of his hymns. Arthur Paul Davis provides an apt description of this form:

> Watts's hymns generally follow a simple pattern. The opening line
> is striking and appealing: "Our God, our help in ages past." This
> line sets the tone of the complete poem. The hymn progresses
> swiftly from the opening to a strong climax:

---

[32] For a description of hymnic meters, see below.

[33] The omissions were suggested in cases where he considered that the text was "too Poetical for meaner Understandings, or too particular for whole Congregations to sing," but also to avoid leaving the decision "to the Judgment or casual Determination of him that leads the Tune." See Watts, preface to *Hymns and Spiritual Songs* (1709), xiv.

[34] Watts, preface to *Hymns and Spiritual Songs* (1707), viii, ix.

[35] Plett, "The Poetic Language of Isaac Watts's Hymns," 8.

[36] Ibid., 100.

11

Be thou our guide while life shall last,
And our eternal home!

The whole hymn usually contains but one evangelical idea; metre, diction, and imagery all subserve this theme. Each hymn becomes therefore an epitome of some important Christian thought. The net result of these practical considerations made for the permanently simple, but satisfying poetic form of the English hymn.[37]

William Eaton Stephenson pointed out that in Watts's best hymns, "the tension between soaring theme and restrained form results in a rare vibrancy and charm."[38] In essence, though he was certainly not the first to write hymns in English, Watts can be considered the inventor of the English hymn as the term became commonly used and understood because he set the pattern that was followed by later writers.[39]

Watts's hymns fulfilled a liturgical function in that they had a specific role in worship, chiefly as an accompaniment to exhortation and preaching. As he noted in the prefaces to both *Hymns and Spiritual Songs* and *The Psalms of David Imitated*, strict versifications of the psalms often contained concepts that related more to the situation of the ancient Hebrews than that of contemporary Christians.[40] Such ideas did not match the evangelical preaching of Independents (or Anglicans either, for that matter), and he sought to provide material that could illustrate, summarize, or enhance his own sermons and those of others. His publications of sermons accompanied by hymn texts he had written illustrate one way in which Watts envisioned his hymns being used.

The role of song in Watts's own congregation is seen in a surviving account of morning worship from 1723 that lists the following elements:

---

[37] Davis, *Isaac Watts*, 203–204. Davis quoted the line "Be thou our guide while life shall last" as it was often printed in twentieth-century hymnals; Watts's original was "Be thou our guard while troubles last" (see ch. 16).

[38] Stephenson, "The Heroic Hymn of Isaac Watts," 233.

[39] Phillips points out that Watts was the progenitor not only of the English hymn as it is known today but also of the hymnbook itself (*The Hymnal: A Reading History*, 87–88). In this context, "hymnbook" refers to a words-only volume that was often used for purposes beyond singing at church, such as personal devotion and the teaching of reading.

[40] *Hymns and Spiritual Songs* (1707), iv–vi; *The Psalms of David Imitated* (1719), iii–iv.

singing a psalm, short prayer, half-hour exposition of Scripture, singing of another psalm or a hymn, long prayer, sermon, prayer, and benediction. The afternoon service was similar, but without the short prayer and exposition, and with an additional psalm before or after the sermon.[41]

While, as noted above, Watts was concerned that his texts be understandable to the average Christian, his skill as a poet helped him circumvent the defects that afflicted much earlier English congregational song material. He typically avoided enjambments—starting or ending a thought in the middle of a poetic line—which, when sung, could disrupt the continuity of thought, especially when lining out was involved.[42] He was generally consistent in his use of poetic meter, meaning that the stresses for each stanza of a hymn match those of the others and the accent pattern of the tune.[43]

Watts was also sparing in his use of word inversions, the alteration of normal word order. Word inversions often result from a lyricist's attempt to maintain the stress pattern of the text or for purposes of rhyme. The result of word inversions is frequently a line that is awkward to read or sing. Even when Watts does use a word inversion, he does it so skillfully that the sense of the verse is not disrupted or the rhyme forced.

The difference between Sternhold (as one example among his predecessors) and Watts in terms of poetic meter and word inversions can be seen in two lines from their respective versions of Psalm 23. In Sternhold's versification, the first two lines are "My shepherd is the living Lord, / nothing therefore I need." The first line sets up an iambic poetic meter (which is maintained throughout most of the text) but—if read with normal word accentuation—the second line begins with a dactylic foot that, when sung to an iambic tune, awkwardly stresses the "ing" of

---

[41] Cornick, "Looking Back: A Historical Overview of Reformed Worship," 32–33. See also Davies, *Worship and Theology in England*, 101–102.

[42] Lining out was a psalm-singing performance practice in which the leader read or sang a line of text, after which it was repeated by the congregation. The technique became widespread because many congregants could not afford a psalm book (they were not provided by the church) or could not read.

[43] This is not to say that Watts never varied the stress pattern from stanza to stanza, as will be seen several times in the following chapters, but when he did so it was generally for a specific purpose. His most common alteration of meter was the formation of a choriambus. See below for a fuller description of poetic meter and a definition of choriambus.

"nothing." If spoken in prose, the logical order of the second line would be "therefore I need nothing" but Sternhold had to end the line with "need" to rhyme with "feed" in a subsequent line; the result is a verse that is convoluted and unnatural to normal English speech.

Watts's first version of the same psalm begins with an identical first line, "My shepherd is the living Lord," but the next line, "now shall my wants be well supplied," continues the iambic pattern, avoiding the shift of poetic meter as found in Sternhold.[44] Watts's line does involve a word inversion; the sense of the line as normally spoken would be "now my wants shall be well supplied." However, the line given by Watts makes perfect sense; the Sternhold line is awkward to read or sing, but Watts's parallel verse fairly trips off the tongue.[45]

This brings up another feature of Watts's hymns: the sound of the words themselves. He often employs sibilants to suggest the hissing of a snake or the crashing of waves on the seashore and consonants such as "b" or "p" to give roughness to a line or stanza. On the other hand, his use of open vowel sounds and "soft" consonants ("w," "n," etc.) lends an air of comfort and gentleness to portions of text. While he seldom uses true onomatopoeia (a word sounding like what it describes), the sounds of the lyrics both suggest and give life to the intended meaning. More than is the case with most hymn writers, Watts's texts fairly cry out to be read aloud.

Testimony to the quality of Watts's hymn writing has been given by many scholars and fellow poets, including poet laureates of his native land. When Robert Bridges, who served as poet laureate from 1913 to 1930, published *The Yattendon Hymnal* in 1899, he included six texts by Watts, more than any other author except the compiler himself.[46] More recently, when Sir John Betjeman (poet laureate 1972–1984) was inter-

---

[44] In both the Sternhold and Watts examples, the spelling and capitalization have been modernized.

[45] To be sure, as pointed out in Fletcher, "English Psalmody and Isaac Watts," Watts himself was not always free from inverting words to create a rhyme (110–11).

[46] Watts hymns in *The Yattendon Hymnal* included "Come Let Us Join Our Cheerful Songs" (10), "How Bright These Glorious Spirits Shine" (adapted by W. Cameron, 40), "When I Survey" (70), "O God, Our Help in Ages Past" (76), "From All That Dwell Below the Skies" (80), and "Christ Hath a Garden Wall'd Around" (adapted by Bridges, 96).

viewed on television, the interviewer insisted "that hymns were worthless doggerel."

"Ah, I see what you mean," Betjeman said mildly, and quoted this:

> *His dying crimson, like a robe*
> *Spreads o'er his body on the Tree;*
> *Then am I dead to all the globe,*
> *And all the globe is dead to me.*

The young man was silenced.[47]

The lines quoted by Betjeman were the original fourth stanza from Watts's "When I Survey the Wondrous Cross."[48] Considering that Watts was not writing for other poets or even poetry lovers but for common people, such praise is even more remarkable.

Perhaps the best testimony to the quality of Watts's hymns is their continued use in Christian worship more than 250 years after the author's death. Like most prolific authors, Watts's works are not of uniform merit or usefulness; changes in theology, culture, and language have led to the abandonment of most of his hymns and of individual stanzas in some texts that have otherwise survived.[49] Changes in musical taste have caused the tunes to which some texts are traditionally sung to decline in usage, resulting in a parallel abandonment of the words themselves.[50]

Nevertheless, many of his texts continue to appear in contemporary hymnals where they are frequently among the ones that are best known and most often sung. "Joy to the World" is a staple of the Christmas season in shopping malls and elevators, not to mention churches. At least one of his lyrics has even appeared in the context of popular Christian

---

[47] Magnusson, *Glorious Things*, 1–2.

[48] This hymn was evidently a favorite with Betjeman and was sung at his memorial service in Westminster Abbey.

[49] Gordon Rupp observed that "There are hymns [by Watts] about which the fashions have changed, and hymns whose words have become quaint and silly to us. And both of these together perhaps, in his patriotically religious hymns" (*Six Makers of English Religion 1500–1700*, 121).

[50] Davis takes the opposite approach, suggesting that "In a few cases, it is possible that the tunes are now keeping alive poems whose doctrines would otherwise have sent them into oblivion" (*Isaac Watts*, 206).

music.[51] There is no way of calculating how often Watts texts are printed in church worship orders or sung from screens or memory, but the number is surely large.

This Book

Isaac Watts has been the subject of numerous biographies and critical studies ranging from the eighteenth to the twenty-first centuries. The books also run the gamut in their assessment of Watts from laudatory hagiography to outright dismissal of his abilities as a poet, and from retelling undocumented stories about him to serious scholarly scrutiny of the available sources.[52]

---

[51] See Chris Tomlin, J. D. Walt, and Jesse Reeves's "The Wonderful Cross," which incorporates portions of "When I Survey."

[52] The classic biographies and studies of Watts are (in chronological order): Gibbons, *Memoirs of the Rev. Isaac Watts, D. D.* (1780); Milner, *The Life, Times, and Correspondence of the Rev. Isaac Watts, D.D.* (1834); Josiah Conder, *The Poet of the Sanctuary. A Centenary Commemoration of the Labours and Services Literary and Devotional of the Rev. Isaac Watts, D.D.* (London: John Snow, 1851); D. A. Harsha, *The Life and Choice Works of Isaac Watts, D. D.* (New York: Derby & Jackson, 1857); E. Paxton Hood, *Isaac Watts: His Life and Writings, His Homes and Friends* (London: Religious Tract Society, 1875); Thomas Wright, *Isaac Watts and Contemporary Hymn-Writers*, vol. 3 of The Lives of the British Hymn-Writers (London: C. J. Farncombe & Sons, 1914); Benson, *The English Hymn* (1915), chs. 3–4; Bernard Lord Manning, *The Hymns of Wesley and Watts: Five Informal Papers* (London: Epworth Press, 1942); Davis, *Isaac Watts: His Life and Works* (1943); Erik Routley, *Isaac Watts (1674–1748)* (London: Independent Press, 1961); Escott, *Isaac Watts, Hymnographer* (1962); and Selma L. Bishop, *Isaac Watts. Hymns and Spiritual Songs, 1707–1748: A Study in Early Eighteenth-Century Language Changes* (London: Faith Press, 1962) and *Isaac Watts's Hymns and Spiritual Songs (1707): A Publishing History and a Bibliography* (1974). Recent published analyses and critical studies of Watts's hymns can be found in Madeleine Forell Marshall and Janet Todd, *English Congregational Hymns in the Eighteenth Century* (Lexington: Kentucky University Press, 1982); Donald Davie, *The Eighteenth-Century Hymn in England* (Cambridge: Cambridge University Press, 1993); J. R. Watson, *The English Hymn: A Critical and Historical Study* (Oxford: Oxford University Press, 1999); Isabel Rivers and David L. Wykes, eds., *Dissenting Praise: Religious Dissent and the Hymn in England and Wales* (Oxford: Oxford University Press, 2011); Richard Arnold, *Trinity of*

So, it might be asked, why yet another book on Watts? Simply put, I take a different approach to the subject. Whereas previous studies have traced Watts's biography or analyzed and summarized the entire corpus of his hymnic works, pointing out their strengths and weaknesses as poetry, I concentrate on a selected body of some of his best-known works, providing reflections and commentaries on them that are partly historical, partly analytical, and partly devotional.[53]

The hymns for the present study have been chosen from those that seem to be the ones by Watts most often published in United States hymnals, based primarily on an admittedly unscientific survey of texts cataloged on the website www.hymnary.org.[54] While there are other worthy Watts texts that are thus excluded from the discussion, those considered here will probably be the ones that will be the most familiar and therefore of the most interest to the majority of hymn singers.

As has been true with hymns by many other authors, Watts's texts have been subjected to various alterations over the course of time. Apart from the chapter titles, quotations from other authors, and where other-

---

Discord: The Hymnal and Poetic Innovations of Isaac Watts, Charles Wesley, and William Cowper (New York: Peter Lang, 2012); Douglas Bond, *The Poetic Wonder of Isaac Watts* (Sanford, FL: Reformation Trust, 2013); and Graham Beynon, *Isaac Watts: Reason, Passion and the Revival of Religion* (London: Bloomsbury T&T Clark, 2016). See also the doctoral dissertations listed in the bibliography.

[53] It will be readily apparent, however, that this book relies heavily upon the work of the writers on Watts mentioned earlier.

[54] Hymnary.org incorporates the Dictionary of North American Hymnology, a project of the Hymn Society in the United States and Canada. The dictionary indexes more than 5000 congregational song collections published in North America since the first edition of the Bay Psalm Book in 1640. The present book discusses the Watts hymns that were published in at least 500 collections in North America, to which several additional items have been added that were issued fewer than 500 times ("Come Sound His Praise Abroad," "I Sing th'Almighty Power of God," "I'll Praise My Maker with My Breath," "The Heavens Declare Thy Glory, Lord," and "Welcome, Sweet Day of Rest"). It should be noted that in selecting the hymns to be covered in this book, no account has been taken of when the American printings occurred. In some cases, a hymn may have had many printings in the eighteenth, nineteenth, and/or early twentieth centuries but in more recent times has declined in usage, or vice versa; nevertheless, they are included here as representing the Watts lyrics that have historically been among his most widely used texts.

wise noted, each study gives the stanzas of the hymn as they were first published by Watts, including their original spelling, capitalization, punctuation, orthography, and use of generic masculine pronouns (e.g., "Our God, Our Help in Ages Past" rather than "O God, Our Help in Ages Past," "Saviour" instead of "Savior," etc.); exceptions to this general rule are noted in the discussions themselves (see, for example, the chapter on "Before Jehovah's Awful Throne").[55] Important revisions Watts made to the words in later editions are pointed out, publication and technical information are supplied for each lyric, and a commentary accompanies every stanza. Unless otherwise specified, all references to Watts's *Hymns and Spiritual Songs*, *Divine Songs Attempted in Easy Language for the Use of Children*, and *Psalms of David Imitated in the Language of the New Testament* are to the first editions of those books.

The discussions pay special attention to two aspects of Watts's work, their relationship to the Scriptures from which he often drew the ideas and forms for his hymns and the meaning of the words he used as they were understood in the early eighteenth century.[56] To the latter end, frequent use has been made of Nathan Bailey's *An Universal Etymological English Dictionary*, one of the first such books, initially published in

---

[55] Two features of the hymns as given in Watts's early publications are silently changed in this book: (1) the old style "s" has been altered to modern usage and (2) the second letter of the first word in a text, which was often given by Watts (or the printer) as a capital, is lowercased. An example of the latter is "Alas! and Did My Saviour Bleed?": in the first edition of *Hymns and Spiritual Songs*, the initial "a" of "Alas" was in a large font and took up about a line and a half of space; the subsequent letter ("l") was then made a capital, as though it were the beginning letter of the word. In this book, the initial letter is given as a simple capital and the second in lower case.

[56] In his article "Isaac Watts: Father of English Hymnody," Cook aptly observed that "The great genius of Watts lay in his ability to popularize and, unlike most popularizers, to better what he popularized" and that "He needed the stimulus of the thoughts of others, but once he had it his work was marked with his own distinctive genius. This is why his best work is his metrical Psalms and hymns based upon Scriptural passages." We may disagree with the subsequent claim that "His freer compositions are less worthy of notice" without disputing the importance of Watts's reliance upon Scripture for some of his best efforts (31).

1721.[57]

Unless otherwise noted, Scripture references are given from the King James Version (KJV) since this was the one most commonly employed in Watts's own day and was the text that he paraphrased most often in his psalms and hymns.[58] The word "hymn" is used generically to refer both to Watts's paraphrases of the psalms and his freely written texts unless a more technical distinction needs to be made; the context will generally make such exceptions obvious.

The Analysis of Hymns

While this introduction is not the place for a comprehensive discussion of the elements of hymnody, for those who may be unfamiliar with the tools of hymn analysis brief identifications of a few basic items that are included in the discussions may be helpful. Hymns are usually known by the first line of the text. Some authors (Watts included) also give hymns a title that indicates their general subject or background.

Hymns are generally made up of individual lines (verses) that are combined into stanzas (strophes), groups of lines that are intended to be sung to a strophic (repeating) melody.[59] Within a hymn, each stanza usually has the same basic metrical pattern as the one(s) before it. Indications such as "1:3" refer to the stanza of the hymn being referenced and the individual line of that stanza (thus, in the example, stanza 1, line 3).

Hymn texts make use of two types of meter, hymnic meter and poetic meter.[60] Hymnic meter indicates the number of syllables in each line of a stanza. While there can be an almost infinite number of hymnic meters, the most frequent ones in Watts's time were common meter (CM=8686, four lines with the first and third having eight syllables and

---

[57] Bailey's book does not include page numbers but simply lists the terms in alphabetical order. Unless otherwise specified, references are to the first edition of this book.

[58] Fletcher points out at least one instance in which Watts apparently relied upon the Geneva Bible ("English Psalmody and Isaac Watts," 143).

[59] Throughout this book "verse" will be used in two meanings: (1) a verse of Scripture or (2) a single line of poetry. It will not be employed as a synonym for "stanza" except when quoting other writers who use it in that sense.

[60] Hymnic and poetic meters should not be confused with musical meter, which refers to the number of beats and unit of beat in a measure of music.

the second and fourth six syllables), long meter (LM=8888), and short meter (SM=6686). Any of these meters could be doubled (D) to make eight lines, and there were other combinations of eights and sixes that saw some use, often under the name "particular" or "peculiar" meter.

Poetic meter refers to the accent or stress pattern of the text. The most common poetic meters in hymns are iambic (u/), trochaic (/u), dactylic (/uu), and anapestic (uu/).[61] An individual unit of one of these patterns is a foot. Watts uses iambic poetic meter almost exclusively, though, like other hymn writers, he sometimes incorporates one foot of another meter into a hymn. A metric modulation that Watts often used at the beginning of lines was the choriambus, a four-syllable foot that combines a dactyl and an iamb, as in the opening verse of "Joy to the World."[62]

Another important component of hymns is their use of rhyme, the correspondence of sounds. While many fine hymns have been written without rhyme, most hymns—and certainly those of Watts—use this device to enhance the rhythm and memorability of the text. Many rhyming patterns are possible. The most common ones in a four-line text are ABAB (lines 1 and 3 rhyme, as do the lines 2 and 4; also called "cross rhyme") and ABCB. In hymns with long lines (such as LM texts), adjacent lines are often rhymed (AABB). Watts employed both "true" rhymes and "false" rhymes; the latter are words that do not actually correspond but have somewhat similar sounds (near rhymes, e.g., "made" / "Head") or that look like they should rhyme but do not (eye rhymes, e.g., "Word" / "Lord").[63]

---

[61] The symbol "u" represents an unstressed syllable, while "/" stands for a stressed syllable. Examples of poetic meter given in the hymn discussions will use bold type for stressed syllables and plain type for unstressed syllables.

[62] In an essay titled "The Cadence of Verse" published in *Reliquiæ Juveniles* (1734), Watts noted that "It has been an old and just Observation, that English Verse generally consists of Iambick Feet" (311) but that "there are some parts of the Line which will admit a Spondee, that is, a Foot made of two long Syllables; or a Trochee, where the first Syllable is long, and the latter short" (312). He commented further that "Trochees are frequently used for the first Foot [of a line of poetry]" (313). This is another way of describing a choriambus.

[63] The examples are from "Jesus Shall Reign Where'er the Sun" (see 3:3-4 and 4:1-2). William Eaton Stephenson points out that false rhyme "is a device employed in the hymns [by Watts] to take the everlasting jingle out of the short

Watts made frequent use of parallelism in his writing, a feature that is common in the psalms. The three principal types of parallelism are synonymous (saying essentially the same thing in other words: "our help" / "our hope"), antithetical (saying the opposite: "ages past" / "years to come"), and complementary (extending the thought: "Our shelter from the stormy blast / And our eternal home").

While, as noted above, Watts strove consistently for simplicity in his texts, he also had frequent recourse to poetic devices that make the hymns more vivid and memorable. In fact, it is part of Watts's genius that his art is often hidden behind a veil of simplicity. Since these devices often have a profound impact on the way the hymn is constructed and understood, they are pointed out individually as they occur in each lyric.[64]

Watts's hymns, like all lyric poems, are designed primarily for singing and are technically incomplete until they are accompanied by music. However, the present discussion is restricted almost exclusively to the words themselves. There are three principal reasons for this: (1) with very few exceptions, we cannot know exactly which tunes—if any—Watts had in mind when he was writing his texts[65]; (2) while there are currently certain relatively standard pairings ("Joy to the World" with ANTIOCH, for example), the texts can be (and often are) sung to a variety of tunes; and (3) in the actual singing of hymns, the full meaning and understanding of the text is often lost in the enjoyment or labor of performance. If it is the music that gives life to the hymn, it is the text that gives meaning to the music and is ultimately the reason for its being sung.

Singing many of these texts throughout the course of my life and living with all of them for an extended period has deepened my love and appreciation for them as spiritual expressions of a faithful Christian from

---

form, to let some lines sweep on without interruption while perfect rhyme closes others off"; see Stephenson, "The Heroic Hymn of Isaac Watts," 175.

[64] Important discussions of poetic devices in hymn texts can be found in Lovelace, *The Anatomy of Hymnody* (New York: Abingdon Press, 1965), and Gray, *Hermeneutics of Hymnody: A Comprehensive and Integrated Approach to Understanding Hymns* (Macon: Smyth & Helwys Publishing, 2015), especially chapter 5.

[65] Watts wrote his texts to fit the standard psalm tunes of the time, but whether or not he had specific ones in mind is unknown, except in a few cases (see, for example, the discussion of "I'll Praise My Maker with My Breath," chapter 11).

a previous era. It is my firm conviction that these hymns still have much to say to Christians and their churches in the twenty-first century, that they will continue to do so, and that a close study of them can be both inspirational and rewarding. It is hoped that this book will result in a greater appreciation for and understanding of the hymns, leading to more effective singing and use of them in public worship and private devotion, and that such appreciation and understanding will help "the Redeemer's name be sung / through every land, by every tongue."[66]

---

[66] "From All that Dwell Below the Skies," 1:3-4. See chapter 8.

1

ALAS! AND DID MY SAVIOUR BLEED?

It is particularly fitting that both the first and last hymns discussed in this book have as their subject the cross of Christ. The crucifixion and resurrection formed the crux (pun intended) of Watts's thinking and ministry. In one of his sermons, he used the "voice" of a generic believer to answer the question of how someone who was not "a Great King, a Governor of the Earth" and was put to death could be the Messiah.

> I have seen my Sins nailed to the Cross of this Redeemer; I have found a way for the Pardon of all my Iniquities, and the Satisfaction of my Conscience, (which was before full of Anguish) in and from the Cross of this Messiah; I have found Holiness wrought in my Soul by the Belief of this Gospel; I have felt such Virtue proceeding from this Saviour, that I, who was before all over unclean and defiled, am, in some degree, made holy: this Gospel therefore must be from God, and this is the Messiah his Son.[1]

The centrality of Jesus' sacrifice to Watts's faith is nowhere more evident than in the hymns that open and close this volume, "Alas! and Did My Saviour Bleed?" and "When I Survey the Wondrous Cross."

"Alas! and Did My Saviour Bleed?" is the ninth text in Book II of *Hymns and Spiritual Songs* (1707), where it is titled "Godly Sorrow arising from the Sufferings of Christ." This part of the volume contains hymns "Composed on Divine Subjects"; though "Conformable to the Word of God," very few of the lyrics in this section are given a specific

---

[1] Watts, "Sermon III. The Inward Witness to Christianity," in *Sermons on Various Subjects* (1721), 69–70.

scriptural reference, in contrast to Books I and III, in which nearly every hymn has one. "Alas! and Did My Saviour Bleed" is a common meter text in iambic poetic meter, uses cross rhyme, and is one of Watts's greatest hymns on the cross.

The first two and a half stanzas are cast in the form of questions, for which iambic meter is particularly suited since it has a supplicatory nature and pulls the singer forward toward the question mark. These stanzas suggest a Christian's internal debate, contemplating the divine mystery of the cross and asking if it—and particularly the singer's own role in the crucifixion—can all be true. In a sense, the questions are rhetorical; the singer already knows the answers through biblical witness and personal experience. By casting his thoughts as rhetorical questions, Watts makes the text both more vivid and more personal.[2]

Stanza 1
    Alas! and did my Saviour bleed?
        And did my Sovereign dye?
    Would he devote that Sacred Head
        For such a Worm as I?

While, as noted above, the initial stanza of Watts's hymn is cast in the form of a question, the first word is an exclamation, complete with exclamation point: "Alas!" The first edition of Nathan Bailey's eighteenth-century *An Universal Etymological English Dictionary* (1721) included the term (as "Alass") and its derivation but did not give a definition. However, in the second edition (1724), Bailey noted that the word is "an Interjection of Grief" and defined "interjection" as "an undeclinable Word, used to express the Affections or Passions of the Mind." Thus, from the very first word of Watts's hymn, the singer is plunged into a world of passion (Latin "passio"="suffering"), despair, sorrow, and grief. Watts's use of this expression can be likened to the phrase employed by the Old Testament prophet in Isaiah 6:5, "Woe is me! for I am undone."

The reasons for the singer's despair are expressed through synonymous and antithetical parallelisms: "Saviour bleed" / "Sovereign die" (synonymous) and "Sacred Head" / "Worm" (antithetical). The starkness

---

[2] See chapter 2 ("Am I a Soldier of the Cross?") for a similar use of rhetorical questions.

of the singer's grief is enhanced by the many "d" and "s" sounds: "did," "bleed," "die," "would," "devote," "sacred," and "head"; "alas," "saviour," "sovereign," "sacred," and "such." In line 3, Watts uses synecdoche, in which part of an object is used to stand for the whole; in this case, Jesus' "Sacred Head" is symbolic of his whole body.

Modern hymnal compilers and congregations are generally uncomfortable with Watts's "worm" language in line 4 (as well as in other hymns), and it is frequently altered. The original is often taken to reflect an extreme Calvinist view of humanity as totally depraved and worthless, while more recent cultural and theological tenets hold that humanity is at least worth saving. Watts was certainly a Calvinist in most respects, but his purpose in referring to himself as a "worm" was probably less to express the worthlessness of humanity than to remind "the singer of his fallen condition" and to establish "the gulf between an Infinite God and his creation."[3] Here, the "worm" language sets up a contrast between the majestic "Sacred Head" of Christ and the hymn writer's (and singer's) own status as a creature that falls far short of the glory of God. The writer may also have had in mind Job 25:6 ("How much less man, that is a worm? and the son of man, which is a worm?") or Psalm 22:6 ("But I am a worm, and no man").

Stanza 2
> Thy Body slain, sweet Jesus, thine,
> > And bath'd in it's [*sic*] own Blood,
> While the firm mark of Wrath Divine
> > His Soul in Anguish stood?

In the second edition of *Hymns and Spiritual Songs* (1709), this stanza was marked for possible omission—a suggestion that has been followed by most hymnal editors—but the author also made several changes to it, implying that he still considered it to be an integral part of the hymn. Watts corrected "it's" to "its" and revised lines 3 and 4 to read "While all expos'd to Wrath divine / The glorious Sufferer stood?" The reasons for the revision are probably both poetic and theological: the second version avoids an accent on the word "the" in the third line, as well as the problematic line about Jesus' "Soul" being "in Anguish."

---

[3] Plett, "The Poetic Language of Isaac Watts's Hymns," 117.

Still, in contrast to the surrounding stanzas, the second strophe seems to lack focus, which may be one reason why it was marked for omission. It continues the questioning found in stanza 1 but does not have an action verb to give a sense of direction. Note, for instance, in stanza 1, the verbs "did" (used twice) and "devote," which provide momentum, as well as the absence of such verbs in stanza 2. The stanza also rather abruptly (and strangely) changes the line of communication from the human-to-human focus of the first stanza—and almost all the rest of the hymn—to a direct address to Jesus (lines 1-2), followed by just as sudden a return to a human-to-human design.[4]

Stanza 3
> Was it for Crimes that I had done
> > He groan'd upon the Tree?
> Amazing Pity! Grace unknown!
> > And Love beyond degree!

Stanza 3 marks a shift in the hymn from rhetorical questions (lines 1-2) to declarative statements (lines 3-4) and can be viewed as the pivotal point of the text. Watts's use of the word "Crimes" suggests the seriousness of human offenses against God; not merely misjudgments, mistakes, or errors, these are flagrant violations of the law. Crime demands punishment, but, in this case, it is not the offender who is punished; instead, it is the One who "groan'd upon the Tree."

The wonder of Christ's sacrifice leads Watts to abandon both question and explanation in favor of simple ejaculations of astonishment over the "Pity," "Grace," and "Love" that are "Amazing," "unknown," and "beyond degree." Watts here uses ecphonesis, in which an exclamation mark is used to give emphasis or emotion to a word or phrase. In his later *A Guide to Prayer* (1715), Watts pointed out that such exclamations "serve to set forth an affectionate Wonder, a sudden Surprize [*sic*], or violent Impression of any thing on the Mind."[5]

---

[4] A human-to-God line of communication is also found in the last two lines of the hymn, but in that place it makes a great deal more sense than in the second stanza.

[5] Watts, *A Guide to Prayer*, 113. See chapter 19 ("Sweet Is the Work") for another Watts hymn that makes significant use of this device.

Another point to be made about this stanza is the author's use of the words "had done" instead of "have done." In effect, Watts has transported himself into the past to a time before the crucifixion, asking if that awful event occurred because of "Crimes" he had committed. In using this wording, Watts links himself directly with those who crucified Jesus and shows that he is just as guilty of Christ's death as were they.

It is interesting to compare this stanza with the third strophe from another text in *Hymns and Spiritual Songs*, "And Now the Scales Have Left Mine Eyes."

> Was it for Crimes that I had done
>> My dearest Lord was slain,
> When Justice seiz'd God's only Son
>> And put his Soul to Pain?

Which of these hymns was written first cannot now be determined. At any rate, Watts knew when he had written a good line and felt free to reuse it as needed.

Stanza 4
> Well might the Sun in Darkness hide,
>> And shut his Glories in,
> When God the mighty Maker dy'd
>> For Man the Creature's Sin.

In stanza 4, Watts places himself at the scene of the crucifixion as a witness to the darkness that descended at the death of Christ (Matt 27:45; Mark 15:33). Lines 3 and 4 use one of Watts's favorite poetic devices, antithesis, contrasting "God the mighty Maker" (the Creator) with "Man the Creature"; these lines parallel the "Sacred Head" and "Worm" of stanza 1. Jesus is directly identified as "God the mighty Maker," an orthodox view of Christ, not the Arianism with which Watts's later writings are sometimes tagged: the Creator is also the Crucified.

Stanza 5
> Thus might I hide my blushing Face
>> While his dear Cross appears,
> Dissolve my Heart in Thankfulness,

And melt my Eyes to Tears.

The opening word, "Thus" (="therefore"), links stanza 5 with the previous strophe: just as the sun hid itself on the day of the crucifixion, we should hide our blushing faces when contemplating the cross. Implied in this statement is that *we* are the ones who are responsible for the crucifixion; we should be ashamed when we see the sacrifice Christ had to make on our behalf. "While" implies something that is still happening; the image of the cross is not something that appears only once and can now be forgotten, it is (metaphorically speaking, at least) a continuing vision of which we are constantly reminded.

The appearance of the cross causes more than mere blushing, however. Because of the recognition of what Christ has done, the singer's heart is "dissolved," eaten away as if by acid, but here the acid is "Thankfulness." Further dissolution appears in the singer's eyes, which are melted to tears. The next stanza makes it clear that these are not tears of joy (paralleling the "Thankfulness" of 5:3) but of sorrow. The order of these lines is significant: thankfulness for Christ's sacrifice for us does not dispel the grief of knowing what he had to go through to accomplish his mission.

Stanza 6
> But drops of Grief can ne'er repay[6]
> The debt of Love I owe,
> Here, Lord, I give my self away,
> 'Tis all that I can do.

Watts links the first line of stanza 6 with the end of stanza 5 by the word "drops," corresponding to the "Tears" of the previous strophe. At the same time, "But" sets up an antithesis with the previous stanzà, suggesting that tears, while an appropriate response to the sacrifice of Christ, are not enough. We owe a "debt of Love" that we can only begin to repay by giving ourselves away: after all, this is the only thing we have to give.

---

[6] In the first edition of *Hymns and Spiritual Songs* "ne'er" was spelled "ne're." This was corrected in the second edition, and the correction has been adopted here.

What does it mean to give oneself away? In worship? In service? In all one's being? Removing "self" and putting Christ in its place? Watts is not specific at this point, and appropriately so: it is up to each singer as inspired by God to decide how they will give themselves away.

Watts's words have often been sung to a Scottish folk melody titled MARTYRDOM (or AVON). During the nineteenth century, an American gospel song publisher and composer named Ralph E. Hudson wrote a new tune for the stanzas and added a refrain, "At the cross, at the cross, where I first saw the light, / And the burden of my heart rolled away, / It was there by faith I received my sight / And now I am happy all the day." The words and music of the refrain were a parody of a nineteenth-century popular song, "Take Me Home to the Place Where I First Saw the Light."[7] The refrain, of course, was not part of Watts's original concept for the hymn.

In his *Isaac Watts: Reason, Passion and the Revival of Religion*, Graham Beynon quotes stanzas 1, 5, and 6 of the hymn and notes the progression of "themes of contemplation of truth, arousing of appropriate passions, and commitment to live for God."[8] In many ways this is a typical Watts hymn on the cross, with the contemplation of the crucifixion leading to a text that is full of stark reminders of Christ's sacrificial death and the role that each person played in the horrors of that event. The hymn is filled with vivid language and raw emotion. However, the text is not gratuitous, for it does not stop with the ugliness nor, conversely, does it lead the singer to contentment, but rather to a commitment of all of one's being to the love and service of God. There is not much more that a hymn, a sermon, or a prayer can do.

---

[7] Spell, *Music in Texas*, 65–68.
[8] Beynon, *Isaac Watts*, 107.

2

AM I A SOLDIER OF THE CROSS

"Am I a Soldier of the Cross" was first published in Watts's *Sermons on Various Subjects, Divine and Moral: With a Sacred Hymn Suited to Each Subject* (1729), the final book of a three-volume set of sermons the preacher issued between 1721 and 1729.[1] The initial appearance of the hymn in a congregational song collection was in the London Baptist pastor John Rippon's *A Selection of Hymns from the Best Authors, Intended to Be an Appendix to Dr. Watts's Psalms and Hymns* (1787).[2]

As noted in the title of Watts's book, each of the fourteen sermons in the third volume is linked with a hymn. The hymns were not printed adjacent to the sermons they were intended to accompany but were grouped together at the end of the book; however, each text was clearly labeled as to which sermon it belonged.

"Am I a Soldier of the Cross" was written for the first sermon in the volume, titled "Holy Fortitude, or Remedies against Fear" and based on 1 Corinthians 16:13: "Stand fast in the faith, quit you like men, be strong."[3] According to the preface, this sermon and one other, "The Universal Rule of Equity,"

---

[1] In *Isaac Watts and Contemporary Hymn-Writers*, Wright speculated that "Am I a Soldier of the Cross" and other hymns that were published after *The Psalms of David Imitated* had probably already been written by 1719 (133). No evidence has been located to corroborate this theory.

[2] J. R. Watson, "Am I a Soldier of the Cross," *The Canterbury Dictionary of Hymnology*, https://hymnology.hymnsam.co.uk/ (accessed June 24, 2017). In the nineteenth century, the text was sometimes appended to another hymn, "Do I Believe What Jesus Saith?" first published in Watts's *Sermons on Various Subjects*, 2:471–72, with the first line altered to "Are we the soldiers of the cross?"

[3] The same title was used for the second sermon in the volume (the two discourses formed a pair), but each had a different accompanying hymn.

were transcrib'd and prepared for the 2d Volume [of sermons, 1723]; but the Printer was constrain'd to exclude them for want of Room. And had I not given Notice of them in the 10th and 16th Sermons of that Volume, I question whether I should have printed them now; the World having since that Time been so well furnish'd with Discourses on those Subjects in that excellent Treatise on the Christian Temper, which my worthy Friend Mr. Evans hath sent Abroad, and which is, perhaps, the most compleat Summary of those Duties which make up the Christian Life, that hath been publish'd in our Age.[4]

Thus the sermon on "Holy Fortitude" appears to have been preached (and the hymn probably written) at least six years before it was printed. Fortunately, Watts did not withhold the sermon from publication, for it gave the church "Am I a Soldier of the Cross."

The Sermon

A summary of the sermon may be helpful in setting the context for the hymn. Watts acknowledges with gratitude that "The Land where our Lot is cast [England], is honoured with the Christian Name," and thus the people to whom he was preaching do not suffer the sort of physical persecution that was characteristic of some other times and places. Nevertheless, Christians must be courageous because of the "growing Temptation" of infidelity, the natural depravity of humanity, and the "Malice and Rage of Satan with his evil Angels."[5]

The preacher distinguishes between what he calls "Active Valour or Courage," which "enables us to attempt and venture upon any bold act of Duty," and "Passive Valour," "an habitual Firmness and Constancy of Soul, as enables us to bear what Sufferings we fall under."[6] Watts observes that active valor is called for in the following circumstances.

(1) When the Christian professes and practices "strict Piety, even

---

[4] Watts, *Sermons on Various Subjects*, 3:vi–vii. The reference is to John Evans's two-volume *Practical Discourses concerning the Christian Temper: Being Thirty Eight Sermons upon the Principal Heads of Practical Religion* (1723).

[5] Watts, *Sermons on Various Subjects*, 3:2–3.

[6] Ibid., 3.

under the special View and Notice of profane Sinners";[7]

(2) in "the Company of Infidels and Apostates from Christianity [among whom Watts specifically names 'Deists and Scoffers'], who throw their impious Jests on the Gospel of Christ";[8]

(3) in the temptation "to practise an unfashionable Virtue, or to refuse Compliance with any fashionable Vice";[9]

(4) when a person must "undertake the Cause of the Oppressed, to plead for the Poor against the Mighty, or to vindicate the Innocent against the Men of Slander or Violence";[10]

(5) if it becomes necessary to admonish other Christians who "depart from the Ways of Righteousness";[11]

(6) when a reformation of "vicious Customs of a City or a Nation" is needed;[12]

(7) when one is confronted by persons in a higher station of life [e.g., a rich person or a servant's master] to act in or agree with non-Christian ways;[13]

(8) on occasion to give one's very life, even "to a bloody Death."[14]

Passive valor applies in the case of "Sickness, Pain, Shame, Losses, Disappointments, all the sorrowful Changes of Life, or Death itself from the mere Hand of God,"[15] or when encountering "Persecutions of all Sorts...for the sake of God," that is, when one suffers for the faith or simply as part of the human condition but remains faithful.[16] For both active and passive valor, Watts gives specific examples of ways in which Christians must show "holy fortitude" in their dealings with other people and various circumstances.

---

[7] Ibid., 6.
[8] Ibid., 7.
[9] Ibid., 10.
[10] Ibid., 12–13.
[11] Ibid., 14.
[12] Ibid., 16.
[13] Ibid., 19.
[14] Ibid., 20–21.
[15] Ibid., 22.
[16] Ibid., 24.

The Relationship between the Sermon and the Hymn

It might be expected that the hymn Watts wrote to accompany the sermon would correspond directly to the principal points of the latter. That, however, is not the case, and the relationship between the two writings is more oblique than direct. Certainly, there are words, phrases, and thoughts common to both writings, as can be seen by a comparison of the following phrases from the sermon and the hymn.

1) "losing the heavenly Prize"—"While others fought to win the Prize"
2) "enables us to attempt and venture upon any bold act of Duty, which may endanger our present Ease"—"Must I be carry'd to the Skies / On flow'ry Beds of Ease"
3) "we must not be afraid to own, that we fear the great God, and that [we] worship that awful Name"—"And shall I fear to own his Cause, / Or blush to speak his Name?"
4) "Christians have need of holy Fortitude, to venture their Lives at the Demand of Providence, and expose themselves to Violence, and to a bloody Death"—"While others fought to win the Prize, / And sail'd thro' bloody Seas?"
5) "because they can bear the Wounds, the Reproaches, or Death it self"—"I'll bear the Toil, endure the Pain."

Despite these loose parallels, the hymn is not merely a metrical version of the sermon but a reflection of its general message of courage in the face of challenges and difficulties. The purpose of "Am I a Soldier of the Cross" is not primarily didactic—to summarize the homily—but liturgical: to give the hearers of the sermon an opportunity to reflect upon and respond to it.[17]

The Structure of the Hymn

"Am I a Soldier of the Cross" is given the same title as the sermon "Holy Fortitude" and is laid out in six common meter stanzas of iambic poetic

---

[17] See also the discussion of this sermon and hymn in Stephenson, "The Heroic Hymn of Isaac Watts," 214–17.

meter. Like "Alas! and Did My Saviour Bleed?" Watts couches the opening stanzas as a series of rhetorical questions.[18] As is common with Watts, cross rhyme (ABAB) is employed for the hymn, including several false rhymes (cross/cause, flood/God, Lord/Word, war/afar).[19]

The first three stanzas are terse and direct; they seem almost clipped or rapid-fire. In part, this directness results from Watts's characteristic use of short words, a feature that is especially prominent in stanza 3, which consists entirely of monosyllabic words and three separate questions in the space of four lines. The sense of directness is also created by the nature of the questions in the first three stanzas, which are bold (though implied) calls to action.

Stanza 1
> Am I a Soldier of the Cross,
> > A Follower of the Lamb?
> And shall I fear to own his Cause,
> > Or blush to speak his Name?

The first two lines of stanza 1 set up an implied antithesis between the (war-like) "soldier" and the (peaceful) "Lamb" that suggest Watts's sermonic categories of "active valor" and "passive valor" In the sermon, Watts observes that "Sometimes in the Cause of our Country, Divine Providence calls us to expose our Blood, and to assist or guard the Nation against Invasions from abroad, or Tumults at home, and to quell the Rage of a brutal Multitude." Also, he notes, "there are Seasons when we may be called to venture our Lives for our Christian Brethren."[20] Such instances call for soldier-like courage and (active) valor. At the same time, Christians are followers of "the Lamb," one who was led as a sheep to the slaughter (Acts 8:32), a model that we are to emulate (Rom 8:36);

---

[18] In his *A Guide to Prayer. Or, a Free and Rational Account of the Gift, Grace and Spirit of Prayer* (1715), 113, Watts called these "Interrogations, when the plain Sense of any thing we declare unto God is turned into a Question to make it more Emphatical and affecting."

[19] However, the words "war" and "afar" were true rhymes rather than eye rhymes in eighteenth-century England. See Bysshe, "A Dictionary of Rhymes" in *The Art of English Poetry*, 5.

[20] Watts, *Sermons on Various Subjects*, 3:21.

this is perhaps the ultimate model of passive valor.

The next two lines (1:3-4) contain a tripartite synonymous parallelism: "fear / own / Cause" and "blush / speak / Name." To some degree, these parallelisms correspond with the first two lines: the "soldier of the cross" should not "fear to own the cause" and the follower of the Lamb should not "blush to speak God's name." Nathan Bailey's *An Universal Etymological English Dictionary* gives one of the meanings of "own" as "belonging to"; thus, to "own [God's] Cause" means to belong to the cause. The metaphor of blushing to speak God's name is a reminder that fortitude is required not only when the Christian is physically or emotionally threatened but also in the ordinary run of daily life when the cause of Christ might cause personal embarrassment. Perhaps Watts is here alluding to 2 Timothy 1:8 ("Be not thou therefore ashamed of the testimony of our Lord") or similar New Testament passages.

Stanza 2
>   Must I be carry'd to the Skies
>   On flow'ry Beds of Ease,
>   While others fought to win the Prize,
>   And sail'd thro' bloody Seas?

Stanza 2 uses vivid metaphors to paint contrasting pictures of different approaches to following Christ: will we be content with "flow'ry Beds of Ease" or will we be like the martyrs who "sail'd thro' bloody Seas"? Watts sets up both antithetical and synonymous parallelisms to make his point: "carry'd / fought" and "flow'ry Beds" / "bloody Seas" present contrasting pairs, while "Skies" and "Prize" both suggest heaven. "Bloody Seas" is a particularly powerful metaphor: how much blood has to be shed for the seas to become bloody?

Watts, a Calvinist, is careful not to suggest that a person's lack of fortitude endangers their salvation: both the "flow'ry Beds of Ease" and the "bloody Seas" will lead to the same goal as far as redemption is concerned. However, according to Watts, personal comfort is not the goal of the valorous Christian. Instead, like the martyrs, Christians must strive to "win the Prize," not simply have it handed to them.

Stanza 3
> Are there no Foes for me to face?
> > Must I not stem the Flood?
> Is this vile World a Friend to Grace,
> > To help me on to God?

Though, as Watts acknowledged in the sermon, English Christians of his time were not subject to official persecution, the rhetorical question that begins stanza 3 implies that there are still "foes" with which to deal—mockers, scoffers, infidels, Deists, atheists, Christians who have strayed from the truth, etc. It is important to understand that Watts is using militant language metaphorically to suggest that such "foes" should be resisted, but—as the sermon makes clear—it is by standing up for the truth of the gospel whatever the cost, not by taking up arms. The second line of the stanza reminds the singer that while he or she may be only a single individual, each person is responsible for helping "stem the flood" of ungodliness by courageous action, whether active or passive.

In 3:3-4, the hymn writer, perhaps reflecting John 3:20 ("For every one that doeth evil hateth the light, neither cometh to the light, lest his deeds should be reproved"), makes it clear that the "World" is not the Christian's friend. A Christian who holds a posture of righteousness stands in judgment of the world (even when no words are spoken or written), something that the world abhors. Thus, the world is always seeking to bring Christians down to its level, not to elevate them to greater goodness and godliness ("to help me on to God"). This is as true in the present day as it was in Watts's, when he and his kind were given the "scandalous Names of Puritan and Precisian."[21]

Stanza 4
> Sure I must fight if I would reign:
> > Increase my Courage, Lord:
> I'll bear the Toil, endure the Pain,
> > Supported by thy Word.

---

[21] Watts, *Sermons on Various Subjects* (1729), 3:11. N. Bailey, *An Universal Etymological English Dictionary* (1721), defines "Precisian" as "one who is over-scrupulous in Point[s] of Religion."

With stanza 4, the approach of the hymn changes from rhetorical questions to declarative statements. The first word might be taken as a substitute for "yes" ("Yes, I must fight if I would reign"), connecting it with the previous stanza. However, Bailey defines "sure" as "safe, secure, trusty, faithful." It is probably the last-named meaning that Watts had in mind and thus the stanza should probably be understood as "I must fight faithfully if I would reign."

The stanza is a prayer to God, but it is not the request of someone asking for deliverance from troubles. Instead, the petition is that God will "increase my courage" so that I (the singer) can "fight," "bear the Toil," and "endure the Pain"—a further contrast with the "flow'ry Beds of Ease" of stanza 2. The fourth line names the source of the singer's courage, the Word of God. This may refer to God's answer to the singer's prayer, the Bible, Jesus, or—more likely—to all three.

Stanza 5
>   Thy Saints in all this glorious War
>   Shall conquer tho' they die;
>   They see the Triumph from afar,
>   And seize it with their Eye.

Stanzas 5 and 6 are frequently deleted in hymnal publications of this lyric. There are probably several reasons for this omission. The last two stanzas alter the voice from singular (I) to plural (saints, they, etc.) and change the focus from courage to face hardships to the eternal reward for having endured them. They also contain some concepts that are a bit awkward to sing: how exactly do saints "seize" something "with their Eye"?[22] The stanzas simply do not rise to the level of the first four and seem anticlimactic. Since the fourth stanza makes a fitting conclusion to the text with its turn from questioning toward resolution and the positive emphasis in the last line, the final stanzas have generally been treated as superfluous by hymnal editors.

Stanza 5 points out that the result of faithfulness "in all this glorious War" may well be the death of the saints, but that they will ultimately

---

[22] The phrase is obviously metaphorical and is parallel to the previous line; "Seizing" triumph with the eye means that one will keep his or her focus on the triumph, but the metaphor seems a bit forced.

"conquer" with a vision of "Triumph" in "their Eye." The last two lines present a rhetorical chiasmus between "see / eye" and "triumph / it."

> Stanza 6
>> When that illustrious Day shall rise,
>>> And all thy Armies shine
>> In Robes of Victory thro' the Skies,
>>> The Glory shall be thine.

The last stanza turns the focus of the Christian's victory back where it belongs: to God. The shining armies phrase probably refers to Revelation 19:14 ("And the armies which were in heaven followed him upon white horses, clothed in fine linen, white and clean"), while the "Robes of Victory" also allude to the garments of those who "came out of great tribulation, and have washed their robes, and made them white in the blood of the Lamb" (Rev 7:14).

Watts and Military Imagery

"Am I a Soldier of the Cross" and other hymns have been criticized in some quarters for their use of military imagery. While this is not the place for a full discussion of the issue, it should be noted that this imagery is just that—imagery: metaphorical language in which one word or concept is used as a replacement for another. In this case, the ideas of soldiering, fighting, war, etc. are employed in the same sense as Paul's description of the "whole armour of God" (Eph 6:11-17), with particular notice of v. 12: "For *we wrestle not against flesh and blood*, but against principalities, against powers, against the rulers of the darkness of this world, against spiritual wickedness in high places" (emphasis added).

Warfare is an unfortunate fact of human existence, one that hymn writers have frequently drawn upon, just as they have drawn upon imagery from farming, athletics, banking, etc. Using military metaphors does not encourage killing other people or glorification of war any more than using these other metaphors encourages growing vegetables, playing baseball, or financial dealings.[23] Rather, military imagery, when used

---

[23] Some critics seem to take military imagery in hymnody literally but do not interpret other metaphorical references in the same manner.

properly, suggests exhibiting the characteristics of a good soldier: courage, obedience, and cooperation in mission. Watts's hymn is not a call to arms but a call to constancy and dedication. We must be careful not to take a too literal and too facile understanding of such metaphorical language.[24]

---

[24] For further discussion of this issue see Music, "War and Peace in Christian Hymnody," 97–110.

3

BEFORE JEHOVAH'S AWFUL THRONE

"Before Jehovah's Awful Throne" began as a poem, "Sing to the Lord with Joyful Voice," in Watts's 1706 *Horæ Lyricæ,* where it was titled "Praise to the Lord from All Nations" and given in five stanzas.[1] Watts then reprinted it without change in *Hymns and Spiritual Songs* (Book I, no. 43). When he published the second editions of *Horæ Lyricæ* and *Hymns and Spiritual Songs* in 1709, he dropped this hymn from both collections. He then incorporated it into *The Psalms of David Imitated* in 1719, where it served as the second of his versions of Psalm 100. The author took this opportunity to revise the text, adding a stanza ("We are his people, we his care") and amending all the others except the first and last.[2]

As published in *The Psalms of David Imitated,* the text demonstrates a remarkable improvement over the original. In the words of Harry Escott,

> The recension (1719) shows that Watts had made considerable progress in the mastery of his craft. The experience of writing hymns for a particular congregation had assisted him in this regard. The Psalm is now more of a unity, the rhymes are better managed, the individual stanzas more compact, the language less self-conscious and literary, the rhythm smoother, and the whole composition simpler and more stately.[3]

---

[1] Watts, *Horæ Lyricæ,* 59–60.
[2] This is the version of the text that is used in the present book.
[3] Escott, *Isaac Watts, Hymnographer,* 142. Escott gives all three versions of the text and discusses them on pp. 140–42.

It has also been pointed out that three lines seem to have been borrowed from or modeled after the version of Psalm 100 by John Patrick, whose *A Century of Select Psalms* had first been published in 1679.[4]

Both Psalm 100 versions in *The Psalms of David Imitated* employ long meter and are iambic in accent pattern. The first version of the psalm, "Ye Nations Round the Earth, Rejoice," is labeled "a Plain Translation," suggesting that it is intended to be a literal versification, and the second (the current text) is "a Paraphrase," implying a freer approach. "Ye Nations Round the Earth, Rejoice" is also headed by the phrase "Praise to our Creator," but this was undoubtedly meant to apply to both versions of the psalm.

As will be noted further below, Watts did not write the line "Before Jehovah's Awful Throne." This was an alteration by John Wesley when he included stanzas 2–6 in his *A Collection of Psalms and Hymns* (1737), usually nicknamed the "Charlestown Collection" from its place of publication, Charlestown (Charleston), South Carolina. This volume, issued while John was serving as a missionary in the British colony of Georgia, was the first of the more than sixty hymn collections published by John Wesley and his brother Charles.

Stanza 1
    Sing to the Lord with joyfull [*sic*] Voice;
    Let every Land his Name adore;
    The *British* Isles shall send the Noise
    A-cross the Ocean to the Shore.

This first stanza illustrates one of Watts's techniques in trying to make the psalms relevant for eighteenth-century British Christians by specifically mentioning his native country in the text. The first two lines are a relatively straightforward versification of the opening of Psalm 100: "Make a joyful noise unto the Lord, all ye lands." Lines 3 and 4 then specify how this praise is going to be accomplished—Britain will have the responsibility for making it happen.

During the eighteenth century, the British people often identified themselves with the biblical nation of Israel. This can be seen in both the hymns of Watts and the librettos of the oratorios by Watts's younger

---

[4] Benson, "The Evolution of a Great Hymn," 334–35.

contemporary, George Frederick Handel. In stressing the nationhood of Israel (as reflected in the oratorio *Israel in Egypt*) and biblical heroes and deliverers such as Samson and Judas Maccabeus,[5] Handel and his librettists captured what was widely believed (by the British, at least) to be the special character of Great Britain: Israel was the "chosen nation," and Britain—if perhaps not "chosen" in the same sense—was (or could become) a "new Israel" that had been specially blessed as the predominant superpower of the time. Such thinking was common among Englishmen during the eighteenth century.[6]

However, while Watts was as loyal to his country as any other Briton of his era, his reference to the British Isles, at least in this hymn, is not patriotic chest-beating but an acknowledgment that his country has an obligation to lead other nations in praise. From Watts's point of view, the favors of God have fallen on every nation ("Let every Land his Name adore"), but because of God's special blessings, Britain above all others should be first in the act of glorifying the Lord. As a kingdom surrounded by the sea, it would only be natural to send the "Noise" "A-cross the Ocean."

Wesley did not include this stanza in the "Charlestown Collection," instead beginning the hymn with stanza 2. Since his collection was compiled in and for the American colony of Georgia, perhaps he considered the reference to the British Isles to be out of place, though the colonies were, of course, at that time a part of the British Empire. At any rate, Wesley's revision became the standard form of the text for many later

---

[5] Judas Maccabeus is not a biblical character but appears in the intertestamental Apocrypha.

[6] For a full discussion of Handel's oratorio librettos in their eighteenth-century background, see Ruth Smith, *Handel's Oratorios and Eighteenth-Century Thought* (Cambridge: Cambridge University Press, 1995). Note especially p. 10: "special church services and special sermons…time and again…delivered their messages by comparing the British nation with the biblical Israelites," and p. 92: "the oratorio Israelites were of real interest to [Handel's audiences] as images of themselves." See also her chapter 12. Watts himself made a direct connection between the chosen people of the Old Testament and Britain in his paraphrase of Psalm 67: "Our God will crown his chosen Isle / With Fruitfulness and Peace" ("Shine, Mighty God, on Britain Shine," st. 6). On Watts's patriotism as reflected in his congregational songs see Escott, *Isaac Watts, Hymnographer*, 222–23.

collections, and Watts's original first stanza fell out of common use.[7]

> Stanza 2
> Nations, attend before his Throne
> With solemn Fear, with sacred Joy;
> Know that the Lord is God alone;
> He can create, and he destroy.

Watts's second stanza paraphrases Psalm 100:2-3a:

> [2]Serve the LORD with gladness:
>   come before his presence with singing.
> [3]Know ye that the LORD he is God:
>   it is he that hath made us, and not we ourselves.

Believers are to "serve the LORD" by "attend[ing] before his Throne" in a particular manner, which Watts describes in paradoxical fashion as "solemn Fear" and "sacred Joy."

Modern people are sometimes put off by the idea of "fearing" God, but the biblical witness shows that people who had a direct encounter with the Almighty often had to be admonished not to be afraid (Gen 15:1), professed their unworthiness (Isa 6:5), or fell at his feet (Rev 1:17). Fear is but a natural response to an encounter with an omnipotent God, the Maker of heaven and earth and all that is. As Hebrews 10:31 puts it, "It is a fearful thing to fall into the hands of the living God."

However, for Watts, it is not only with fear but also with joy that Christians are to come before the throne—as the psalmist puts it, "with singing." This joy is not mere happiness or being in good spirits; it is "sacred Joy," joy that is deep-seated and derived from knowing God and holy things. Coming to the Lord with joy does not take away the fear of God, but neither does fear of the Lord take away the joy of knowing him.

---

[7] The deletion of the first stanza and the alteration of the first two verses of the second stanza were the principal changes Wesley made in Watts's hymn. On Wesley's deletion of nationalistic stanzas from Watts's hymns, see Kolodziej, "Isaac Watts, the Wesleys, and the Evolution of 18th-Century English Congregational Song," 242–43.

The third line of the stanza is a nearly exact quotation of the opening of Psalm 100:3. Watts summarizes the second clause of the verse in three words, "He can create." He then adds something not found in the psalm, "and he destroy." The juxtaposition of "create" and "destroy" is reminiscent of Genesis 6:7, the prologue to the sending of Noah's flood: "And the Lord said, I will destroy man whom I have created from the face of the earth." Another scriptural parallel is Psalm 104:29b-30a, referring to both animals and humans: "thou takest away their breath, they die, and return to their dust. Thou sendest forth thy spirit, they are created." It is to the grace of God that we owe our very existence, a fact of which Watts reminds us in straightforward, unadorned language.

In the version of this stanza that John Wesley provided for the "Charlestown Collection," he restated the opening lines as "Before Jehovah's awful Throne / Ye Nations, bow with sacred joy," and it was in this form that Watts's hymn became best known in later times. At first glance, it appears that Wesley merely rearranged Watts's thoughts, substituting "awful" for "fear" and describing God's throne in that way.

However, there is a difference between "awful" and "fear," a distinction that might be lost to modern singers. Nathan Bailey defines "fear" as "Apprehension of Evil, Dread, Fright," which certainly fits with modern usages of the term. His definition of "awful" is "terrible, apt to strike a Terror into; to be feared, or revered." Using these definitions (and for modern folk), the word "awful" suggests a disastrous occurrence, as in "he had an awful illness" or "that was an awful car wreck."

However, Bailey gives two other synonyms for the word "aw[e]," "Observance" and "Respect," and later defines "Reverent" and "Reverential" with the terms "respectful" and "awful." Thus, while "awful" can have a negative meaning, it can also have the connotation of "respectful" or "reverential," and that is probably the sense in which Wesley used it. Wesley's point was that God's throne is awe-inspiring, not dreadful. The word could probably better be expressed in modern times as "aweful" (full of awe), or perhaps a completely different word should be substituted to avoid misunderstanding.

Stanza 3
> His sovereign Power without our Aid
> Made us of Clay, and form'd us Men:

And when like wand[e]ring Sheep we stray'd,
He brought us to his Fold again.

Watts's third stanza extends his paraphrase of v. 3 of the psalm, cit-
ing more directly than in stanza 2 the content of the second clause, "it is
he that hath made us, and not we ourselves." The reference to humans
being made of "Clay" alludes to several other Scripture passages, including Genesis 2:7 ("And the Lord God formed man of the dust of the
ground") and Isaiah 64:8 ("O Lord, thou art our father; we are the clay,
and thou our potter; and we all are the work of thy hand").

The psalmist's mention of God's people being "the sheep of his pasture" led Watts into a technique he used often in *The Psalms of David
Imitated* of bringing references from other parts of the Bible into a psalm
version. Note that there is no mention in the psalm of the sheep going
astray or being led back into the fold. The going astray is derived from
Isaiah 53:6a ("All we like sheep have gone astray") and Matthew 18:12
("if a man have an hundred sheep, and one of them be gone astray, doth
he not leave the ninety and nine, and goeth into the mountains, and see-
keth that which is gone astray?"). John 10 mentions sheepfolds (e.g., v. 1)
but Watts drew from this merely a passing allusion to the "Fold."

Stanza 4
We are his People, we his Care,
Our Souls and all our mortal Frame:
What lasting Honours shall we rear
Almighty Maker, to thy Name?

The last portion of v. 3 of the psalm forms the background for the
first line of stanza 4, "we are his people, and the sheep of his pasture,"
but the remainder of the stanza does not depend upon the psalm. God's
"Care" extends not only to "Our Souls" but to our bodies ("mortal
Frame") as well, providing us with food, the amazing healing power of
the human body, and even the very air we breathe. God's graciousness to
his people leads Watts to question what we can give back to God that
will be "lasting" (4:3-4). These lines may be an allusion to Psalm 116:12,
"What shall I render unto the Lord for all his benefits toward me?" With
this question, Watts changes the line of communication in the hymn
from human-to-human to human-to-God by addressing it directly to the

Lord.

Stanza 5
    Wee'll croud thy Gates with thankfull Songs,[8]
    High as the Heavens our Voices raise;
    And Earth with her ten thousand Tongues
    Shall fill thy Courts with sounding Praise.

Stanza 5 answers the question posed in the last lines of the previous stanza: our "lasting Honours" will consist of crowding God's (heavenly) gates "with thankfull Songs" while all the earth echoes the song "with sounding Praise." This is Watts's version of v. 4 of the psalm: "Enter into his gates with thanksgiving, and into his courts with praise: be thankful unto him, and bless his name." Watts likely drew the "ten thousand Tongues" from a combination of Revelation 5:11 ("I heard the voice of many angels round about the throne and the beasts and the elders: and the number of them was ten thousand times ten thousand, and thousands of thousands") and 7:9-10 ("I beheld, and lo, a great multitude, which no man could number, of all nations, and kindreds, and people, and tongues, stood before the throne.... And cried with a loud voice, saying, Salvation to our God which sitteth upon the throne, and unto the Lamb").

The stanza is remarkable for its parallelisms and contrasts: "croud thy Gates" / "fill thy Courts," "thankfull Songs" / "sounding Praise," "Heavens" / "Earth," and "Voices" / "Tongues." Note that these parallelisms pair the two outer lines with each other and the two inner lines together.

Stanza 6
    Wide as the World is thy Command,
    Vast as Eternity thy Love;
    Firm as a Rock thy Truth must stand
    When rolling Years shall cease to move.

---

[8] In the second edition of *The Psalms of David Imitated*, the spellings of "Wee'll" and "thankfull" were corrected, but "croud" was retained.

47

Watts concludes his hymn by expanding upon the last two clauses of the psalm's fifth verse, "his mercy is everlasting; and his truth endureth to all generations." The author sets this stanza apart from the others by beginning each of the first three lines with a choriambus. Each line also features a trio of strong nouns and adjectives that describe God's power, mercy, and steadfastness: "Wide / World / Command," "Vast / Eternity / Love," and "Firm / Rock / Truth."

It is interesting that in line 3 Watts used the word "must" instead of "will" or "does" or something similar. In essence, the author says that there is no choice in the matter: because God is God, his truth *has* to stand both now and "When rolling Years shall cease to move." The last line is reminiscent of the description in "Our God, Our Help in Ages Past" of time being "like an ever-rolling Stream."

In another publication, Watts wrote that praise is "a Part of that Divine Worship which we owe to the Power that made us: 'Tis an Acknowledgment of the Perfection of God, ascribing all Excellencies to him, and confessing all the Works of Nature and Grace to proceed from him." He went on to describe how inadequate is human praise of God, though it be "dress[ed] up…in Magnificence of Language…shining Figures, and sounding Words." Even the "holy Psalmist" could only say "Thou art good, and thou doest good" (Ps 119:63). "How inconsiderable an Offering is this for a God!" Watts exclaimed, "and yet so condescending is his Love, that he looks down, and is well pleased to receive it."[9]

In his paraphrase of Psalm 100, Watts provided a hymn that gives believers a vehicle for singing praise directly to God, something that is not found in the original passage. Thus he turns an admonition to praise into an act of praise itself. As Watts acknowledged, the result may indeed be an "inconsiderable Offering for a God," yet, as he also noted, "so condescending is his Love, that he looks down, and is well pleased to receive it."

---

[9] Watts, *Reliquiæ Juveniles*, 28–29.

4

COME HOLY SPIRIT, HEAVENLY DOVE

"Come Holy Spirit, Heavenly Dove" is the thirty-fourth text in Book II of *Hymns and Spiritual Songs* (1707). Watts titled the hymn "Breathing after the Holy Spirit: or, Fervency of Devotion desir'd." The text consists of five common meter stanzas in an iambic pattern using cross rhyme.

In a lengthy sermon on "The Doctrine of the Trinity, and the Use of it" published twenty-two years after the first edition of *Hymns and Spiritual Songs*, Watts devoted a section to a discussion of the work of the Holy Spirit under the following heads.

1. The Spirit "convinces us of Sin."
2. "The Spirit discovers the Mercy of God the Father to us, and assures us that he is willing to be reconciled."
3. It is the Spirit "who effectually reveals Christ Jesus to the Soul as the great Reconciler."
4. The Spirit "makes us willing to return to God in this Way of his own Appointment"; that is, it is the Spirit who "powerfully persuades and inclines us to part with every Sin."
5. "The Holy Spirit preserves and carries on his own divine Work in the Soul."[1]

In a statement that is particularly relevant to "Come Holy Spirit, Heavenly Dove," Watts further observed that

---

[1] Summarized from Watts, *Sermons on Various Subjects, Divine and Moral*, 445–48.

In our Approaches to God in order to obtain Peace and Favour with him, we must pray, and wait, and hope for the divine Influences of this blessed Spirit, to convince us of Sin, to make us sincerely willing to be reconciled to God, to give us a clear and affecting Sight of Christ in all the Power and Glory of his mediatorial Office, and to enable us to apply our selves to Christ by a living Faith, that we may by him be brought into the Favour of God.[2]

He also discussed the appropriateness of addressing the Holy Spirit directly in praise and prayer.

Now tho' it be generally agreed that there are no plain and express Precepts or Examples of Prayers or Praises so directly addressed to the Holy Spirit in all the New Testament, yet since the Holy Spirit is true God, since he is represented in Scripture in a personal manner, or as a divine Person, and since in the sacred Œconomy he is appointed to enlighten, to sanctify, and to comfort us, I think we may by just Inference derive sufficient Ground from Scripture upon some Occasions to offer Petitions to the Holy Spirit for his sacred Influences, and to give him Praise when we have receiv'd them.[3]

Watts's hymn particularly reflects the "hope for the divine Influences of this blessed Spirit" referred to above, as well as his view that the Spirit can be addressed directly.

Stanza 1
> Come Holy Spirit, Heavenly Dove,
>> With all thy quick[e]ning Powers,
> Kindle a Flame of sacred Love
>> In these cold Hearts of ours.

In the first stanza, Watts incorporates two biblical symbols of the Holy Spirit, the dove and the flame. The dove image derives from the baptism of Jesus as recorded in Matthew 3:16 ("he saw the Spirit of God descending like a dove, and lighting upon him"), and the flame from the

---

[2] Ibid., 448–49.
[3] Ibid., 451–52.

account of the day of Pentecost in Acts 2:3 ("And there appeared unto them cloven tongues like as of fire, and it sat upon each of them").

The stanza is a prayer to the Spirit to warm the hearts of believers with "a Flame of sacred Love." The "quickening" work of the Holy Spirit is a reflection of several New Testament passages, including John 6:63, Romans 8:11, and 1 Peter 3:18. According to Bailey's *An Universal Etymological English Dictionary*, the verb "to quicken" means "to make or become alive, as a Child in the Womb; also to hasten." In the gerund form used by Watts, the line should be understood as "with all thy enlivening powers," but the rich imagery of being made alive like "a Child in the Womb" should not be missed; in essence, the singers are calling upon the Spirit to give them a new birth. For Watts, this was not a reference to salvation but to a rebirth of spirituality.

In the last two lines, believers confess that their hearts are "cold" and ask God to enflame them with "sacred Love." Watts breaks the iambic pattern in the third line, beginning it with a choriambus, which gives a sense of eager anticipation of the warming to come.

Stanza 2
>Look, how we grovel here below;
>>And hug these trifling Toys;
>Our Souls can neither fly nor go
>>To reach Eternal Joys.

The idea of "groveling" is not a popular one in a twenty-first century democracy but undoubtedly it was not any more pleasant an image in the eighteenth century when Watts wrote this text. To "grovel" suggests abject humiliation before a person who has complete control over the individual.[4] But that is not the sense of this stanza. It is not that we are groveling before God; rather, it is that we *voluntarily* grovel on the earth with our "trifling Toys" instead of living where the "Flame of sacred Love" could be kindled in our hearts. Perhaps we might better understand the term "grovel" in this context as "wallow," because this is something we are doing willingly. And while we are groveling (or wallowing), we hug

---

[4] To be sure, N. Bailey's definition in *An Universal Etymological English Dictionary* does not have a particularly negative connotation, simply noting that the word means "lying on the Face or with the Face to the Ground."

the "trifling Toys" of possessions, position, reputation.[5]

In lines 3 and 4, Watts notes that our groveling condition prevents us from either "fleeing the scene" or ascending to the "Eternal Joys" that should rightfully be ours. Since Watts was writing for believers, he probably means that we cannot get away from the Holy Spirit (cf. Ps 139:7-12) but that without the warming of the Spirit neither can we experience the full joy of our salvation. Thus we are caught in a wretched state.

Stanza 3
>In vain we tune our formal Songs,
>>In vain we strive to rise,
>*Hosannas* languish on our Tongues,
>>And our Devotion dies.

In stanza 3, Watts turns from our miserable everyday condition to observe that without the Holy Spirit things are no better in our worship. The first two lines use anaphora—beginning successive lines with the same word or phrase—to emphasize the vanity (emptiness) of our "formal Songs" and our attempts to "rise." According to Bailey, "formal" can mean simply "belonging to form," or "punctual," "affected," or "precise." Watts probably had no pejorative intent in using "formal" here; after all songs have to have a form of some kind for humans to sing them, but he notes that while our songs may be timely (punctual), well sung (affected), or say the right things (precise), they are ineffective without the presence of the Holy Spirit. The evidence of this is that "Hosannas [our songs of praise] languish"—"grow faint or weak," "droop," "fall away," "consume or pine away" (Bailey)—we grow mute, and our attempts at devotion ("religious Zeal") are killed.

In eighteenth-century British congregational song practice, to "tune a song" meant to set the pitch and line out the verses; since the singing was completely a cappella, this task was the responsibility of the precentor or song leader. The picture that Watts imaginatively draws is of a precentor striving to find an appropriate pitch and lead the congregation

---

[5] In the second edition of *Hymns and Spiritual Songs*, Watts altered line 2 to read "Fond of these trifling Toys." While this change perhaps makes the stanza a bit "nicer," it loses the vividness of the original and creates a couple of mismatched poetic accents.

but without success: the congregation begins half-heartedly and finally gives up in the middle of the song.

Stanza 4
> Dear Lord! and shall we ever lye
>> At this poor dying rate?
> Our Love so faint, so cold to thee?
>> And thine to us so great?

In stanza 4, Watts asks with the psalmist "How long, O Lord?" (cf. Ps 13:1): will we lie forever in this miserable state? The phrase "dying rate" does not refer to the number of people dying at a particular time. Bailey derives "rate" from a Saxon word for "condition," and that is probably the sense in which Watts uses it. The author returns to the theme of the first stanza about the coldness of believer's hearts, but now it is a question of how this freeze can happen, particularly since the "Flame of sacred Love" that God has for his children is "so great." This suggests more than merely that the fire has not reached the cold; rather, the cold is making active resistance against the warmth of the flame.

Stanza 5
> Come Holy Spirit, Heavenly Dove,
>> With all thy quick[e]ning Powers,
> Come, shed abroad a Saviour's Love,
>> And that shall kindle ours.

Watts's last stanza repeats the initial lines from stanza 1 but changes the last two lines, at the same time retaining two important words from the earlier strophe, "Love" and "kindle." Here the poet calls upon the Holy Spirit to "shed abroad" the love of Jesus, which will in turn ignite the singers' love. Bailey gives one definition of "to shed" as "to send forth as to shed Tears." Thus, the line should probably be understood as asking the Holy Spirit to "send forth" or "spread" the Savior's love; the latter term is sometimes substituted for Watts's "shed."

There is a sense in which this hymn is not so much about the Holy Spirit as it is about the need for spiritual warmth. It will be noted that the Spirit is mentioned directly only in the first and last stanzas of the hymn while the interior stanzas describe the sorry state in which the believers find themselves.

However, for Watts, the third person of the Trinity is the source from which the Christian derives his or her desire for close communion with God. If our hearts and our worship are cold it is because we choose to "grovel" here below without the indwelling of the Spirit. Saying and singing the right words are not enough—the Holy Spirit must inhabit our actions for them to be efficacious. And since the Spirit is mentioned explicitly in the outer stanzas, it is evident that for Watts spiritual warmth both begins and ends with the Holy Spirit.

5

COME LET US JOIN OUR CHEERFUL SONGS

Isaac Watts seems to have had a particular fondness for the Book of Revelation. He opened his *Hymns and Spiritual Songs* with a text based on Revelation 5, "Behold the Glories of the Lamb." This hymn was followed by thirteen others in Book I that were based on the Apocalypse.[1]

One of these hymns was "Come Let Us Join Our Cheerful Songs" (no. 62 in Book I). Watts headed the hymn "Christ Jesus the Lamb of God Worshiped by all the Creation" and provided the scriptural reference Revelation 5:11-13.

In a later sermon, Watts observed "that all our Appearances before God in this World in his Sanctuary, are but Means to prepare us to stand before God in the World that is to come."[2] This hymn and others like it were designed for that very purpose—to model the way worship is and will be carried out in heaven, and thus how it should be exercised on earth in the present. As James Wendall Plett expresses it,

> According to Watts the singing of songs is necessary in the Christian's movement toward heaven. It is as though the bounds between earth and heaven can be diminished through song. In Watts's hearing, the Christian church unites with the angels in singing the songs of universal praise to God.[3]

---

[1] See numbers 8, 21, 25, 40, 41, 49, 56, 58, 59, 61–63, and 65.

[2] "Sermon XIV. Appearance before God here and hereafter," part 2, in *Sermons on Various Subjects* (1721), 441.

[3] Plett, "The Poetic Language of Isaac Watts's Hymns," 80–81.

The author cast the text of "Come Let Us Join Our Cheerful Songs" in five stanzas of common meter and an iambic pattern. One interesting feature of this hymn is the varied spelling of several words, only some of which were altered in the second edition.[4]

Stanza 1
Come let us joyn our chearful Songs
    With Angels round the Throne;
  Ten thousand thousand are their Tongues
    But all their Joys are one.

Stanza 1 is a relatively straightforward rendering of Revelation 5:11, "And I beheld, and I heard the voice of many angels round about the throne and the beasts and the elders: and the number of them was ten thousand times ten thousand, and thousands of thousands." Watts adds the line "But all their Joys are one" to fill out the stanza but also to emphasize that despite their myriad tongues, the angels are all singing for the same purpose—to glorify the Lamb.

Another change from the scriptural passage is that Watts alters the focus from a mere description of heavenly worship to an invitation for humans to join in the singing. This may be an allusion to earlier verses in Revelation 5 in which "the four beasts and four and twenty elders" (representing humanity) "sung a new song" for having been redeemed by the blood of the Lamb (vv. 8-9). It is possible to see the phrase "chearful Songs"—which does not occur in the Revelation passage—as a reflection of James 5:13b, "Is any [among you] merry? let him sing psalms."[5]

Two poetic features of this stanza stand out. As observed above, in the last two lines Watts sets up an antithesis between the myriad tongues of the "Angels round the Throne" and the fact that they are all in unison in their "Joys." The third line is remarkable in the fact that every word but one begins with the same letter (t).

---

[4] The second edition corrects "joyn" to "join" in stanzas 1 and 5, and "Skie" to "Sky" in stanza 4, but not "dy'd" in stanza 2 or "Glorys" in stanza 4.
[5] Several English translations—such as the American Standard Version—give the word "merry" in this passage as "cheerful."

Stanza 2
> "Worthy the Lamb that dy'd," they cry,
>> "To be exalted thus;
> "Worthy the Lamb," our Lips reply,
>> "For he was slain for us."[6]

In stanza 2, Watts splits the first part of the hymn in Revelation 5:12 ("Worthy is the Lamb that was slain") between two groups, the angels and the redeemed, again perhaps echoing the earlier passage in this chapter and also Revelation 5:14 ("And the four beasts said, Amen. And the four and twenty elders fell down and worshipped him that liveth for ever and ever"). Lines 1 and 3 employ a choriambus to give a lilt to the song of the angels and the redeemed.

Significantly, Watts is careful to keep the angels and the redeemed separate in this stanza. Whereas the angels sing a more or less generic praise to God, the redeemed are specific in the reason for their praise: "he was slain for us," something of which the angels cannot boast (see 1 Pet 1:12).

Stanza 3
> Jesus is worthy to receive
>> Honour and Power divine;
> And Blessings more than we can give,
>> Be, Lord, for ever thine.

The third stanza completes the paraphrase of v. 12, reducing the list of terms ascribed to the Lamb from "power, and riches, and wisdom, and strength, and honour, and glory, and blessing" to just three, "Honour," "Power," and "Blessings." Watts observes that after we have given everything we possibly can to honor the Lamb, he still deserves more. He also abandons the Lamb metaphor to name specifically who the Lamb is—Jesus. Both of the first two lines open with a choriambus, giving them an exuberance that matches their message of praise.

---

[6] In the first edition of *Hymns and Spiritual Songs*, quotation marks appeared only at the beginning of the first three lines. The opening quotation mark in the last line and the closing quotation marks have been supplied. In the second edition, Watts gave the quotations in italics.

The first two stanzas of the hymn maintain a human-to-human line of communication, as do the first two verses of stanza 3. In the third line of the stanza, the voice shifts to a human-to-God orientation in which Jesus is addressed directly. This line of communication will continue in the following stanza.

Stanza 4
> Let all that dwell above the Skie,
>> And Air, and Earth, and Seas,
> Conspire to lift thy Glorys high,
>> And speak thine endless Praise.

Revelation 5:13 forms the framework for stanzas 4 and 5, with stanza 4 mainly emphasizing the first part of the verse: "And every creature which is in heaven, and on the earth, and under the earth, and such as are in the sea, and all that are in them, heard I saying, Blessing, and honour, and glory, and power, be unto him that sitteth upon the throne, and unto the Lamb for ever and ever."

It is interesting to note the similarity between the first line of this stanza and the opening line of the hymn "From All that Dwell below the Skies" (see chapter 8). As he did in stanza 1, Watts turns the emphasis from reporting an observation to calling for a response.

The word "conspire" has a negative connotation in modern times, suggesting an agreement between people to engage in illegal activity or do someone else harm. However, the word literally means to "breathe together," and one of the definitions given by Bailey is "to agree together." Thus, in this context, Watts is calling upon the angels, saints in heaven, and all the earth to "agree together" to "speak [God's] endless Praise."

Stanza 5
> The whole Creation joyn in one,
>> To bless the Sacred Name
> Of him that sits upon the Throne,
>> And to adore the Lamb.

Watts concludes the hymn by emphasizing the second part of v. 13. Since this stanza is essentially a continuation of stanza 4 it should be understood that this is still part of the call for a response from "The whole Creation," but the author once again changes the voice, this time back to the human-oriented line of communication with which the hymn opened.[7]

While there is no evidence that Watts ever did so, it is easy to see how this hymn could have been used in association with a sermon on Revelation 5:11-13, given its change of focus from the scriptural description of heavenly worship to an invitation for the redeemed to join in that worship. The preacher could explicate the meaning of the passage in an expository sermon, after which the congregation would sing the hymn to make application of it to their own lives, much as is the case with "Am I a Soldier of the Cross." Whether or not Watts himself actually did this, use of the hymn in this way would certainly be a good idea for preachers today.

"Come Let Us Join Our Cheerful Songs," which Lionel Adey called "the most healthy-minded of all [hymns] on heaven,"[8] is a remarkably compressed version of the scriptural passage on which it is based. Though it uses five stanzas to paraphrase the three verses of the focal text, and though it includes some repetition of ideas,[9] the hymn is actually two words shorter than its model (115 words versus 117). Watts makes every word count, but, for all this economy, still vividly portrays John's vision of the innumerable host of heaven praising the Lamb who was slain that the people of earth might have salvation.

---

[7] Whenever God is referred to in third-person singular, the line of communication will almost invariably be human to human or human to inanimate object.

[8] Adey, *Class and Idol in the English Hymn*, 176.

[9] For example, the line "The whole Creation joyn in one" essentially repeats "Let all that dwell above the Skie / And Air, and Earth, and Seas" from the previous stanza.

6

COME SOUND HIS PRAISE ABROAD

Watts published "Come Sound His Praise Abroad" in *The Psalms of David Imitated* as the second of three paraphrases of Psalm 95, one each in common meter, short meter, and long meter. The three versions differ not only in their metrical schemes but also in the emphasis that is given to each text, as can be seen by their titles. Two of the titles indicate a suggested liturgical usage: the common meter rendering is called "A Psalm before Prayer," while the short meter paraphrase is "A Psalm before Sermon." The title of the long meter version is a summary of its subject matter, "Canaan lost thro' Unbelief; or, a Warning to Delaying Sinners."

"Come Sound His Praise Abroad" is the short meter arrangement of the psalm. It is given in six iambic stanzas employing cross rhyme.

Stanza 1
>   Come sound his Praise abroad,
>   And Hymns of Glory Sing:
> *Jehovah* is the sovereign God,
>   The universal King.

The opening stanza is based on Psalm 95:1-3:

> [1]O come, let us sing unto the LORD:
>   let us make a joyful noise to the rock of our salvation.
> [2]Let us come before his presence with thanksgiving,
>   and make a joyful noise unto him with psalms.

> [3]For the LORD is a great God,
>   and a great King above all gods.

In his first two lines, Watts maintains the parallelism of the Hebrew psalm but combines the first two verses into one, using as his cue for doing this the words "come" (in the first half of each verse) and "joyful noise" (in the second half of each verse). Perhaps significantly, the author changed the "psalms" of v. 2 into "Hymns"; that, indeed, was what Watts was doing in *The Psalms of David Imitated*—altering psalms into hymns.

In Watts's time, the term "Jehovah" as a translation of "Yahweh" in the Old Testament was a common name for God. This form of the Hebrew Tetragrammaton (YHWH) has fallen out of favor with biblical scholars but is difficult to replace in a hymn text because of its three syllables.[1] Perhaps it can continue to be sung with a "mental asterisk." At any rate, lines 3 and 4 are a clear summary of Psalm 95:3—there is no other god beside the Lord God, who is not only "sovereign" but "universal"; the latter word is an unusually long one for Watts.

Watts's opening stanza represents a slight change of focus from that of the psalm. Whereas the psalm calls on the faithful to "sing unto the Lord," Watts's text tells them to "sound his Praise abroad," suggesting that the singing is to be directed horizontally rather than vertically; that is, we are to sing God's praises to other people, or at least sing in their hearing. This perhaps implies that there is to be a missionary motive to the singing. To be sure, Watts was a Calvinist who believed that people were either elected by God to salvation or not, and to suggest that he felt the same imperative as that demonstrated in the missionary movements of the late eighteenth and nineteenth centuries would be anachronistic. However, Watts had a lifelong interest in spiritual conversion, as can be seen, for example, by his role in the publication of *A Faithful Narrative of the Surprizing [sic] Work of God in the Conversion of Many Hundred Souls in Northampton* [Massachusetts], *and the Neighbouring Town and Villages of New-Hampshire in New-England* (1737), an abridgement of a letter by Jonathan Edwards about the Great Awakening taking place in the American colonies.[2] At the very least, in his hymn, Watts supports the

---

[1] See chapter 15.
[2] *A Faithful Narrative of the Surprizing Work of God in the Conversion of Many Hundred Souls in Northampton, and the Neighbouring Towns and Villages of*

idea that believers are to proclaim the praises of the Lord in a public manner, hoping to lead others into joining in that praise.

Stanza 2

> He form'd the Deeps unknown;
> He gave the Seas their Bound;
> The watry [*sic*] Worlds are all his own,
> And all the solid Ground.

Having established that God's praise should be spread abroad because of who God is (sovereign and universal), Watts moves on to note that he is also worthy of praise because of what he has done, specifically, his work in creation. This stanza paraphrases vv. 4 and 5 of the psalm.

> [4]In his hand are the deep places of the earth:
> the strength of the hills is his also.
> [5]The sea is his, and he made it:
> and his hands formed the dry land.

The stanza is a relatively straightforward version of the psalm except that Watts omits the reference to the "strength of the hills," apparently subsuming this concept into the second half of v. 5 ("his hands formed the dry land"). As he sometimes did in preparing his version of a psalm, the author seems to allude to passages from other psalms in the text. For instance, "He gave the Seas their Bound"—an idea that is not directly noted in Psalm 95—is reminiscent of Psalm 104:9, which observes that God "hast set a bound [for the waters] that they may not pass over; that they turn not again to cover the earth." The use of anaphora ("He") reiterates exactly who can be credited with the creation of land and sea. In lines 3 and 4, the alliterative "watry Worlds" and the predominance of vowels and "soft" consonants to begin the other words suggest the gentle lapping of waves on the shore, but when one gets to "solid Ground" the very sound of the words suggests the firmness of earth.

New-Hampshire in New-England. In a Letter to the Revd. Dr. Benjamin Colman of Boston. Written by the Revd. Mr. Edwards, Minister of Northampton, on Nov. 6, 1736. And Published, with a Large Preface, by Dr. Watts and Dr. [John] Guyse (London, 1737).

Stanza 3

> Come, worship at his Throne,
> Come, bow before the Lord:
> We are his Works and not our own;
> He form'd us by his Word.

Stanza 3 reflects Psalm 95:6-7a.

> [6]O come, let us worship and bow down:
> let us kneel before the LORD our maker.
> [7]For he is our God;
> and we are the people of his pasture, and the
> sheep of his hand.

As he did in stanza 2, Watts uses an anaphora to open the stanza. Beginning consonant sounds also play an important role in the strophe, with lines 1 and 2 featuring plosive "k" and "b" sounds ("come" [twice], "bow," "before"), while the last two lines mainly glide through vowel and soft consonant sounds ("w," "n," "f").

Also like stanza 2, the author adds a thought that is not in the source verse, in this case setting up an antithesis by adding that we can take no credit for our creation ("We are his Works and not our own"). Here again, the author appears to draw upon a psalm other than the one he is ostensibly paraphrasing, in this case using not only Psalm 95:7 but also the very similar verse found at Psalm 100:3: "Know ye that the Lord he is God: it is he that hath made us, and not we ourselves; we are his people, and the sheep of his pasture."

Stanza 4

> To Day attend his Voice,
> Nor dare provoke his Rod;
> Come, like the People of his Choice,
> And own your gracious God.

To this point in the text Watts has remained relatively close to the ideas and even the actual wording of Psalm 95, with occasional insertions from other psalms. Beginning with stanza 4, he begins to depart more significantly from the literal psalm text. The stanza is based loosely on the last clause of Psalm 95:7–8.

> [7]To day if ye will hear his voice,
> [8]Harden not your heart, as in the provocation,
>   And as in the day of temptation in the wilderness:

The first line is obviously a close versification of v. 7b, but the second line is only tenuously related to v. 8, primarily through the word "provoke" ("provocation" in the psalm). In that verse, "the provocation" and "the day of temptation in the wilderness" are references to the nearly continual backsliding and complaining—not to mention the lapse into idolatry with the Golden Calf—of the people of Israel as they wandered in the desert after their delivery from Egyptian bondage. This identification is reflected in Watts's third line, when he admonishes "the People of his [God's] Choice" (i.e., the chosen people; see Deut 7:6, 14:2) to "own" (acknowledge) the God whose graciousness has been poured out upon them by freeing them from slavery and promising them a new land. Here Watts has inserted a new thought into the psalm: whereas the original contains only the idea of judgment for the hard hearts of the people, Watts inserts God's grace into the mix. There is still hope, if the people will only realize their status as the chosen ones and acknowledge their God.

Stanza 5

> But if your Ears refuse
> The Language of his Grace,
> And Hearts grow hard like stubborn Jews,
> That unbelieving Race.

The fifth stanza also draws part of its imagery from v. 8, particularly the idea of hearts growing hard. At the end of stanza 4, Watts has just held out hope that the people will return to their "gracious God." He then begins the next stanza with the small but important word "But": if you acknowledge God, all will be well, *but* if you "refuse" there will be consequences. Note that it is the "Ears" that refuse God; in other words, the people will not even listen to the One who created them and chose them for his own. If the ears refuse to hear "The Language of his Grace," the result will be hardened hearts.

It is uncomfortable to read or sing about the "stubborn Jews" being an "unbelieving Race." Two features of these lines should be observed. God is upbraiding his own beloved people for their stubbornness and hardness of heart. The problem is not so much with Watts as it is with the psalm itself, though of course he could perhaps have omitted this reference as he did in the common meter version of the psalm.

Second, and more importantly, the lines are not about the Jews but about the Christians who are singing the hymn. Note the simile: if *your* "Hearts grow hard" *like* the "stubborn Jews." Christians are being admonished to learn from the Old Testament Hebrews not to let their "Hearts grow hard." By "That unbelieving Race" Watts is referring to the fact that the Jews did not believe in Jesus as the Messiah.

Still, the language is problematic. As Stephen Orchard observed of similar references in other Watts texts, "This was not a conscious antisemitism in the modern sense but it is still anti-semitic." He then explains, "In his enthusiasm for the new Israel, and for protestant Britain's providential role, Watts lost sight of the Jews as a people. In this he was no different from most of his contemporaries who, if they thought about the different faiths to be found in the world at all, regarded them as unenlightened and at the mercy of God."[3] When Watts and other Christians of his time thought of the Jews, it was primarily as the people of the Old and New Testaments, not as an ethnic group living during the eighteenth century. Unfortunately, without this awareness, a phrase such as "That unbelieving Race" is certainly open to misunderstanding or mischaracterization, and the stanza is usually omitted.[4]

Though Watts ended stanza 5 with a period, it is not complete in itself, a fact that he acknowledged in the second edition of *The Psalms of David Imitated* (1719) by replacing the period with a semicolon. Thus stanzas 5 and 6 form a unit that cannot be broken without jeopardizing their meaning.

---

[3] Orchard, "The Hymns of Isaac Watts," 161.

[4] Note also the last stanza of Watts's short meter version of Psalm 106 (part 2): "Let *Israel* bless the Lord, / Who lov'd their antient Race; / And *Christians* join the solemn Word / *Amen* to all the Praise," and his note to this psalm that "*Tho'* the Jews *now seem to be cast off, yet the Apostle* Paul *assures us that* God hath not cast away his People whom he foreknew. *Rom.* 11. 2. *their unbelief and Absence from God is but for a Season, for they shall be recalled again.* v. 25. 26."

Stanza 6

> The Lord in Vengeance drest
> Will lift his Hand and swear,
> *"You that despise my promis'd Rest,*
> *"Shall have no Portion there.["]*

Watts closes his hymn by paraphrasing the last verse of the psalm (v. 11), "Unto whom I sware in my wrath that they should not enter into my rest." The author's imagination paints for us a scene in a courtroom. The Lord is "drest" in "Vengeance" (suggesting a judge's robe). He then raises his hand and pronounces sentence on the accused. Though God has "promis'd Rest" to his people they have not listened to him and will be condemned to miss the "Portion" of blessing and grace he has prepared for them. The legal language reflects the seriousness of the offense in refusing God's mercy.

"Come Sound His Praise Abroad" maintains a closer relationship to its source psalm than some of Watts's other "imitations." Like its antecedent, the hymn moves from a call to praise God both for who he is and for what he has done into warnings about how God's people should relate to him. Since, as noted above, Watts suggested that the hymn was intended to be sung "before Sermon," presumably the preacher would pick up the idea of judgment in the last two stanzas to begin his homily.

Without the sermonic or psalmodic context, the hymn appears to end on a "down" note. It is probably at least partly for this reason that the hymn is no longer as widely anthologized as it once was. The website www.hymnary.org provides a chart tracking the appearance of this and other texts in American hymnals. Between 1750 and approximately 1875, the lyric seems to have been printed quite frequently. After 1875, the number of publications drops off dramatically until the late twentieth century, when it seems to have seen a resurgence of interest, without, however, returning to the peaks it experienced in the eighteenth and early nineteenth centuries.[5] It should also be pointed out that most of the American anthologies have—probably appropriately—dropped the last two stanzas (sometimes the last three). This leaves a short but very useable hymn of praise and admonition.

---

[5] www.hymnary.org. Accessed February 7, 2018.

While there is little reason to regret the loss of the last two stanzas, it must be remarked that we should not eliminate all hymns or stanzas that deal with judgment. Admittedly, this is not a popular or pleasant subject to sing about; it is much easier to sing praise or prayer. Still, judgment is a reality that needs expression in our worship. If, perhaps, these particular stanzas by Watts are no longer considered suitable for singing, this does not mean that they cannot be used in private devotion. After all, if the subject of judgment was good enough for the psalmist, it should be good enough for us.

7

COME, WE THAT LOVE THE LORD

As is noted in various chapters throughout this book, Isaac Watts wrote about several subjects that either appealed to him more directly than others or in which he achieved greater than ordinary heights of hymn writing. Among these topics are the creation and sustaining of the natural order, the sacrificial death of Jesus on the cross, the joy that comes from knowing God, and heaven and the life to come. One thinks, for instance, of "I Sing th'Almighty Power of God," "When I Survey the Wondrous Cross," "Joy to the World, the Lord Is Come," and "There Is a Land of Pure Delight," respectively. However, while Watts generally dealt with a single central subject in his lyrics, in several of them he at least touched upon two or more of these themes. "Come, We That Love the Lord" is one of these texts.

"Come, We That Love the Lord" is titled "Heavenly Joy on Earth" in Watts's *Hymns and Spiritual Songs* (no. 30 in Book II). Since the hymns in the second book were not based on specific Scriptures, Watts did not provide a biblical reference for it.

Watts chose short meter and an iambic poetic pattern for the text. Iambic meter is often used for texts of an inviting or supplicatory nature such as this one. The brevity of lines 1, 2, and 4 in each stanza, the consistent forward pull of the iambs, and the preponderance of true rhymes give the hymn a sense of directness and vigor.[1]

---

[1] The only false rhymes in the forty lines of the text are "Place" and "less" (st. 2), and "rise" and "bliss" (st. 7).

Stanza 1

> Come, we that love the Lord,
> And let our Joys be known;
> Join in a Song with sweet Accord,
> And thus surround the Throne.

The first stanza is a good example of the basic simplicity of Watts's hymnic writing. Except for "Accord" and "surround," the words are all monosyllables and ones that would largely be familiar from everyday speech.

This strophe is a straightforward invitation for those who "love the Lord" to express their joys in him. But the purpose is more than simply to articulate personal feeling; the singers are to make these joys "known," to make others aware of their love for and joy in the Lord. Furthermore, they are to be in "Accord" with one another—to be in "Agreement or Contract."[2] The last line is slightly ambiguous: are the singers to surround the throne or are their songs to surround the throne? The answer is probably "yes"!

Stanza 2

> The Sorrows of the Mind
> Be banisht from the Place;
> Religion never was design'd
> To make our Pleasures less.

In the second edition of *Hymns and Spiritual Songs*, stanza 2 was bracketed, indicating that it could be omitted. Perhaps the stanza is less suited to congregational singing than its surroundings, but it still has some important things to say.

In the first place, Watts says that the "Sorrows of the Mind" should be banished from the place of worship. This is not the same thing as saying that there is no place in worship for sorrow. How else should we react to our sins or to the crucifixion of Christ? As human beings, we cannot but be sorrowful in our spirits and emotions at times. What the author probably intended by the phrase "Sorrows of the Mind" is sorrow on which we dwell inordinately, sorrow that we keep mulling over and

---

[2] N. Bailey, *An Universal Etymological English Dictionary*.

that comes between us and God. It is also important to note that these "Sorrows" are contrasted with the "Joys" (not happiness) of the first stanza. Happiness is shallow and fleeting; joy is more deep-seated and long-lasting. Watts is telling us that sorrow is wrong only when it gets in the way of the basic, deep-seated, long-lasting joy of the redeemed.

The author also comments on the role of religion: religion was not designed to take away pleasure but to redirect it. As the psalmist put it, "Thou wilt shew me the path of life: in thy presence is fulness of joy; at thy right hand there are pleasures for evermore" (16:11). Watts expounded further on this idea in one of his sermons.

> Christianity does not abridge us of the common Comforts of Flesh and Blood, Nor lay an unreasonable Restraint upon any natural Appetite; but it teaches us to live like Men, and not like Brutes; to regulate and manage our animal Nature with its Desires and Inclinations, so as to enjoy Life in the most proper and becoming Manner; to eat and drink, and taste the Bounties of Providence, to the Honour of our Creator, and to the best Interest of our Souls.[3]

As Watts sees it, religion does not take pleasure away from Christians but simply diverts it from the things of the world to the things of God.

Stanza 3

> Let those refuse to sing
> That never knew our God,
> But Favorites of the heavenly King
> May speak their Joys abroad.

One of the "Pleasures" of which Watts speaks in stanza 2 is singing, and in the third stanza he gives direct attention to the matter. In 1690, a Baptist named Isaac Marlow published a book titled *A Discourse Concerning Singing in the Publick Worship of God in the Gospel-Church* in which he questioned "Whether David's Psalms, or any humane prescribed, or precomposed Matter, may or ought not to be vocally sung by all the Church together, as part of the publick, constant and ordinary worship of God,

---

[3] *Sermons on Various Subjects*, 2:23.

instituted in his Gospel-Church."[4] Marlow followed the earlier example of Ulrich Zwingli in claiming that New Testament references to singing (e.g., Col 3:16) referred to an "inward expression," not to a vocal utterance, and that singing aloud should be excluded from Christian worship. Marlow was answered by the London Baptist pastor Benjamin Keach in *The Breach Repaired in God's Worship* (1691), and a pamphlet war soon erupted among Baptists over the issue and lasted through much of the 1690s.

All this was going on during Watts's teens and early adult years, and while he was not a Baptist but a Congregationalist, his own denomination probably experienced some of the same division over the issue, though perhaps not in as public a manner. It could well be that Watts had that situation in mind as he was writing this stanza, perhaps taking a sly dig at the nonsingers.

At any rate, the implication of the stanza is clear: one way we can identify those who know God is by whether they sing to him or not. Not every believer has a beautiful voice, but each one should have a song. In the last line, the idea is again expressed that our joy (singing) is not simply for our own pleasure or expression but is a means to tell others of the Lord. The word "Favorites" is now often changed to "children" and "That" to "who."

The thoughts in this stanza from "Come, We that Love the Lord" are paralleled to a remarkable degree by the first stanza of another text from *Hymns and Spiritual Songs*.

> Let them neglect thy Glory, Lord,
>   Who never knew thy Grace,
> But our loud Song shall still record
>   The wonders of thy Praise.

Titled "*Praise to God for Creation and Redemption*," "Let Them Neglect Thy Glory, Lord" goes on to give "All Glory to th'UNITED Three, / The Undivided One" who "form'd us by a word" and—in language that is reminiscent of the later "Joy to the World"—calls on "Earth and Skies" to "Repeat the joyful Sound" and let "Rocks, Hills and Vales reflect the Voice / In one Eternal Round."

---

[4] Marlow, *A Discourse Concerning Singing*, 5.

Stanza 4

> The God that rules on high,
>   And thunders when he please,
> That rides upon the stormy Skie,
>   And manages the Seas.

Like stanza 2, stanza 4 was marked in the second edition for possible omission.[5] Perhaps the deletion was suggested because this stanza seems abruptly to change the focus from encouraging the saints to express their joy to describing some of the attributes of God's power. The stanza is also an incomplete sentence, the thought of which is not finished until stanza 5. There is also a grammatical problem (at least for modern singers) in that "please" should be plural.

The stanza is essentially a cento of quotations from the psalms, with each line drawing upon a specific verse for both its content and much of its language.

1) The Lord hath prepared his throne in the heavens; and his kingdom ruleth over all (Ps 103:19).
2) The voice of the Lord is upon the waters: the God of glory thundereth (Ps 29:3a).
3) Extol him that rideth upon the heavens (Ps 68:4b; see also v. 33a and 104:3).
4) Thou rulest the raging of the sea: when the waves thereof arise, thou stillest them (Ps 89:9).

There is a marked similarity between the last two lines of this stanza and the end of the first stanza of William Cowper's later hymn, "God Moves in a Mysterious Way," initially published in John Newton and Cowper's *Olney Hymns* (1779) though the sea and sky images are reversed.

> God moves in a mysterious way,
>   His wonders to perform;
> He plants his footsteps in the sea,
>   And rides upon the storm.

---

[5] Watts also corrected the spelling of "Skie."

Perhaps this is an instance of one great hymn writer either consciously or unconsciously echoing another one.

Stanza 5

> This awful God is ours,
>   Our Father and our Love,
> He shall send down his heav'nly Pow'rs
>   To carry us above.

The fifth stanza was not designated for potential omission but if the fourth stanza is omitted, retention of this one makes little sense: describing God as "awful" fits better after describing him as ruling on high, thundering, riding on the storm, and controlling the seas than it does after an invocation to speak of joy in his presence (as in stanza 3). As noted in a previous chapter, Bailey defined "awful" as "terrible, apt to strike a Terror into; to be feared, or revered." The concept of God's being "awful" is not a popular one in the twenty-first century, but when one thinks of a being who has the characteristics listed in stanza 4 one cannot help but respect and revere—and yes, even fear—that Deity.

Watts does not leave matters there, however, for in the very next line he calls God "Our Father and our Love." Our relationship with God is one of honor for his might and power but also one of love as our caring Parent. While lines 3 and 4 seem poetically weak, they do carry an important message: one of the marks of God's care for us is that he will use his divine power to take us to himself.

Stanza 6

> There we shall see his Face,
>   And never, never sin:
> There from the Rivers of his Grace
>   Drink endless Pleasures in.

The sixth stanza continues the thought from stanza 5 of being swept up into God's presence. Watts uses epizeuxis—immediate repetition of a word ("never")—to emphasize that there will be no more sin in heaven. The last two lines allude to Revelation 22:1 ("pure river of water of life, clear as crystal, proceeding out of the throne of God and of the Lamb") and to Psalm 36:8b ("thou shalt make them drink of the river of thy pleasures").[6]

Stanza 7

> Yes, and before we rise
> To that immortal State,
> The Thoughts of such amazing Bliss
> Should constant Joys create.

In stanza 7, Watts observes that, while a future in heaven will be "amazing Bliss," contemplation of the reward to come should bring us "constant Joys" while we are still on earth. The stanza opens somewhat ungracefully with awkward accentuation of the first two syllables, "**Yes, and** be-**fore** we **rise**." The first four syllables should probably be thought of as a choriambus ("**Yes**, and be-**fore**") but there seems to be no reason in the text for Watts to have used this modulation. The rhyming of "Bliss" with "rise" is frankly bizarre. Perhaps because of this awkwardness and the fact that three successive stanzas say essentially the same thing the stanza is generally omitted.

Stanza 8

> The Men of Grace have found
> Young Glory here below,
> Young Glory here on earthly Ground
> From Faith and Hope may grow.

The eighth stanza seems to have given Watts a good bit of trouble. As printed in the first edition of *Hymns and Spiritual Songs*, the stanza seems ungainly and the meaning is unclear. "Young" is too strong a word to be sung on an unaccented note in an iambic tune. And what exactly is "Young Glory," used not once but twice in an anaphora?

---

[6] Note the similarity of this stanza to the first strophe of a later hymn that is sometimes attributed to the American John Leland: "O when shall I see Jesus, / And dwell with him above, / To drink the flowing Fountains, / Of everlasting Love. / When shall I be deliver'd, / From this vain World of Sin? / And with my blessed Jesus / Drink endless Pleasure in" (quoted from *The Christian's Duty*, 2nd ed., 1801). Leland's hymn was first published in Eleazar Clay's *Hymns and Spiritual Songs* (1793).

Watts recognized these difficulties and, in the second edition, revised the middle lines as "Glory begun below / Celestial Fruits on earthly Ground." These changes help clarify the meaning of the stanza, but the awkward accentuation is not helped by the revision to the second line. Perhaps because of these problems, in the second edition Watts indicated by brackets that the stanza could be omitted.

The stanza does have some important things to say, however. The first half indicates that the joys that should come from knowing about a future in heaven (mentioned in stanza 7) have indeed already been found on earth by "Men of Grace." And how is this "Young Glory" (or these "Celestial Fruits") to be found? By "Faith and Hope": if we want to gain a foretaste of heaven, it will be by exercising our faith and our hope.

Stanza 9

> The Hill of *Zion* yields
> A thousand sacred Sweets
> Before we reach the heavenly Fields,
> Or walk the golden Streets.

In stanza 9, Watts continues the emphasis of the previous two strophes on the foretaste of glory to be had here on earth. Since, however, stanzas 7 and 8 are often omitted, this one frequently serves as the only reference to the subject in modern congregational singing.

"Zion" has often been used by hymn writers in three different senses: as a reference to the earthly city of Jerusalem (built on Mount Zion), as a synonym for the church, or as a metaphor for heaven. The first meaning was employed by Watts in his version of Psalm 76 from *The Psalms of David Imitated*: "In Judah God of Old was known; / His Name in Israel great; In Salem stood his holy Throne, / And Zion was his Seat" (st. 1). In his hymn "How Honourable Is the Place" (*Hymns and Spiritual Songs*), titled "The Safety and Protection of the Church," Watts employed it in the second sense when he called the church "Zion the Glory of the Earth, / And Beauty of the Land." In "Come, We That Love the Lord," Zion appears as a reference to heaven. However, as noted also in stanzas 7 and 8, this heaven yields its "sacred Sweets" even before we arrive there. The phrase "Hill of Zion" may be a reflection of Psalm 2:6 ("Yet have I set my king upon my holy hill of Zion").

The Bible never uses the phrase "heavenly Fields" to describe paradise. In constructing this expression, Watts perhaps had in mind Jesus' parable in Matthew 13, where he likens the "kingdom of heaven" to a "treasure hid in a field" (v. 44).[7] The reference to "golden Streets" is from Revelation 21:21: "and the street of the city [the new Jerusalem] was pure gold, as it were transparent glass."

Stanza 10

> Then let our Songs abound,
> And every Tear be dry;
> We're marching thro' *Immanuel's* Ground
> To a more joyful Sky.

Watts's beginning the last stanza with the word "then" implies that songs should "abound" and "tears be dry" as a consequence of the "heaven on earth" that Christians can experience through their faith and hope (st. 9). J. R. Watson points out that the linkage between "abounding songs" and the drying of tears contains "echoes of the magnificent Chapter 35 of Isaiah," especially v. 10, "And the ransomed of the Lord shall return, and come to Zion with songs and everlasting joy upon their heads: they shall obtain joy and gladness, and sorrow and sighing shall flee away."[8] Watts reused the phrase "And every Tear be dry" to conclude a hymn in the second edition of *Hymns and Spiritual Songs* (1709), "How Are Thy Glories Here Display'd" (6:4).

Even as we tread this world, we know that it is "Immanuel's Ground." "Immanuel" is a Hebrew word meaning "God with us" and is used twice in Isaiah (7:14 and 8:8). Because of its presence in Isaiah's prophecy of the Messiah, the term is often applied to Jesus.

Watts's employment of the term "marching" is interesting. Bailey defines "to march" as "to go, to set forwards as an Army does." "Marching" adds an element of color that would not be present if the "tamer" term "walking" (which would fit metrically) were used. The movement through "Immanuel's Ground" is neither a mere stroll nor a frantic run—it is a purposeful, orderly, confident setting out on a journey. Though, as noted by Bailey, "march" often has a military context, that is not invariably the case

---

[7] Matthew 13 includes two other comparisons of heaven to a field (vv. 24, 31).

[8] Watson, *An Annotated Anthology of Hymns*, 129.

(consider, for example, the "freedom marches" of the American civil rights movement), and Watts probably did not have in mind the idea of soldiering so much as that of determination and unity.

In the second edition, Watts altered the last line to "To fairer Worlds on high." While the change improved the poetry and made the line more singable (by replacing the unaccented second syllable with an accented one), it upset Watts's original balance with the opening stanza by removing the word "joy" ("And let our Joys be known"—"To a more joyful Sky").

If one word could be used to describe this hymn, it would be "joy." Some form of the word is used in four of the ten original stanzas, the emphasis in every stanza is on the bliss that can be experienced in the present life as well as that to come, and even the short meter and iambic metrical patterns seem to reflect a sense of joyful expectation.[9] At the same time, the hymn touches upon God's control of the natural order (st. 4) and the anticipation of heaven (st. 10).

One more word should be said about the hymnic meter Watts chose for this text. Short meter is often a difficult one for a hymn writer because the brevity of the lines does not give much scope for elaboration. Every word has to be carefully chosen and placed to attain both meaningfulness of content and beauty of diction while avoiding "filler" words and pious platitudes. In truth, Watts was not entirely successful with this hymn. The fact that he provided ten stanzas suggests that he felt the need for a broader scope, but since three of them say much the same thing, the reason for his use of this expanded palette is unclear. Furthermore, several of the original stanzas are awkwardly written.

Watts recognized some of these deficiencies. The revisions to and suggestions for deletion of stanzas he made in the second edition of *Hymns and Spiritual Songs* considerably improved the piece. Subsequent editors have made judicious selections of the remaining strophes (usually the original stanzas 1, 3, 9, and 10), and the result is an exuberant, pithy, and joyous invitation for God's people to raise their voices in praise. One cannot ask for much more from 104 syllables.[10]

---

[9] In addition to stanzas 1 and 10, the word appears in stanzas 3 and 7.

[10] In the nineteenth century, the American gospel song author and composer Robert Lowry added a chorus, "We're marching to Zion, beautiful, beautiful Zion; we're marching upward to Zion, the beautiful city of God," to Watts's text and wrote the accompanying tune MARCHING TO ZION.

8

FROM ALL THAT DWELL BELOW THE SKIES

Psalm 117 forms part of the Egyptian Hallel (Pss 113–118) and is the shortest chapter in the Bible, consisting of only two verses.[1] Watts included three paraphrases of the psalm in *The Psalms of David Imitated*, one each in common meter, long meter, and short meter. "From All That Dwell Below the Skies" is the long meter version. Austin C. Lovelace called Watts "The most successful [hymn] writer in Long Meter" because "a large canvas was suited to his lofty theme of God as Creator and Sovereign Lord," naming this hymn, as well as "High in the Heav'ns, Eternal God," "Jesus Shall Reign Where'er the Sun," and "When I Survey the Wondrous Cross," as prime examples of his claim.[2]

"From All That Dwell Below the Skies" is in iambic poetic meter. In the first stanza, however, reading lines 2 and 3 as iambic means that the unimportant word "the" receives a stress. If the opening of these verses is read as a choriambus (e.g., **Let** the Cre-a-tor's **Praise** a-**rise**) this not only solves the accent problem but emphasizes the celebratory nature of the lines through the opening dactylic foot.

The rhyme scheme of the hymn is AABB. This rhyming pattern is particularly characteristic of hymns that have long lines, such as this one; its purpose is to aid the reader or singer in anticipating the next rhyme and memorizing the text.

---

[1] See chapter 22 for a description of the Egyptian Hallel.
[2] Lovelace, *The Anatomy of Hymnody*, 26.

Stanza 1
> From all that dwell below the Skies
> Let the Creator's Praise arise:
> Let the Redeemer's Name be sung
> Thro' every Land, by every Tongue.

Stanza 1 of Watts's hymn paraphrases Psalm 117:1. In the KJV, the verse contains only twelve words:

> O praise the LORD, all ye nations:
>> Praise him all ye people.

Watts uses exactly twice that number for his first stanza.

The overall structure of this stanza is interesting. The synonymous parallelism of the psalm verse is matched by the parallel structure of the two halves of the stanza, but the British author changes the order of the thoughts in the first two lines (essentially making a chiasmus with the psalm text) while keeping the order the same for the following lines.[3]

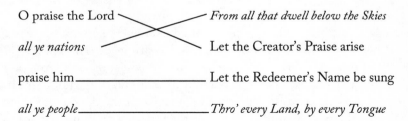

This change in the order of the ideas also creates a *chiasmus* within the first stanza.

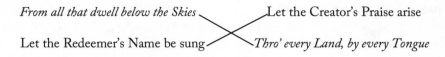

Thus, the thoughts in the psalm verse might be diagrammed as ABAB, while in the Watts stanza they are ABBA. The parallelism of the

---

[3] In the following examples, lines containing similar thoughts are marked by plain or italic type.

two B lines in Watts's stanza is made more explicit through anaphora, both lines beginning with "Let the."

Watts fleshes out the psalmist's word "Lord" by naming two of God's characteristic and important roles as Creator and Redeemer (note the position of these words in the center of the middle lines). Many Old Testament passages refer to God (the Father) as a Redeemer, but the word is not used in that form in the KJV of the New Testament. Nevertheless, it is tempting to see in the use of "Creator" and "Redeemer" an allusion to both the Old and the New Testament, the Father as the Creator and the Son as the Redeemer.

Three factors support such an interpretation: (1) While "redeemer" is not used directly in the New Testament (KJV), "redeem" or some other form of the word appears several times in reference to Jesus (for example, Gal 3:13; Titus 2:14); (2) one of Watts's goals was to make the psalms fit into the New Testament dispensation; and (3) the term "redeemer" was commonly applied to Jesus both by Watts and by his contemporaries.[4] Of course, it should be stressed that Watts and other orthodox Christians see the Father and Son each as being active in *both* the creation and redemption.

Stanza 2
    Eternal are thy Mercies, Lord;
    Eternal Truth attends thy Word;
    Thy Praise shall sound from Shore to Shore
    Till Suns shall rise and set no more.

Verse 2 of the psalm on which Watts based his hymn makes use of complementary parallelism, in which the second line extends the thought

---

[4] Two examples of Watts's usage will suffice. The preface to *The Psalms of David Imitated* asks "What need is there that I should wrap up the shining Honours of my Redeemer in the dark and shadowy Language of a Religion that is now for ever abolished; especially when Christians are so vehemently warned in the Epistles of St. *Paul* against a Judaizing Spirit in their Worship as well as Doctrine?" The first part of Watts's long meter version of Psalm 8, stanza 4, applies the psalm to Jesus' triumphal entry into Jerusalem with these lines: "Children amidst thy Temple throng / To see their great Redeemer's Face; / The Son of David is their Song, / And young Hosanna's fill the Place."

of the first:

> For his merciful kindness is great toward us:
> and the truth of the LORD endureth for ever.

Watts picks up the two important words in these half verses, "merciful" and "truth," to structure the opening lines of the stanza, but through another use of anaphora ("Eternal") he changes the focus slightly by making it not only God's "truth" but also God's "merciful kindness" ("Mercies") that "endureth for ever."

The last half of stanza 2 covers the closing words of the psalm ("Praise ye the Lord") and expands further upon the "endureth for ever" idea. The change expresses that God's mercy and truth are not only eternal ("Till Suns shall rise and set no more") but are also universal ("from Shore to Shore"), a concept that is not found directly in Psalm 117. There is a striking similarity between these lines and the last two lines in stanza 1 of "Jesus Shall Reign Where'er the Sun": "His Kingdom stretch from Shore to Shore, / Till Moons shall wax and wane no more." Comparable lines can also be found in other psalm versions: "Where e'er the Sun shall rise or set, / The Nations shall his Praise repeat" and "His Mercies ever shall endure / When Suns and Moons shall shine no more."[5] One thing that sets line 3 in "From All That Dwell Below the Skies" apart from these others is its extensive use of sibilants ("Thy Praise shall sound from Shore to Shore"), perhaps suggesting the breaking of waves on a coastline.

There is no way of being sure in what order Watts versified the psalms and thus it is impossible to say which of these similar lines came first. However, the comparisons do reveal that, when Watts wrote a good phrase, he did not hesitate to use it again in a different context.

Another aspect of the second stanza that is worthy of note is the change Watts made in the line of communication. Whereas both verses of the psalm consist of human-to-human communication—people calling on other people to praise the Lord, with an explanation of why they should do so—the second stanza alters this to a human-to-God orientation. Instead of being merely a *call* to praise, the stanza is now an *expres-*

---

[5] See, respectively, "Ye Servants of th'Almighty King" (Ps 113, LM, st. 1) and "Give to Our God Immortal Praise" (Ps 136, LM, st. 4).

sion of praise. The hymn thus makes an excellent beginning to a service of worship, in which people call upon one another to praise God (st. 1) and then join in doing so (st. 2).

In many of his psalm versions, Watts's task was to compress and summarize the thoughts expressed in the Old Testament passage. Because of its brevity, Psalm 117 presented him with a different challenge: how to write a text that is long enough to make a hymn that is satisfying to sing but is not padded with irrelevant words and thoughts. That he succeeded admirably is evident from the widespread use the hymn has received over the past three hundred years.

9

HOW BEAUTEOUS ARE THEIR FEET

"How Beauteous Are Their Feet" is a short meter, iambic hymn that was first printed as number ten in Book I of *Hymns and Spiritual Songs* (1707). One feature that sets this text apart from many of the others in this study is that it does not use cross rhyme but a rhyme scheme of ABCB.

Watts titled the hymn "The Blessedness of Gospel-Times Or, The Revelation of Christ in Jews and Gentiles" and listed the Scripture basis as "Isa. 5. 2, 7, 8, 9, 10. Matt. 13. 16, 17." However, the Isaiah reference was misprinted and should have read "Isa. 52. 7, 8, 9, 10."[1]

In some respects, "How Beauteous Are Their Feet" is similar in procedure to Watts's paraphrasing of the psalms, in which he incorporates New Testament verses and allusions into an Old Testament text. As in the psalm versions, the basic framework for the hymn is the Old Testament passage (Isaiah, in this case) but some of the lines and stanzas point more directly toward New Testament texts (here, the Gospels of Matthew and, as will be shown below, Luke).

Stanza 1
> How beauteous are their Feet
> Who stand on *Zion*'s Hill,
> Who bring Salvation on their Tongues,
> And Words of Peace reveal!

---

[1] Interestingly, the error was not corrected in the second edition (1709).

The first stanza paraphrases Isaiah 52:7: "How beautiful upon the mountains are the feet of him that bringeth good tidings, that publisheth peace; that bringeth good tidings of good, that publisheth salvation; that saith unto Zion, Thy God reigneth!"

The stanza sets up a pattern that will be seen in the next three strophes. Each begins with the word "How," followed by a descriptive adjective, then a noun that stands for a physical attribute. In the present stanza, the noun is "Feet," which, closely following the Isaiah passage, are described as "beauteous." Watts retains the exclamation mark that closes the Scripture verse, giving a heightened sense of the joy brought by salvation. The verse from Isaiah was quoted in Romans 10:15, but, unlike his procedure in some of the psalm versions, the author does not appear to have referred directly to the New Testament passage. Nevertheless, it was undoubtedly in the back of his mind as he wrote this stanza.

Stanza 2
>How charming is their Voice!
>How sweet the Tidings are!
>"*Zion*, behold thy Saviour-King,
>"He Reigns and Triumphs here.["]

Stanza 2 emphasizes the preacher's voice, which is described as "charming" and the source of "sweet Tidings." Like stanza 1, it is based on Isaiah 52:7, focusing particularly on the last clause, "that saith unto Zion, Thy God reigneth!" and again retaining the exclamation marks.

It seems likely that Watts did not rely solely upon the Isaiah 52 verse for this stanza but also had in mind the similar passage in Isaiah 40:9. Here one finds a specific reference to the word "voice" ("lift up thy voice with strength"), which is not found in Isaiah 52:7, and the phrase "Behold your God," which accords more closely with line 3 of the hymn; the last line is obviously derived from the principal source for the hymn. Essentially, Watts has melded two verses from Isaiah into a single reference.

The rhyming words of stanzas 1 and 2 are worthy of notice. Both stanzas make use of dissonance, in which only the consonant sounds that end the words are alike ("Hill" / "reveal" and "are" / "here"). This looseness contrasts with the remaining stanzas, which all contain true rhymes.

Stanza 3

> How happy are our Ears
> That hear this joyful Sound
> Which Kings and Prophets waited for,
> And sought, but never found!

The third stanza turns from describing the preacher to characterizing the hearers of the message. It is at this point that Watts departs from the Old Testament to insert passages from the New Testament into the hymn. The reference he gives in the title is Matthew 13:16-17: "But blessed are your eyes for they see: and your ears, for they hear. For verily I say unto you, That many prophets and righteous men have desired to see those things which ye see, and have not seen them; and to hear those things which ye hear, and have not heard them." From v. 16 he derives the "Ears"—which are not mentioned in the Isaiah passage—that are the focus of the stanza. The opening lines are also similar to Psalm 89:15a, "Blessed is the people that know the joyful sound" ("blessed" and "happy" are synonyms), which Watts might have used as source material not only for this hymn but for "Salvation! O the Joyful Sound!" as well (see ch. 17). The "Ears" of the listeners are "happy" to "hear this joyful Sound" that the preacher is proclaiming.

Watts's apparently encyclopedic knowledge of the Scriptures is well demonstrated by this stanza, for, though he claimed the Matthew passage as his source, he appears to have drawn also from Luke 10:24, where the "righteous men" of Matthew are replaced by "kings," as in Watts's text: "For I tell you, that many prophets and kings have desired to see those things which ye see, and have not seen them; and to hear those things which ye hear, and have not heard them." In keeping with the "Ears" of the opening line, lines 3 and 4 emphasize the portions of the verses from Matthew and Luke that describe "those things...which ye...have not heard."

Stanza 4

> How blessed are our Eyes
> That see this Heav'nly Light;
> Prophets and Kings desir'd it long
> But dy'd without the sight!

Watts now moves to the eyes of those to whom the gospel message is proclaimed. The gospel has been transformed from words into light; this is not just any light, it is "Heav'nly Light." The author repeats the "Kings and Prophets" from stanza 3 but, in good chiastic fashion, reverses them to "Prophets and Kings" (this is actually the order of the words in Luke 10:24).

Stanza 5

> The Watchmen join their Voice,
> And tuneful Notes imploy [*sic*];
> *Jerusalem* breaks forth in Songs,
> And Desarts [*sic*] learn the Joy.

Watts returns to the Isaiah passage for stanza 6, paraphrasing Isaiah 52:8-9:

> [8]Thy watchmen shall lift up the voice; with the voice together shall they sing: for they shall see eye to eye, when the LORD shall bring again Zion.
> [9]Break forth into joy, sing together, ye waste places of Jerusalem: for the LORD hath comforted his people, he hath redeemed Jerusalem."

An important feature of this stanza is the change that the hymn writer makes in the verb tenses from the future to the present. The watchmen *do* (not *shall*) "join their Voice," they *do* "imploy" "tuneful Notes," etc. The implication is that Isaiah's prophecy has now been fulfilled: the gospel is being proclaimed through the itinerancy and voices of preachers and witnessed to by the ears and eyes of the people. This is cause for breaking out into song. Even the "Desarts" will "Break forth" into song once they "learn the Joy."

Stanza 6

> The Lord makes bare his Arm
> Thro' all the Earth abroad,
> Let ev'ry Nation now behold
> Their Saviour and their God.

Stanza 6 paraphrases Isaiah 52:10: "The Lord hath made bare his holy arm in the eyes of all the nations; and all the ends of the earth shall see the salvation of our God." Watts equates the Lord's baring of "his holy arm" with the spread of the gospel message. Baring the arm implies that a person is making clear his or her intention and preparing for action. In modern terms, it might be said that the person is "rolling up their sleeves." This phrase is used to show that the person is preparing to engage in some activity and is getting out of the way anything that might interfere with the activity. The implication of the hymn (and the Isaiah passage) is that the Lord has revealed his intentions to "all the Earth," calling for a response for "ev'ry Nation" to acknowledge "Their Saviour and their God."

As noted above, a part of Watts's title for "How Beauteous Are Their Feet" was "The Revelation of Christ in Jews and Gentiles." Perhaps a better way of expressing the title would have been "The Revelation of Christ *to* Jews and Gentiles," for the hymn is more about the proclamation of the gospel than it is about the reflection of the gospel in "Jews and Gentiles." It is also rather curious that, in a hymn text about the telling of the gospel message, there is not a single mention of "Jesus" or "Christ." To be sure, the word "Saviour" appears twice and "Christ" is found in the title, giving the hymn the appropriate context. However, the title has generally been omitted in publications other than editions of Watts's own *Hymns and Spiritual Songs*. The hymn works more by allusion and metaphor than by direct statement, which is perhaps an important corrective for our overly prosaic age.

It can be imagined what the Isaiah passage—and consequently the hymn he wrote based on it—must have meant personally to Watts, a preacher and pastor himself, who probably equated "Zion's Hill" with the pulpit of his own church from which he sought to proclaim "Salvation" and "Words of Peace." One wonders how much this hymn might have meant in particular to Watts during the period of his extended illness in 1712–1716 when he was unable to preach in his own church. Watts was determined to serve in whatever capacity he could, whether that meant through his pulpit ministry or his writing ministry. When one door was closed to him, he found another. That is a good model for Christians in all ages and stations in life.

10

I SING TH'ALMIGHTY POWER OF GOD

"I Sing th'Almighty Power of God" was published in Watts's *Divine Songs Attempted in Easy Language for the Use of Children* (1715). This book was the first English-language collection of sacred songs designed specifically for children. It became spectacularly successful, by one reckoning achieving more than 660 editions.[1]

Watts dedicated the volume to Sarah, Mary, and Elizabeth Abney, the daughters of Sir Thomas Abney, with whose family he resided for thirty-six years. In the dedication, which is dated June 18, 1715, Watts acknowledges the ministrations of the girls' father and mother—as well as the daughters themselves—during his illness and compliments the girls for their "Knowledge of Religion" and "Memory of Divine things both in Verse and Prose." He further commends them for honoring him by "learning by heart so large a number of the Hymns I have publish'd."

According to the preface, "The greatest part of this little Book was composed several Years ago, at the request of a Friend, who has been long engag'd in the Work of Catechising a very great Number of Children of all kinds, and with abundant Skill and Success." As he had in

---

[1] This figure is based on the bibliography of *Divine Songs* editions by Stone, *The Divine and Moral Songs of Isaac Watts*, 45–93, and its 1929 unpublished supplement. Pafford observes that Stone's bibliography must be used with caution, both because of what is included and what is not (Pafford, 1–2, 61–63, 275–78). For a more recent and more focused bibliography, see Tielke Uvin, *A Descriptive Bibliography of British and Irish Editions of Isaac Watts's Divine Songs (1715-ca. 1830)*, https://biblio.ugent.be/publication/8633724 (accessed February 9, 2020), which catalogs 264 items (p. 3) but does not include any from the US.

Hymns and Spiritual Songs, the author noted his attempt to "sink the Language," in this case "to the Level of a Child's Understanding." That this was a volume that was intended for singing, not merely reading, is evident from his observation that the poems were written in such a way that they could be sung "to the most usual Psalm Tunes."

At the conclusion of the preface Watts indicated that he had appended some "Sonnets on Moral Subjects for Children" in the hope that "some fitter Pen" would be thus challenged "to write a little Book of them." "My Talent doth not lie that way," he noted, and—though he was to live another thirty-three years—he claimed to be "a Man on the Borders of the Grave" who "has other Work" to do. Besides, if he were to engage in more verse writing, he would spend it "in finishing the Psalms, which I have so long promised the World"; four years later he kept this promise by publishing *The Psalms of David Imitated in the Language of the New Testament* (1719).[2]

To modern eyes and ears, *Divine Songs* is a curious blend of very adult-like sensibilities and subjects on the one hand, and childlike (even childish) naïveté on the other. In part, this results from Watts's attempt to treat profound theological concepts in as simple a manner as possible. For example, the third song, "Blest be the Wisdom and the Pow'r," traces the story of salvation from the fall in the garden of Eden through the incarnation, crucifixion, resurrection, ascension, and second coming of Jesus in eight common meter stanzas. Something of their tone can be seen in stanza 2.

> Our Father eat [*sic*] forbidden Fruit,
>   And from his Glory fell;
> And We his Children thus were brought
>   To Death, and near to Hell.

Other songs attempt to put in verse form admonitions for children to engage in proper behavior but often come across as preachy, overly judgmental, or simply morbid, such as song fifteen, "O 'Tis a lovely thing for Youth," titled "Against Lying."

---

[2] Watts, *Divine Songs Attempted in Easy Language for the Use of Children* (1715), n.p.

> Then let me always watch my Lips,
> Lest I be struck to Death and Hell,
> Since God a Book of Reckoning keeps
> For every Lye that Children tell. (st. 6)

It should be emphasized that, though these poems are mostly religious in orientation and are designed to be sung, it was not Watts's purpose that they be used in the worship services of the church. Rather, they were intended for catechizing children into the Christian faith and teaching them moral and proper behavior.

While it is easy to critique items such as those quoted above, it should be remembered that Watts was writing during a time when children were seen as miniature adults and well before the romanticized nineteenth-century view of them as sweet, innocent little lambs.[3] Furthermore, the book contains many individual pieces and stanzas that reach a high level of inspiration, such as the first stanza from song seven.

> Great God, with Wonder, and with Praise,
> On all thy Works I look;
> But still thy Wisdom, Pow'r and Grace,
> Shine brighter in thy Book.

"I Sing th'Almighty Power of God" is just such a piece, and it has been widely anthologized in congregational song collections and heartily sung by people of all ages. The hymn is the second song in the collection and is titled "Praise for Creation and Providence." Based primarily upon the first chapter of Genesis, Watts wrote the text in eight stanzas of cross-rhymed common meter with an iambic accent pattern.

As might be expected in a hymn written for children, the text is full of concrete images and references to familiar objects. However, unlike some of the other poems in the book, this one was not "written down" to children and certainly met the author's goal of writing simple poems that

---

[3] For a near-contemporary view of children that was similar to that of Watts, note the following stanza from the American Puritan Michael Wigglesworth's poem *The Day of Doom* about children who died in infancy: "A crime it is [original sin], therefore in bliss / you may not hope to dwell; / But unto you I shall allow / the easiest room in Hell" (st. 181).

93

could be kept "above Contempt" and "profit all (if possible) and offend none."[4]

> Stanza 1
> I Sing th'Almighty Power of God,
>> That made the Mountains rise,
>> That spread the flowing Seas abroad,
>>> And built the lofty Skies.[5]

Stanza 1 is the first of three strophes that celebrate the creation by referring to one of the attributes of God and two or three of his works. Each stanza begins with the same two words, "I sing," making this a personal expression of praise.

Structure of Stanzas 1–3 in "I Sing th'Almighty Power of God."

Opening	Attribute of God	Elements
I Sing…	Power	Mountains, Seas, Skies
I Sing…	Wisdom	Sun, Moon, Stars
I Sing…	Goodness	Food, Creatures

The attribute dealt with in stanza 1 is God's "Almighty Power," which created the mountains, the seas, and the skies. However, the mention of the created things is no mere matter-of-fact listing, for the language Watts employs characterizes each of them in a particular way through the use of alliteration and specific word choices. The alliteration of "made the Mountains" gives the line a sense of strength and solidity (like a mountain), while that of "spread the…Seas abroad" suggests the expansiveness of the ocean; the sibilants could even be likened to the

---

[4] Watts, preface to *Divine Songs Attempted in Easy Language for the Use of Children* (1715), n.p.

[5] In the first edition of *Divine Songs* this stanza ended with a semicolon, which was corrected in the second edition (1716) to a period. Note too the similarity of the last line to ones in the later *Psalms of David Imitated*, "He fram'd the Globe, he built the Sky" ("Let All the Earth Their Voices Raise," Ps 96, "As the 113th Psalm," st. 3) and "He built the Earth, he spread the Sky" ("Give to Our God Immortal Praise," Ps 136, LM, st. 3).

hissing of waves on the shore, and the word "flowing" gives a sense of the continual motion of the sea, as do the internal near-rhymes "spread" and "abroad." Note, too, how each of these elements is described: God made the mountains "rise," the seas are "flowing," and the skies are "lofty," words that express the nature of the items themselves.

There are remarkable similarities of thought between this strophe and the opening stanza of part two of Watts's paraphrase of Psalm 65 in *The Psalms of David Imitated*, which he titled "The Providence of God in Air, Earth and Sea; or, The Blessing of Rain."

> 'Tis by thy Strength the Mountains stand,
> > God of Eternal Power;
> The Sea grows calm at thy Command,
> > And Tempests cease to roar.

Both stanzas deal with the mountains and the sea, but "I Sing th'Almighty Power of God" emphasizes their *creation* while the psalm version focuses on God's *control* and *sustaining* of them. The "Tempests" reference in the psalm version appears in stanza 5 of the present hymn (see below), but with a different context.

While the elision in the opening line ("th'Almighty") is not particularly awkward to sing, such constructions have become relatively rare in recent English usage, and it is sometimes revised slightly to "I Sing the Mighty Power of God."

Stanza 2
> I sing the Wisdom that ordain'd
> > The Sun to rule the Day;
> The Moon shines full at his Command,
> > And all the Stars obey.

The last word of stanza 1, "Skies," leads Watts to turn his attention further upward in stanza 2 to celebrate God's creation of the universe, specifically, the sun, moon, and stars. The creation of these objects is attributed to God's "Wisdom," rather than his "Power," though of course Watts does not mean to exclude either one. In addition to Genesis 1:16, the author probably had Psalm 136 in mind as he wrote this stanza: the second line is practically a direct quote from 136:8a ("The sun to rule by day") and lines 3 and 4 reflect 136:9a ("The moon and stars to rule by night").

In this stanza, the stress is on both God's *creation* and *control* of the elements: he "ordain'd" the Sun, the Moon shines "at his Command," and the "Stars obey" his will. The stanza has a further (though indirect) parallel with his paraphrase of Psalm 65 in the initial lines of the latter's second stanza: "Thy Morning-Light and Evening-Shade / Successive Comforts bring." Here the sun and moon are translated into "Morning-Light and Evening-Shade."

> Stanza 3
>> I sing the Goodness of the Lord,
>>> That fill'd the Earth with Food,
>> He form'd the Creatures with his Word,
>>> And then pronounc'd them good.

In the third stanza, Watts "returns to earth" to sing God's "Goodness" in making the "Creatures" of the planet (presumably including humans) and providing food for their sustenance. The Lord's generosity toward his creatures is evident in the fact that he did not merely furnish them with food but "fill'd" the earth with it. This aspect of God's care for his creatures reflects several passages from the Psalms, including 145:15 ("The eyes of all wait upon thee; and thou givest them their meat in due season") and 147:9 ("He giveth the beast his food, and to the young ravens which cry"). It is enlightening to observe some of Watts's rhapsodic musings on God's provision of food in an essay on "Divine Goodness in the Creation," published in his *Reliquiæ Juveniles* (1734).

> What is more necessary for the Support of Life, than Food? Behold the Earth is cover'd with it all around; Grass, Herbs and Fruits for Beasts and Men, were ordain'd to overspread all the Surface of the Ground, so that an Animal could scarce wander any where, but his Food was near him. Amazing Provision for such an immense Family![6]

---

[6] Watts, *Reliquiæ Juveniles*, 36.

It might seem odd that Watts acknowledged God's provision of food before he mentioned the formation of the creatures that would eat that food. Two factors perhaps explain this order. First, the animals would have needed a food supply immediately upon their coming into being. Second, and perhaps more importantly, this is the order implied in Genesis 1:11-12 ("the third day"), which describes the creation of grass, herbs, and fruit trees. It is not until the fifth day that sea life and birds are made, and land animals and humans do not appear until day six. Thus, it appears that Watts simply followed the outline of the Genesis story in writing this stanza. The last line of the stanza paraphrases the refrain that runs throughout Genesis 1, "and God saw that it was good" (e.g., v. 25).

Stanza 3 does not contain a true rhyme (both of the rhyming pairs are eye rhymes) but it should be noted that all four of the words end with the same "d" consonant ("Lord," "Food," "Word," "good"). This identity helps call attention to these important words and increase their memorability. The interior lines of the stanza are also characterized by alliterative "f" sounds ("fill'd," "Food," "form'd"). Note too that "fill'd" and "form'd" come second in their respective lines.

Stanza 4
> Lord, how thy Wonders are display'd
>> Where'er I turn mine Eye,
> If I survey the Ground I tread,
>> Or gaze upon the Sky.

The fourth stanza serves as a summary of the first three. No matter where Watts (or the singer) looks—on earth or in the heavens—God's "Wonders are display'd." The stanza is reminiscent of several passages from the psalms, including 19:1 ("The heavens declare the glory of God") and 102:25 ("Of old hast thou laid the foundation of the earth: and the heavens are the work of thy hands").

This stanza also marks a change of voice. The first three strophes maintain a human-to-human line of communication, in which Watts "sings" *about* God. With stanza 4, he shifts to direct address *to* God. This is a familiar pattern in Watts texts, including "Am I a Soldier of the Cross?" and "When I Survey the Wondrous Cross."

Two words in the final lines of the strophe are of particular interest.

Nathan Bailey's eighteenth-century *An Universal Etymological English Dictionary* defines "survey" as "to view or look about on all Sides, to oversee," or "to measure Land," and "gaze" as "to stare, look about or look earnestly upon." These definitions suggest not just a casual glance but rather a thorough examination of all parts of an object and continuous looking at it.

During Watts's time, the modern sciences were developing, probing as fully as possible all the observable phenomena of the heavens and the earth. Like his contemporary namesake, Sir Isaac Newton—though approaching the subject from a different perspective—Watts saw in the creation and the operations of nature the handiwork of God. There is a childlike sense of delight in the stanza, as might be expected in a hymn written for children, but some of the same wonder bubbles to the surface in certain of Watts's later psalm paraphrases, suggesting that he had a special "joy in the created world" as a reflection of its Maker.[7]

Stanza 5
> There's not a Plant or Flower below
>   But makes thy Glories known;
> And Clouds arise and Tempests blow
>   By Order from thy Throne.

The change of voice in stanza 4 continues in stanza 5 as Watts engages in celebrating less permanent aspects of God's creation, plants, flowers, clouds, and storms. Though "the grass withereth" and "the flower fadeth" (Isa 40:7), Watts reminds us that every type of plant and flower makes known the Lord's "Glories."

Some have objected to the last two lines of the stanza as implying that God sends hurricanes, tornados, or other natural disasters as punishment on humans for their sinfulness—or worse, simply as some sort of cruel pleasure. However, there is no such suggestion in Watts's lines. His point is that through clouds and storms God waters the earth, which makes the plants and flowers mentioned in the first line grow. In the context of a hymn that deals with the many ways that God provides for

---

[7] Watson, *The English Hymn*, 134. See Watts's many versions of Psalms 147 and 148, and his description of the wonders of nature in *Death and Heaven*, 102–105.

98

his creation, it cannot have been Watts's meaning to attribute the potentially destructive power of storms to God's wrath.

Several further considerations present themselves. First, the "Tempests [that] blow / By Order from thy Throne" are probably not meant to refer to specific storms but to a general "Order" that "there shall be storms," in much the same way that God at first commanded "let there be light" without indicating a specific source of or target for the light. Second, while people tend to focus on the negative aspects of storms (as "disasters"), they are also beneficial in replenishing the earth.[8] Third, humans' tendency to build their habitations in places that are regularly visited by severe environmental events is not God's fault but ours. Finally, there is no mention of humans in the stanza, so it cannot have been Watts's purpose to suggest God's using storms as punishment for them.[9]

One of the lessons of this instance is that it is important to read individual words and phrases of hymns in the context of the whole, not in isolation. In almost any hymn, a word or line can be taken out of context and made to seem antithetical to Christian faith. It is important to understand both what the hymn writer is saying and what he or she is *not* saying.

Stanza 6

Creatures (as numerous as they be)
    Are subject to thy Care:
There's not a Place where we can flee,
    But God is present there.

The immense variety of plants and flowers that "makes [God's] Glories known" is paralleled by the "numerous" animals that are "subject to [God's] Care." The last two lines are a direct reference to Psalm 139:7-8: "Whither shall I go from thy spirit? or whither shall I flee from

---

[8] See "5 Things Hurricanes Can Do That Are Actually Good" at https://weather.com/storms/hurricane/news/hurricane-landfall-benefits-2016 (accessed December 5, 2017).

[9] In another hymn, Watts observes that God does not only send storms, he causes them to cease, a fact that should also be considered. See "'Tis By Thy Strength the Mountains Stand" (Ps 65, CM, part 2): "The Sea grows calm at thy Command, / And Tempests cease to roar."

thy presence? If I ascend up into heaven, thou art there: if I make my bed in hell, behold, thou art there." These lines also mark a subtle transition back to the human-to-human line of communication of stanzas 1–3.

This stanza has received considerable alteration at the hands of later editors though the exact chronology of these changes is not certain. In Thomas Hastings and William Patton's *The Christian Psalmist* (1836), the first line appeared as "Creatures that borrow life from thee," and this version was repeated in some later hymnals.[10] Over a century after Hastings and Patton's book, the line was further altered to "While all that borrows life from Thee" in *The Hymnal* of the Presbyterian Church in the U.S.A. (1950)[11] and the succeeding lines were revised as "Is ever in Thy care, / And everywhere that man can be, / Thou, God, art present there," with the marking "Stanza 3 alt."[12] The version in *The Hymnal* has been widely adopted, with "man" sometimes being changed to "we."

Stanza 7
> In Heaven he shines with Beams of Love,
>> With Wrath in Hell beneath:
> 'Tis on his Earth I stand or move,
>> And 'tis his Air I breath[e].

The initial lines of stanza 7 continue the reference to Psalm 139 by further paraphrasing v. 8: "If I ascend up into heaven, thou art there: if I make my bed in hell, behold thou art there." In the KJV of the psalm verse, "hell" translates the Hebrew word *Sheol*, which referred to the abode of the dead, not necessarily to a place of punishment. However, Watts interpreted "hell" as it became commonly understood in post-New Testament times, as a place where God's wrath was poured out on unre-

---

[10] Hastings and Patton, *The Christian Psalmist*, 255.

[11] Dickinson, ed., *The Hymnal* of the Presbyterian Church in the U.S.A., 107.

[12] These sources were not necessarily the first to use these alterations but are merely the earliest of these particular changes I found. *The Hymnal* was edited by Clarence Dickinson. In this book (as in many others), Watts's stanzas were combined to fit a CMD tune; thus, the original stanza 6 was the last half of stanza 3, accounting for the notation that it was the third stanza that was revised.

pentant sinners.[13]

The hymn writer observes that, while God is everywhere, even in heaven or hell, the singer is currently "betwixt and between"—on the earth—but, in a manner reminiscent of Psalm 24:1, Watts is clear that this earth belongs to God ("The earth is the Lord's, and the fullness thereof; the world, and they that dwell therein"). Even the very air we breathe is God's possession, a gift that he gives us to sustain life (see Ps 104:29b).

This fact suggests two further thoughts. First, while the earth is our home and was given to us by God (Gen 1:28-30), we are but tenants—or, perhaps better—stewards of its true owner; thus, any sense of it belonging to us to do with as we please is misplaced. Second, and related to the first point, God gave us the earth to care for, much as he gave Adam the garden of Eden to "dress it and to keep it" (Gen 2:15). This imposes upon us a responsibility to use nature wisely and respectfully.

The rhymes of this stanza are characterized by dissonance, in which only the final consonant sound is identical: "Love" / "move"; "beneath" / "breathe." The first pair consists of an eye rhyme, while in the second pair the first word uses an unvoiced and the second a voiced "th" sound.

> Stanza 8
> His Hand is my perpetual Guard,
> He keeps me with his Eye:
> Why should I then forget the Lord
> Who is for ever nigh?

Watts's final stanza turns from wonderment at and celebration of creation to consideration of the singer's personal state. Here again the author turns to the psalms for inspiration: "thy right hand upholdeth me" (63:8), "Keep me as the apple of the eye" (17:8), "forget not all his benefits" (103:2), "I will remember the works of the Lord" (77:11), "The Lord is nigh unto them that are of a broken heart" (34:18; or "that call upon him," 145:18).

---

[13] But see his note to the common meter paraphrase of Psalm 16, part two, in *The Psalms of David Imitated*: "'Tis now agreed by the Learned that...Sheol, which is render'd Hell, signifies only the State of the Dead, i. e. the Grave for the Body, and the Separate State for the Spirit."

Scotty Gray has pointed out that this hymn contains "allusions to the omnipotent ('almighty'), omniscient ('the wisdom that ordained'), [and] omnipresent ('the Lord is forever nigh') care of God as Watts rejoices in both the reason and revelation of creation."[14] A similar analysis by Herbert J. Roth led him to claim that despite Watts's vociferous denunciations of Deism, the hymn "could be considered unequivocally Deistic" because of its emphasis on God's omnipotence and omnipresence, as well as the fourth stanza's implication that humans "may learn of God through the study of nature."[15] While Roth makes an important point that the hymn uses some of the language of eighteenth-century Deism, he admits that the "portrayal of God in [this hymn], of course, would appeal to the orthodox Christian as well as to many of the moderate Deists who reconciled Deism with Christianity on the premise that reason and revelation were merely two different approaches in the discovery of truth."[16]

Today, stanzas 7 and 8 of Watts's original text are generally omitted and the first six are combined into three stanzas and sung to a common meter double tune, most often ELLACOMBE or FOREST GREEN. Both pieces are sturdy, straightforward melodies that well express the exuberance and childlike wonder of the text.

In 1789, an Englishwoman named Sarah Trimmer published *A Comment on Dr. Watts's Divine Songs for Children*, which contained brief statements on each poem and questions to be asked about them as an aid to parents and teachers. Her brief opening statement on "I Sing

---

[14] Gray, *Hermeneutics of Hymnody*, 78.

[15] Roth, "A Literary Study," 65.

[16] Ibid., 62. It must be said that an interpretation of the hymn as Deistic is possible only by ignoring the original seventh stanza, the many scriptural echoes in the text, and the fact that the hymn was written originally for children (though, as noted above, this did not necessarily stop Watts from introducing complex theological ideas). Unfortunately, Roth seems to have been aware of only the first six stanzas of the hymn, probably because his source for the text, a reprint of Hastings and Patton's *The Christian Psalmist* (1839), omitted the last two. The seventh stanza, with its mentions of heaven and hell (the latter as an expression of God's wrath), contradicts Roth's statement that "there is a noticeable absence...of the belief or conception of the Deity who enforces obedience to his absolute will by particular rewards and punishments" ("A Literary Study," 62).

th'Almighty Power of God" serves as a good summary of Watts's text: "This Hymn helps you to words in which you may praise God properly for three things, namely, His Power, His Wisdom, and His Goodness."[17] Watts's simple yet profound hymn reminds us that when we try to understand God's power, wisdom, and goodness, we are all still children.

---

[17] Trimmer, *A Comment on Dr. Watts's Divine Songs for Children, with Questions*, 4.

11

I'LL PRAISE MY MAKER WITH MY BREATH

"I'll Praise My Maker with My Breath" is Watts's second version of Psalm 146 in *The Psalms of David Imitated*. It is titled "Praise to God for his Goodness and Truth" and is laid out in six stanzas of 888888 hymnic meter. The text's iambic poetic meter gives it a march-like flavor that accords well with the resolute character of the message it proclaims. The rhyme scheme is AABCCB.

It is interesting to observe the relationship between the two paraphrases of this psalm in *The Psalms of David Imitated*. The first version is in long meter and is nearly identical to the present one except that the latter adds two lines in each stanza, sometimes transfers lines between stanzas, and provides a completely new first (and last) stanza. Watts's general procedure can be seen by a comparison of stanza 4 in the 888888 text with stanza 6 of the long meter version.

888888	LM
The Lord hath Eyes to give the Blind;	The Lord hath Eyes to give the Blind;
The Lord supports the sinking Mind;	The Lord supports the sinking Mind:
He sends the labouring Conscience Peace:	
He helps the Stranger in Distress,	He helps the Stranger in Distress,
The Widow and the Fatherless,	The Widow and the Fatherless.
And grants the Prisoner sweet Release.	

Watts noted the relationship between the two texts in a statement at the end of the first (LM) version: "This Psalm consists so much of single Sentences that a small and easy Transposition of the Verses with a very few Lines added will afford a Metre to the Tune of the 113th Psalm, with a Repetition of the first Stanza at the End to compleat the Tune, as follows."[1]

It seems apparent from Watts's note that the long meter version was written first, and the 888888 paraphrase was developed from it. Thus, the same text has essentially been given twice but in distinctive meters to allow for the use of different tunes.

The "Tune of the 113th Psalm" refers to the melody used with Psalm 113 in Sternhold and Hopkins's Old Version, "Ye Children Which Do Serve the Lord" by William Kethe. The tune, today usually called OLD 113TH, was originally composed by Matthäus Greiter for a German text and was adopted into John Calvin's French-language Genevan Psalter of 1539 as the setting for Psalms 36 and 68, from which it was borrowed for the English psalter. Since Kethe's lyric and Greiter's melody (in its original version) were both laid out in 888888D, Watts had to provide an even number of stanzas to make the lyrics fit the tune; this is the reason for the repetition of the opening stanza at the conclusion of the hymn.[2]

Stanza 1
> I'll praise my Maker with my Breath;
> And when my Voice is lost in Death
> > Praise shall employ my nobler Powers:
> My Days of Praise shall ne'er be past
> While Life and Thought and Being last,
> > Or Immortality endures.

Watts's first stanza expands upon the ideas presented in Psalm 146:2: "While I live will I praise the LORD: / I will sing praises unto my God while I have any being." (Verse 1, "Praise ye the Lord. Praise the Lord, O my soul," is essentially ignored.) Note that the psalmist pledges to praise God "while I have any being" but Watts emphasizes that praise will occur not only while he has "Breath" but even when his voice is silenced by death, at which time his "nobler Powers" will take over. The praise of his "Maker" will extend from now into and throughout eternity.

The broad, striding rhythm of the lines is enhanced by the many

---

[1] Watts, *The Psalms of David Imitated* (1719), 383.

[2] The version of OLD 113TH that is usually sung today is an abridgement of the original from 888888D to 888888, which makes the repetition of the opening stanza unnecessary, though it is still often printed and sung.

"p," "b," and "d" plosive consonants: "praise" (three times), "breath," "death," "employ," "nobler," "powers," "days," "past," "being," and "endures." This feature is particularly prominent in line 3. A remarkable number of "s," "sh," and "z" sounds are also found in the stanza: "praise" (three times), "voice," "lost," "shall" (twice), "powers," "days," "past," "last," and "endures." Another important feature in the rhythm of the stanza is the five-fold repetition of the word "my," all appearing in the first four lines.

Wording similar to that of the initial lines can be found in two other psalm versions by Watts: "I Love the Lord: He Heard My Cries" (Ps 116, pt. 1, st. 6: "Now to his Praise I'll spend my Breath") and "In God's Own House Pronounce His Praise" (Ps 150, st. 3: "Yet when my Voice expires in Death").

Stanza 2
    Why should I make a Man my Trust?
    Princes must die and turn to Dust;
        Vain is the Help of Flesh and Blood;
    Their Breath departs, their Pomp & Power
    And Thoughts all vanish in an Hour,
        Nor can they make their Promise good[.]

Psalm 146:3-4 of the psalm forms the basis for Watts's second stanza:

    [3]Put not your trust in princes, nor in the son of man, in
      whom there is no help.
    [4]His breath goeth forth, he returneth to his earth; in that
      very day his thoughts perish.

In lines 2 and 3, Watts departs momentarily from iambic poetic meter to begin each line with a choriambus.[3] This stanza has a link with stanza 1 in the reuse of the word "breath" (line 4), but whereas the poet's loss of "breath" (at death) will be substituted for by his "nobler Powers,"

---

[3] When sung to most iambic tunes, this choriambus might cause awkward accents on the second syllable of "princes" and on "is," but the long notes at the beginning of these phrases in OLD 113TH obviate this difficulty, as Watts would have anticipated.

the departure of breath from the "Princes" results only in silence; they cannot even help themselves, much less others, when they are in the grave. Again, "b" and "p" sounds are prominent, though in this stanza they are restricted principally to line 4, mocking the empty "Pomp & Power" of the "Princes."

Stanza 3
> Happy the Man whose Hopes rely
> On *Isral's* God: He made the Sky,[4]
> > And Earth and Seas with all their Train:
> His Truth for ever stands secure;
> He saves th'Opprest, he feeds the Poor,
> > And None shall find his Promise vain.

Stanza 3 paraphrases from v. 5 through the first sentence of v. 7 of the psalm:

> [5]Happy is he that hath the God of Jacob for his help, whose hope is in the LORD his God:
> [6]Which made heaven, and earth, the sea, and all that therein is: which keepeth truth for ever:
> [7]Which executeth judgment for the oppressed: which giveth food to the hungry.

In contrast to those who put their trust in earthly rulers (st. 2) are the happy ones who place their hope in God. Watts poetically illustrates the happiness of hoping in God by using a choriambus in the first line, giving a joyful lilt to the beginning of the stanza. The enjambment in the second line is a rather unusual occurrence in Watts. The many plosives of the first two stanzas are here largely replaced by softer, smoother "m," "n" and aspirate ("h") sounds, though "s" and "z" consonants are still found frequently. This gentler mood continues until the last stanza.

Stanza 4
> The Lord hath Eyes to give the Blind;

---

[4] In the second edition of *The Psalms of David Imitated* (1719), Watts corrected "Isral's" to "Israel's."

The Lord supports the sinking Mind;

> He sends the laboring Conscience Peace:
> He helps the Stranger in Distress,
> The Widow and the Fatherless,
>   And grants the Prisoner sweet Release.

Watts paraphrases v. 8 and the first part of v. 9 to form the fourth stanza:

> [8]The LORD openeth the eyes of the blind: the LORD raiseth them that are bowed down: the LORD loveth the righteous:
> [9]The LORD preserveth the strangers; he relieveth the fatherless and widow...

Whereas the psalm talks about the Lord opening the eyes of the blind, Watts's stanza implies that the blind do not even have eyes but that they will receive them from Lord. He also changes the idea of raising those who are bowed down to supporting "the sinking Mind." This stanza demonstrates one of Watts's common psalm paraphrasing techniques, transferring ideas from one part of a psalm to another. In this case, the last line of the stanza is a paraphrase of the last part of v. 7 ("The Lord looseth the prisoners"), most of which was dealt with in stanza 3.

Stanza 5
    He loves his Saints; he knows them well,
    But turns the Wicked down to Hell:
        Thy God O *Zion* ever reigns:
    Let every Tongue, let every Age
    In this exalted Work engage;
        Praise him in everlasting Strains.

Stanza 5 is equivalent to Psalm 146:9b-10:

> [9b]...but the way of the wicked he turneth upside down.
> [10]The LORD shall reign for ever, even thy God, O Zion,

unto all generations. Praise ye the LORD.

The first line, about God loving his saints and knowing them well, is an insertion not found in the psalm and sets up an antithesis with the following line. The phrase "In this exalted Work engage" is also an addition. The "exalted Work" is identified in the following line: "Praise." Watts's practice of expanding the focus of a psalm is evident in this verse: whereas v. 19 claims that it is the God of Zion who will reign "unto all generations," the poet suggests that this God is one who should now be praised not only by "every Age" but also by "every Tongue"; God is not only the God of the Hebrews but of the whole human race. The psalmist's declarative statement ("The Lord shall reign") has also been turned into a command for action ("Let").

Stanza 6
> I'll praise him while he lends me Breath,
> And when my Voice is lost in Death
> > Praise shall employ my nobler Powers:
> My Days of Praise shall ne'er be past
> While Life and Thought and Being last,
> > Or Immortality endures.

As noted previously, stanza 6 is a repetition of stanza 1; however, as is typical with Watts, it is not an exact repeat: line 1 is altered from Watts praising his "Maker with my Breath" to praising God "while he lends me Breath." The change is an important one because it reminds the singer that his or her very breath is on loan from God. Breath can certainly be considered a gift from God, but one is not expected to return a gift. On the other hand, if breath is a loan from God then God expects to receive it back. How do we return our breath to God? For Watts, we do this by praising him.

This hymn was a favorite with John Wesley, who included it in his first hymnal, *A Collection of Psalms and Hymns* (the "Charlestown Collection," 1737). Wesley altered several lines of Watt's original (including the first verse, making it "I'll Praise My Maker While I've Breath") and deleted stanzas 2 and 5. Wesley's changes were well-conceived and have been almost universally adopted.[5]

Watts's version of Psalm 146 is a powerful reminder that the God who created "the Sky, / And Earth and Seas with all their Train" also "saves th'Opprest," "feeds the Poor," "helps the Stranger in Distress," "The Widow and the Fatherless, / And grants the Prisoner sweet Release." No wonder the hymn writer could exclaim that he will praise this omnipotent and loving God both in the present and throughout the age to come.

---

[5] Alan Gaunt, "I'll Praise My Maker While I've Breath," in *Canterbury Dictionary of Hymnology*, https://hymnology.hymnsam.co.uk/ (accessed September 1, 2017). The revisions made by Wesley also included altering lines in stanza 4 to "The Lord pours eyesight on the blind" and "The Lord supports the fainting mind."

12

I'M NOT ASHAMED TO OWN MY LORD

The first edition of Isaac Watts's *Hymns and Spiritual Songs* had a rather long gestation period. Watts was writing hymns at least as early as 1694.[1] A letter from his brother Enoch, dated March 1700, encouraged Isaac to publish his hymns and shows that he was still writing them regularly six years later.[2] The preface to the first edition of *Horæ Lyricæ* (published in late 1705) reveals that by that time he had collected some two hundred texts, and the initial printing of *Hymns and Spiritual Songs* occurred approximately nineteen months later.

When, after at least thirteen years of writing hymns, the first edition of *Hymns and Spiritual Songs* was finally published, Watts did not long rest upon his laurels, for two years later he issued a second edition (1709). This revised version is not a mere reprint; the title page notes that it is "Corrected and much Enlarged." The scope of the enlargement is described in the "Advertisements concerning the second Edition," where Watts states that, in addition to revising texts from the first edition, "There are almost 150 new Hymns added."[3]

---

[1] The earliest dated hymn by Watts, "Shout to the Lord, and Let Our Joys," was published in the first edition of *Hymns and Spiritual Songs* (1707), Book II, no. 92, with the notation "Compos'd the 5th of November, 1694." It has often been said that Watts's first hymn was "Behold the Glories of the Lamb," the text that opens *Hymns and Spiritual Songs* (1707); however, there is no contemporary evidence of this priority. See Music, "Was 'Behold the Glories of the Lamb' Isaac Watts's First Hymn?" 186–92.

[2] For the letter from Enoch, see *The Posthumous Works of the Late Learned and Reverend Isaac Watts, D.D.*, 2:163–67.

[3] Watts, *Hymns and Spiritual Songs* (1709), xiii.

It may be that some of the added hymns were not really "new." In the preface to the first edition, Watts observed that he had been "forc'd to lay aside many Hymns after they were finished, and utterly exclude 'em from this Volume, because of the Bolder Figures of Speech that crowded themselves into the Verse, and a more unconfin'd Variety of Number which I could not easily restrain."[4] While he went on to say that some of these more complex hymns might appear in a subsequent edition of *Horæ Lyricæ*, it is possible that he revised some of them for the 1709 edition of *Hymns and Spiritual Songs*.

Presumably, however, most of the new hymns were written after publication of the first edition, which occurred in July 1707. The second edition was released in April 1709, meaning that it appeared twenty-one months after the initial printing.[5] During this time, he was also in ill health and still serving as senior pastor at his church (though with an assistant); furthermore, the congregation moved to a new meeting house in 1708. This was certainly a remarkable record of productivity—and, of course, it does not include the time needed to make revisions, proofread, and see the second edition through the press.

One of the new hymns added to the second edition was "I'm Not Ashamed to Own My Lord" (Book I, hymn 103). Watts titled the hymn "Not ashamed of the Gospel" and gave the Scripture reference 2 Timothy 1:12 ("For the which cause I also suffer these things: nevertheless I am not ashamed: for I know whom I have believed, and am persuaded that he is able to keep that which I have committed unto him against that day"). Laid out in four stanzas of common meter, the text is in Watts's often-used iambic poetic meter and employs cross rhyme.

Harry Escott characterized "I'm Not Ashamed to Own My Lord" as one of a group of Watts texts that are "a mere RECITAL of God's 'amazing deeds,' or of some theological or ethical doctrine."[6] Here, the "recital" is of God's steadfast support of the believer and the latter's need for trust in the Lord.

---

[4] Preface, *Hymns and Spiritual Songs* (1707), ix.

[5] The dates of these imprints are derived from Watts's "Memorable Affairs in my Life" as transcribed in Hood, *Isaac Watts*, [345].

[6] Escott, *Isaac Watts, Hymnographer*, 244.

Stanza 1
>I'm not asham'd to own my Lord,
>>Or to defend his Cause,
>Maintain the Honour of his Word,
>>The Glory of his Cross.

The opening line of the hymn is drawn directly from the second clause of the source verse, "nevertheless I am not ashamed." The first stanza is similar in several respects to the initial strophe of Watts's later "Am I a Soldier of the Cross."

>Am I a Soldier of the Cross,
>>A Follower of the Lamb?
>And shall I fear to own his Cause,
>>Or blush to speak His Name?

The two stanzas carry an essentially identical message—that Christians should not be "asham'd" or "blush" to claim God—and even employ some of the same key words: own, cause, and cross.[7] However, while the later hymn expresses these thoughts through questions, "I'm not asham'd to own my Lord" does so through strong statements of commitment (emphasis added): "I *will* own my Lord," "I *will* defend his cause," "I *will* maintain the honour of his Word." Since the opening stanzas of the two hymns use the same hymnic and poetic meters, it might be effective to sing them in alternation, first the stanza from "Am I a Soldier of the Cross," then, as a response, the one from "I'm Not Ashamed to Own My Lord."

Another parallel between this stanza and a later writing by Watts can be seen in the second volume of his *Sermons on Various Subjects* (1723). The first sermon in the book was titled "A Rational Defense of the Gospel: Or, Courage in professing Christianity" and was based on Romans 1:16 ("I am not ashamed of the Gospel of Christ, for it is the Power of God unto Salvation to every one that believeth"). Since they are

---

[7] As noted in chapter 3, during the eighteenth century one of the meanings of the word "own" was "belonging to." Thus, the first stanza of the present hymn would mean something like "I'm not ashamed to belong to [or acknowledge] my Lord."

based on different (though similar) Scriptures and were separated in time by at least fourteen years, there is probably no direct link between "I'm Not Ashamed to Own My Lord" and the homily.[8] However, at one point in the sermon, Watts does make a statement that sounds like an echo of his earlier hymn text: "I am not ashamed to contend for it as a good Soldier of Christ; to defend it when it is attack'd, and to vindicate the Cause of my Lord and Master."[9]

In a manner reminiscent of the psalms, Watts structures the first stanza of "I'm Not Ashamed to Own My Lord" as a series of synonymous or complementary parallelisms: "own / defend / maintain" and "my Lord / his Cause / his Word / his Cross." The word of the Lord is further characterized as honorable and his cross as glorious.

Stanza 2
    Jesus, my God; I know his Name,
        His Name is all my Trust,
    Nor will he put my Soul to shame,
        Nor let my Hope be lost.

In the first stanza, Watts went to great lengths to stress his steadfastness in not being ashamed of the gospel of Christ. Stanza 2 opens by giving the source of this strength, "Jesus, my God." This is a bold assertion, particularly in view of how Watts's later writings have been characterized, that identifies Jesus directly as God. There is not a shred of doubt here about the divinity of Jesus. Using an anadiplosis on "his name," Watts links lines 1 and 2, acknowledging that the writer not only "knows" the name of his God but also puts his trust in that name. Watts perhaps had in mind here Psalm 9:10 ("And they that know thy name will put their trust in thee: for thou, Lord, hast not forsaken them that seek thee").

Anaphora ("nor") links lines 3 and 4 of this stanza. The last line carries a thought similar to one expressed in the later sermon mentioned

---

[8] It should be noted that each sermon in the 1723 volume was accompanied by a newly written hymn. The hymn for this sermon, "Shall Atheists Dare Insult the Cross?" bears no resemblance to "I'm Not Ashamed to Own My Lord."

[9] Watts, *Sermons on Various Subjects*, 10.

above, "I am persuaded my Hopes shall never disappoint me."[10] Watts's basic simplicity of vocabulary is evident in this stanza, which contains only a single polysyllable, "Jesus."

Stanza 3
>   Firm as his Throne his Promise stands,
>   And he can well secure
>   What I've committed to his Hands
>   Till the decisive Hour.

Watts extends the message of trust in God begun in stanza 2 into the third stanza. He opens by emphasizing that God keeps his promises; they are as sure as his throne, which "is for ever and ever" (Ps 45:6). The next three lines paraphrase the last clause of the verse from 2 Timothy that serves as the basis for the hymn. In Watts's hands, "that day" has become "the decisive Hour," referring to the hour of death of the believer.

Stanza 4
>   Then will he own my worthless Name
>   Before his Father's Face,
>   And in the new *Jerusalem*
>   Appoint my Soul a Place.

Stanza 4 brings the hymn full circle by repeating the opening thought of the text but with a twist—now it is not the singer who "owns" his Lord, but the Lord who will "own" the singer, despite the latter's "worthless Name." The "worthlessness" of humanity was a common theme among Puritans of the seventeenth and eighteenth centuries but finds little sympathy in the twenty-first. We are, after all, created in the image of God and, as such, are worth *something*.

It is good to be reminded, however, that as a verse from Romans puts it, "There is none righteous, no, not one" (3:10). We are indeed "worthless" when it comes to providing for our own salvation, which can only come from God. Watts typically used the "worthlessness" of humanity as a foil to compare it with Jesus' incomparable glory as a measure

---

[10] Ibid., 8.

of the latter's grace, "in that, while we were yet sinners, Christ died for us" (Rom 5:8).

The author perhaps also drew upon Romans for line 2 of this stanza, "Christ…is even at the right hand of God, who also maketh intercession for us" (8:34). The "new Jerusalem" is, of course, a reference to Revelation 3:12 and 21:2, and the idea of "Appoint[ing] my Soul a Place" suggests John 14:2b-3a ("I go to prepare a place for you. And if I go and prepare a place for you, I will come again, and receive you unto myself"). The many biblical allusions and references in this short stanza make it a truly remarkable conclusion to the text.

One poetic feature of this hymn that stands out is its relative lack of true rhymes. Of the sixteen lines in the text, only six contain a true rhyme. As noted by Scotty Gray, false rhymes "do not indicate a weakness or lack of 'purity.'" He goes on to observe that false rhymes of various types "may well provide a flow and subtlety to the meanings where pure rhyme might be too expected or provide too strong a pulse."[11] Gray's analysis certainly applies to this hymn, in which the absence of true rhyme adds nuances that would be missing with more obvious correspondences of sounds.

Hymns can have many different purposes. Some teach principles and doctrines of the faith. Others proclaim the gospel message to unbelievers. Still others reflect testimonies of the state of the Christian's soul.

Then there are hymns that are sometimes difficult to sing honestly, such as "I'm Not Ashamed to Own My Lord." How many times have we kept silent when we should have spoken boldly, denied (by word or action) knowing our Lord, or been apologetic or ashamed by adherence to Christ? How can we then sing that we are "not ashamed to own" our Lord?

The point of singing a hymn such as this one is not that we will ever measure up to the ideal it presents but that it challenges us to be better than we are. By singing of what we would like to be or become, we are more likely to grow into it. Reading or singing Watts's hymn can help Christians along the road toward imitating those early post-Resurrection disciples who "spoke the word of God with boldness" (Acts 4:31b, NRSV).

---

[11] Gray, *Hermeneutics of Hymnody*, 177.

13

JESUS SHALL REIGN WHERE'ER THE SUN

Isaac Watts's *Psalms of David Imitated* contains a variety of approaches to the paraphrasing of Scripture. Some of his versions, such as "My Shepherd Will Supply My Need," remain relatively close to the message and wording of the biblical text. In others it is sometimes difficult to find exact relationships between the original psalm and the paraphrase for much of the hymn. "Jesus Shall Reign Where'er the Sun" is one that falls into the latter category.

"Jesus Shall Reign" is the second part of Watts's paraphrase of Psalm 72. As noted in the introduction to this book, Watts often broke up the longer psalm paraphrases into shorter hymns. The author gave the second part of his Psalm 72 version the same iambic, long meter metrical scheme as the first part, allowing for flexibility in its singing: the minister or song leader could have the people perform either the entire psalm or only a portion of it, as desired.

The first part of Watts's version, titled "The Kingdom of Christ," covers vv. 1-4, calling for "the king's son" to be given the kingdom and extolling his power and glory.

> Great God, whose universal Sway
> The known & unknown Worlds obey,
> Now give the Kingdom to thy Son,
> Extend his Power, exalt his Throne. (st. 1)

Part two, "Christ's Kingdom among the Gentiles," carries the message of the remaining sixteen verses, that this Messiah is Lord not of a single nation but of all the earth.

Stanza 1

> Jesus shall reign where e'er the Sun
> Does his successive Journeys run;
> His Kingdom stretch from Shore to Shore,
> Till Moons shall wax and wane no more.

Watts's goal of "Christianizing" the psalms to reflect the new covenant God had made with his people is nowhere more evident than in this hymn, in which the very first word is the name of Jesus. Whereas part one of the text began with a generic reference to giving "the Kingdom to thy Son" (drawn more or less directly from v. 1 of the psalm), the beginning of part two gives a specific identification of the "Son" as the Man who was born in Bethlehem, died on a Roman cross, rose from the dead, and ascended into heaven.

Unlike some of Watts's other psalm paraphrases, which proceed more or less from verse to verse in direct order, this one skips around to pick up various bits of verses and combine and reinterpret them in different ways; as Albert Edward Bailey put it, "scarcely a word of the original [psalm] has survived."[1] Thus the first stanza reflects not only v. 5 of the psalm but also parts of vv. 7, 8 and 17:

> [5]They shall fear thee as long as the sun and moon endure,
> throughout all generations
> [7b]...and abundance of peace so long as the moon endureth
> [8]He shall have dominion also from sea to sea, and from the
> river unto the ends of the earth"
> [17a]His name shall endure for ever: his name shall be contin-
> ued as long as the sun.

This stanza gives a two-fold message about the kingdom of Christ: it will be both geographically and temporally all-encompassing. Geographically, as the earth spins and its star appears to "Journey" around it, the light from the sun touches every part of the globe; wherever it does so, Jesus will reign there. To paraphrase a common saying that has been

---

[1] A. E. Bailey, *The Gospel in Hymns*, 53. Incidentally, the pairings of Scripture verse and hymn text given by Bailey often differ from the ones provided here.

applied to a variety of earthly empires, "The sun never sets on the kingdom of Christ." Watts reiterates the point, as does the psalm (v. 8), by observing that the Messiah's kingdom will "stretch from Shore to Shore."

Temporally, Jesus' reign will last until the moon is no more, at which point there will probably not be an earth either. Perhaps it is significant that Watts pluralized "Moons." While he was perhaps referring to the phases of earth's moon, the word might also be construed as applying to moons around other planets. By the time of Watts, four moons had been discovered around Jupiter and five around Saturn, developments of which he was well aware.[2] The implication is that Jesus' reign will last until the solar system—and ultimately the universe and beyond—is no more.[3]

It is important to note that this first stanza is cast in future tense: "Jesus *shall* reign." Of course, Watts would have believed that Jesus already has dominion over the earth but in this hymn, he follows the future tense of the psalm and looks forward to Jesus' universally acknowledged sway.

The impact of this opening stanza is enhanced by its many sibilants ("s" and "z"), especially in line 2. The last line is also remarkable for its balancing of alliterative "m" and "w" sounds, creating a sort of acoustical chiasmus: "*m*oons shall *w*ax and *w*ane no *m*ore."

Stanza 2
[Behold the Islands with their Kings,
And *Europe* her best Tribute brings;
From *North* to *South* the Princes meet
To pay their Homage at his Feet.

Watts marked stanzas 2 and 3 with brackets to indicate that they could be omitted to shorten the hymn, if desired, without doing undue damage to its message. The second stanza is based on Psalm 72:9-11:

---

[2] In his *The Knowledge of the Heavens and the Earth Made Easy*, published seven years after *The Psalms of David Imitated*, Watts mentioned these moons of Jupiter and Saturn (102).

[3] For a discussion of lines from other Watts psalm paraphrases that are similar to the closing of this stanza, see the chapter on "From All That Dwell Below the Skies."

⁹They that dwell in the wilderness shall bow before him;
And his enemies shall lick the dust.
¹⁰The kings of Tarshish and of the isles shall bring presents:
the kings of Sheba and Seba shall offer gifts.
¹¹Yea, all kings shall fall down before him: all nations shall
serve him.

This stanza illustrates another feature of Watts's psalm versions—his attempt not only to Christianize them but also to give them contemporary relevance, in this case by a specific reference to Europe and (in stanza 3) other countries that existed in his day, rather than the Tarshish, Sheba, and Seba of the Old Testament. Since he copied the "Islands" reference from the psalm, it is doubtful that Watts had specific islands in mind, but it is tempting to recall that this was an age of exploration when new islands and continents were being discovered and explored. The English explorer William Dampier had published *A New Voyage Round the World* and *A Voyage to New Holland* (Australia) as recently as 1697 and 1703, respectively, and fascination with exploration of the islands of the South Pacific was to continue with the voyages of Captain James Cook later in the eighteenth century. Watts might even have thought of the British Isles as he was writing this line.

Stanza 3
There *Persia* glorious to behold,
There *India* shines in *Eastern* Gold;
And barbarous Nations at his Word
Submit and bow and own their Lord.]

Stanza 3 continues the "travelogue" of stanza 2, referring specifically to other parts of the known world of Watts's day, Persia (now Iran) and India. The "Eastern Gold" of line 2 is derived from v. 15 of the psalm ("to him shall be given of the gold of Sheba"), and lines 3 and 4 combine v. 9 with the last part of v. 11 ("all nations shall serve him").

Bailey defined "barbarous" as "cruel, fierce, rude, wild." Watts's use of the term is perhaps unfortunate, but he was not referring to Persia and India, which he put in a different category ("glorious" and "Eastern Gold"). He likely had in mind native cultures that had been encountered by explorers, some of which would certainly have been considered barbarous by eighteenth-century European standards. But this also brings an important message in the context of Watts's hymn: Jesus is Lord of every region, culture, language, and ethnic group.

Stanza 4
> For him shall endless Pray'r be made,
> And Praises throng to crown his Head;
> His Name like sweet Perfume shall rise
> With every Morning Sacrifice.

Stanza 4 begins with a close paraphrase of verse 15b: "prayer also shall be made for him continually; and daily shall he be praised." Though Watts's word "For" is more in line with the KJV of the psalm, modern hymnals often alter it to "To": we pray *to* Jesus, not *for* Jesus. These lines could be interpreted as a vision of heaven ("they rest not day and night, saying Holy, holy, holy, Lord God Almighty," Rev 4:8b), but it is more likely that the hymn writer is referring to the hoped-for universal sway of Christ over the earth ("Jesus shall reign where e'er the Sun," i.e., wherever the sun shines). Watts foresees a time when prayer to Christ will never cease and praises will be so numerous that they will surround the Savior like people in a crowd, each trying to place a crown on his head.[4]

Beginning with the last two lines of stanza 4, Watts begins to depart further and further from the actual wording of the psalm on which the hymn is based. He transforms the daily praise of the psalm into "sweet Perfume" and the "Morning Sacrifice." These ideas are not found in Psalm 72 but are packed with other scriptural allusions, including Psalm 141:2 ("Let my prayer be set forth before thee as incense; and the lifting up of my hands as the evening sacrifice"); Exodus 30:7a ("And Aaron shall burn thereon sweet incense every morning"); 2 Chronicles 13:11a ("And they burn unto the Lord every morning and every evening burnt sacrifices and sweet incense"); Song of Solomon 1:3b ("thy name is as ointment poured forth"); Philippians 4:18b ("an odour of a sweet smell, a sacrifice acceptable, wellpleasing to God"); and John 12:3 ("Then took Mary a pound of ointment of spikenard, very costly, and anointed the feet of Jesus...and the house was filled with the odour of the ointment"). As God's people speak the name of Jesus in their "sacrifice of praise"

---

[4] Line 2 is often altered to "And endless praises crown his head."

(Heb 13:15), the name ascends as a sweet-smelling savor, just as the animal sacrifices of the Mosaic Law created a pleasing aroma that rose to the nostrils of God (Exod 29:39-41).

> Stanza 5
>> People and Realms of every Tongue
>> Dwell on his Love with sweetest Song;
>> And Infant-Voices shall proclaim
>> Their early Blessings on his Name.

Watts continues the thought of stanza 4, noting that as people around the globe speak the name of Jesus, they will do so in "every Tongue." Even infants, who presumably cannot yet talk, will be led to proclaim the Savior's name. The first two lines of stanza 5 reiterate the last part of v. 17, "men shall be blessed in him: all nations shall call him blessed," but the reference to blessing the Lord comes only in the last line of the strophe. The only reference to children ("Infant-Voices") in the psalm occurs at the end of v. 4, "he shall save the children of the needy," which is a section of the text covered in part one of Watts's hymn. Perhaps this phrase is an oblique allusion to Matthew 21:15-16, in which Jesus quotes from Psalm 8:2:

> [15]And when the chief priests and scribes saw the wonderful things that he did, and the children crying in the temple, and saying, Hosanna to the son of David; they were sore displeased,
> [16]And said unto him, Hearest thou what these say? And Jesus saith unto them, Yea; have ye never read, Out of the mouth of babes and sucklings thou hast perfected praise?

All these indirect allusions reveal the freedom with which Watts approached the text of the specific psalm he was "imitating" as a source for his hymn.

Donald Rodgers Fletcher criticized this stanza, suggesting that "The expression of 'Infant-Voices' 'proclaiming their early Blessings' shows a straining after effect," when "It would be just as strong and much clearer to say, 'And little children shall sing his praises.'" Fletcher concludes that "The poets of the earlier eighteenth century sometimes forgot that ornamentation which is non-functional is poor art."[5] Without necessarily disputing Fletcher's appraisal of this stanza and his dictum about the value of directness, it should be remarked that one of the beauties of poetry (especially hymnic poetry) is its ability to express truth by suggestion and implication—and, yes, ornamentation—rather than through the prosaically obvious.[6]

Stanza 6
> Blessings abound where e'er he reigns,
> The Prisoner leaps to lose his Chains,
> The Weary find eternal Rest,
> And all the Sons of Want are blest.

Stanza 6 begins with an anadiplosis by picking up the word "Blessings" from the last line of stanza 5. There is no direct parallel to these lines in the psalm, but the "Blessings" are probably a generic summary of those referred to in vv. 6-7 and vv. 12-14:

> [6]He shall come down like rain upon the mown grass: as showers that water the earth.
> [7]In his days shall the righteous flourish; and abundance of peace so long as the moon endureth....
> [12]For he shall deliver the needy when he crieth; The poor also, and him that hath no helper.
> [13]He shall spare the poor and needy, and shall save the souls of the needy.
> [14]He shall redeem their soul from deceit and violence: and precious shall their blood be in his sight.

---

[5] Fletcher, "English Psalmody and Isaac Watts," 124.

[6] It should be noted that Fletcher called the next stanza of this hymn, "Blessings abound where e'er he reigns," "strong, imaginative hymn-writing" (133). On pages 161–62, Fletcher provides a side-by-side comparison of verses from Psalm 72 with the stanzas of Watts's hymn that differs slightly from the analysis given here and reveals both the ambiguity and rich imagery of the poet's work.

Watts then gets specific about who receives these blessings: the "Prisoner," the "Weary," and the "Sons of Want." The reference to the "Sons of Want" may be drawn from vv. 12 and 13 ("the needy"), perhaps with an allusion to v. 4, but there is no exact parallel to the "Weary" and the "Prisoner." Indeed, this stanza seems to correspond as much to Psalm 146:7-8, which Watts paraphrased in "I'll Praise My Maker with My Breath," as it does to Psalm 72.

> [7]Which executeth judgment for the oppressed: which giveth
>   food to the hungry. The LORD looseth the prisoners:
> [8]The LORD openeth the eyes of the blind: the Lord raiseth
>   them that are bowed down: the Lord loveth the
>   righteous

This cross-reference shows yet another procedure that Watts used from time to time by inserting passages from another psalm into one of his paraphrases.

Stanza 7
> Where he displays his healing Power,
> Death and the Curse are known no more;
> In him the Tribes of *Adam* boast
> More Blessings than their Father lost.

The author marked stanzas 7 and 8 for possible omission, perhaps in part because—in spite of a vague similarity to the opening of v. 14 ("He shall redeem their soul from deceit and violence")—he essentially abandons the psalm altogether to make a straightforward theological statement (st. 7) and provide a call to doxology (st. 8). Again, there are indirect references to other Scriptures, this time to 1 Corinthians 15: "For as in Adam all die, even so in Christ shall all be made alive. The first man Adam was made a living soul; the last Adam was made a quickening spirit."

Wherever Jesus reigns and "displays his healing Power" he does away with "Death and the Curse" (original sin). Adam, through his sin, lost Eden, but, thanks to Jesus, his descendants can gain something even better, paradise. Note that Watts returns to the word "Blessings" in the last line, wrapping up the unit of three "Blessings" stanzas that began in stanza 5.

Stanza 8
> Let every Creature rise and bring,
> Peculiar Honours to our King;
> Angels descend with Songs again,
> And Earth repeat the long *Amen.*]

Stanza 8 wraps up "Jesus Shall Reign" with a call on all of creation to honor King Jesus, expanding upon v. 19 of the psalm, "let the whole earth be filled with his glory; Amen, and Amen." The first two lines also reflect Revelation 5:13, from which Watts derives the "every Creature" of the first line and "Honours" in the second: "And every creature which is in heaven, and on the earth, and under the earth, and such as are in the sea, and all that are in them, heard I saying, Blessing, and honour, and glory, and power, be unto him that sitteth upon the throne, and unto the Lamb for ever and ever."

In the eighteenth century, the word "peculiar" did not mean "odd" or "strange" as it is used today, but "particular" or "singular."[7] The implication is that "every Creature" is to bring the "Honours" that are specific to them. These could be objects, abilities, personality traits, or other features, but whatever they are, they are to be our own, not those of someone else; we are to use what God has given *us* to honor the Son.

To choose a simple example, violinists should use their playing to honor Christ; they should not preach a sermon. Pastors should preach their best sermon rather than play the violin. This is neither to say that violinists cannot preach a sermon nor pastors play the violin but that we should not assume that because we have not been blessed with a particular talent or ability we have nothing to give.

The line "Angels descend with Songs again" is an indirect allusion to the song of the angels at the birth of Jesus: "And suddenly there was with the angel a multitude of the heavenly host praising God, and saying, Glory to God in the highest, and on earth peace, good will toward men" (Luke 2:14). The suggestion is that just as the angels descended from heaven to sing at Christ's birth they will descend again, this time to join with the song of the redeemed.

---

[7] N. Bailey, *An Universal Etymological English Dictionary.*

Because of its message of the spread of Jesus' praise around the globe, "Jesus Shall Reign Where'er the Sun" has sometimes been called "the first missionary hymn."[8] Whether or not it merits that designation, it is certainly remarkable that this hymn was written many decades before the beginning of the modern missionary movement in England. Watts's hymn on the universal reign of Christ, a result of the "universalistic spirit of the Hebrew Psalter,"[9] shows that he did not view the faith as being only for England or even for Europe, but that it would eventually encompass "a great multitude…of all nations, and kindreds, and people, and tongues" who would unite in singing "with a loud voice, saying, Salvation to our God which sitteth upon the throne, and unto the Lamb" (Rev 7:9-10).

---

[8] See Routley, *Hymns and the Faith*, 270. The honor of "first missionary hymn" has also been accorded to Martin Luther's version of Psalm 67, *Es wolle Gott uns gnädig sein* ("May God Bestow on Us His Grace"), first published in 1524, nearly 200 years before Watts's hymn. Several other Watts texts also deal with the spread of the gospel and the universal reign of Christ, including some discussed in other chapters of this book (see "The Heavens Declare Thy Glory, Lord").

[9] Escott, *Isaac Watts, Hymnographer*, 160.

14

JOY TO THE WORLD; THE LORD IS COME

"Joy to the World; the Lord Is Come" is one of Isaac Watts's best known and most often sung hymns. It first appeared in *The Psalms of David Imitated* as the second part of his version of Psalm 98. Part one, "To Our Almighty Maker God," was titled "Praise for the Gospel" and consisted of three stanzas. The second part was titled "The Messiah's Coming and Kingdom." Between the two parts, the author placed the following note: "In these two Hymns which I have formed out of the 98th Psalm I have fully exprest what I esteem to be the first and chief Sense of the holy Scriptures, both in this and the 96th Psalm, whose Conclusions are both alike."[1]

What Watts meant by this sentence was that he had extracted a central idea from each of the two psalms and expounded and expanded upon that theme rather than providing a versification or paraphrase of the entire psalm text. It is possible that he took this approach in part to avoid having to deal with Psalm 98:5-6, which mentions playing the harp, trumpets, and cornet before the Lord.

Watts and Musical Instruments

Watts was a Calvinist minister in a Calvinist congregation, and in this tradition musical instruments were not permitted in worship. As the hymn writer pointed out in the preface to *The Psalms of David Imitated*, he thought it was inappropriate for a "Parish-Clerk" in a "Country Church" to "bid all the People joyn with his Words and say, I will praise

---

[1] Watts, *The Psalms of David Imitated*, 253.

thee upon a Psaltery; or, I will open my dark Saying upon the Harp; when even our Cathedrals sing only to the Sound of an Organ," or to assert that "they were to play upon Harp and Psaltery, when Thousands never saw such an Instrument, and know nothing of the Art."[2] Thus, throughout *The Psalms of David Imitated*, he generally omitted references to instruments, interpreted them allegorically (as was common with Calvinists), or cast them in a negative light.

Three examples will illustrate his approaches to the mention of musical instruments in the psalms. In his version of Psalm 150—which is full of references to instruments—Watts omitted every mention of them. In the first part of Psalm 92, he allegorically compares "David's Harp of solemn Sound" to having his "Heart in Tune be found" (see chapter 19). The third part of Psalm 69 speaks negatively of instruments by asserting that Jesus' "dying Groans" and "living Songs / Shall better please my God / Than Harp or Trumpet's solemn Sound." In "Joy to the World," he took the first approach.

Part One of the Psalm

Both parts of the Psalm 98 version use common meter, are iambic in structure, and employ cross rhyme. To provide context for "Joy to the World; the Lord Is Come," part one of the Psalm 98 imitation is quoted below.

> 1. To our Almighty Maker God
>   New Honours be addrest;
> His great Salvation shines abroad,
>   And makes the Nations blest.
> 2. He spake the Word to *Abraham* first,
>   His Truth fulfills the Grace:
> The *Gentiles* make his Name their Trust,
>   And learn his Righteousness.
> 3. Let the whole Earth his Love proclaim
>   With all her different Tongues;
> And spread the Honours of his Name
>   In Melody and Songs.

---

[2] Ibid., xiii–xiv.

The source of part one in Psalm 98 is much more obvious than it is for part two. The initial stanza of part one is a relatively straightforward rendering of Psalm 98:1-2. Verses 2 and 3 form the backdrop for stanza 2, and stanza 3 is a paraphrase of 98:4.

"Joy to the World"

The last clause of the note to Psalm 98 suggests that because the concluding verses of Psalms 96 and 98 are nearly identical (compare Pss 96:11-13; 98:7-9) we should expect some sort of relationship between the two psalms in Watts's paraphrase. Such, indeed, seems to be the case, as will be demonstrated below.

> Stanza 1
> > Joy to the World; the Lord is come;
> > > Let Earth receive her King:
> > Let every Heart prepare him Room,
> > > And Heaven and Nature sing.

As noted above, Watts chose to write "Joy to the World" in iambic meter. However, he gives the reader or singer a surprise at the very opening of the hymn by using a choriambus, followed by two feet of straightforward iambic: "**Joy** to the **World**; the **Lord** is **Come**." This alteration of meter is neither accidental nor incidental but serves as an enhancement of the meaning of the text. Dactylic meter is frequently employed for texts that are of a celebratory or joyful nature (the "chor" in choriambus is the Greek word for "dance"), while iambic meter is often found in lyrics that are supplicating, inviting, or explanatory, the unaccented syllable typically pulling the reader or singer forward into the next thought. By opening with a dactyl, Watts emphasizes the "joy" that is being proclaimed to the world; the turn to iambic then gives the reason for this joy ("the Lord is come") as if to answer an unspoken question, "Why is there joy to the world?"

The iambic meter continues through the rest of the stanza, inviting earth to receive its king, every heart to prepare room for this king, and all of heaven and earth to sing praise. Note the use of anaphora ("Let") and the progression from "earth" (the world) to "heart" (the individual) to "heaven and nature" (all of creation). One of the implications of the stanza is that when human hearts prepare to receive the Lord, the heavens and all of nature join in a song of praise. This idea is reminiscent of Luke 15:7: "joy shall be in heaven over one sinner that repenteth."

Another point to be noted in this stanza is that Watts used the present-tense "is" rather than "has" in line 1: "the Lord *is* come." "Has" would have placed the Lord's coming in the past, i.e., a celebration strictly geared toward the nativity. With "is," Watts located the advent in the present without necessarily excluding it also having occurred at a particular point in history; the implication of this ambiguity is that the arrival of the Lord is not just a long-ago event but also a present and future occurrence.

This opening stanza appears to be an abbreviated version of Psalm 98:4-9, from which Watts picks up the ideas of making "a joyful noise unto the Lord" (v. 4), his coming "to judge the earth" (v. 9), and the response of nature and humanity (as well as heaven) to the Lord's advent. The lines recall other Scripture passages as well. In fact, the phrases "Joy to the world" and "And heaven and nature sing" seem to be derived more directly from Psalm 96:11a ("Let the heavens rejoice, and let the earth be glad") than from Psalm 98.

Line 2, "Let Earth receive Her King," is similar in some ways to Psalm 24:7, "Lift up your heads, O ye gates; and be ye lift up, ye everlasting doors; and the King of glory shall come in," while the idea of the heart preparing room for the Lord reminds the reader or singer that Mary laid Jesus "in a manger; because there was no room for them in the inn" (Luke 2:7). Such a kaleidoscopic employment of the Scriptures was characteristic of many of Watts's psalm versions, and in this case, he used the approach to create an exuberant call on all of creation—including the human heart—to prepare a place for the coming King.

Stanza 2
> Joy to the Earth, The Saviour reigns;
>> Let Men their Songs employ;
> While Fields & Floods, Rocks, Hills & Plains
>> Repeat the sounding Joy.

Stanza 2 is written in parallel fashion to stanza 1: both begin with the same three words, employ a choriambus to express a sense of joy (this time it is "the Earth" that is joyful), then give the reason for the joy and

132

issue an invitation. Whereas the Lord "is come" in stanza 1, now he is celebrated because he "reigns," and therefore, believers (along with all of creation, as in stanza 1) should sing songs of praise.

Here again, Watts seems to have drawn upon both Psalms 96 and 98 for portions of the text. There appears to be little direct relationship between line 1 and any part of Psalm 98, but two half-verses in Psalm 96 show parallel thoughts: "Let the heavens rejoice, and let the earth be glad" (11a) from which the idea of "Joy to the Earth" is drawn; and "Say among the heathen that the Lord reigneth" (10a), from which he derived "The Saviour reigns." Watts then returns to Psalm 98:4-6 for the second line.

Psalm 98 mentions "floods" and "hills" (v. 8) but not "fields," which are alluded to in Psalm 96 (v. 12, "the field"). Watts appears to have added "rocks" and "plains," though for the former he might have had in mind Luke 19:40, "I tell you that, if these should hold their peace, the stones would immediately cry out," and for the latter Isaiah 35:1, "The wilderness and the solitary place shall be glad for them; and the desert shall rejoice, and blossom as the rose."

The idea of natural objects echoing human praise ("Repeat the sounding Joy") is not directly stated in Psalm 98 though it is implied by the order of the verses. Verses 4-6 of the psalm call for humans to "make a joyful noise" to the Lord with harps, psalms, trumpets, and cornets. Verses 7 and 8 then command the sea, the world, the floods, and the hills to join in praise, suggesting that they are responding to what humans have done.

Another point to be made about this stanza is Watts's use of the word "Saviour." Whereas the word "Lord" in stanza 1 could be interpreted as either the Father or the Son, Watts and his contemporaries would have clearly understood "Saviour" in this context as a reference to Jesus. Here again, Watts has directly "Christianized" the psalm.

Stanza 3
> No more let Sins and Sorrows grow,
>> Nor Thorns infest the Ground:
> He comes to make his Blessings flow
>> Far as the Curse is found.

The first two lines of stanza 3 have no direct parallel in Psalm 98 or, for that matter, in Psalm 96. As human beings, we can never do away completely with "Sins and Sorrows" (note the alliteration and the hissing "s" sounds) but Watts observes that at least we do not have to let them "grow." The implication is that "Sins and Sorrows" are like weeds; we may not be able to prevent them, but we can keep them from spreading and ruining the crop. The implied comparison with weeds is made stronger in the second line by the mention of "Thorns infest[ing] the Ground."

The linkage between "Sins and Sorrows" and "Thorns" recalls two Scripture passages, one from the Old Testament and one from the New Testament. Genesis 3:17b-18 tells of the curse that God laid on Adam for his disobedience in eating of the tree of the knowledge of good and evil: "Cursed is the ground for thy sake; in sorrow shalt thou eat of it all the days of thy life; thorns also and thistles shall it bring forth to thee"; that Watts probably had this passage in mind is implied by the mention of "the Curse" in the last line of the stanza. Matthew 13 gives Jesus' parable of the Sower, some of whose seed "fell among thorns; and the thorns sprung up, and choked them" (v. 7), which he likened to a person who hears the word "and the care of this world, and the deceitfulness of riches, choke the word" and the person becomes "unfruitful" (v. 22).[3]

Lines 3 and 4 give the reason why "the Lord is come": to exchange "Blessings" for the "Curse." The blessings are characterized as flowing, in constant movement, washing away the curse. As a Calvinist, Watts perhaps meant the term "Curse" as a reference to original sin, but he could also have had the "curse of the Law" in mind (Gal 3:13).[4] The point, however, is that there is no need for humans to labor under either curse since God has provided a remedy by his salvific work.

---

[3] In his dissertation, "The Heroic Hymn of Isaac Watts," Stephenson linked Watts's mention of "Thorns" to "the crown of the Passion" (the crown of thorns) (199). Stephenson's work points out many similarities in approach between "Joy to the World" and "There Is a Land of Pure Delight" to demonstrate the essential unity between Watts's psalm imitations and his hymns (196–200).

[4] Bond, *The Poetic Wonder of Isaac Watts*, 117.

Stanza 4

> He rules the World with Truth and Grace,
>> And makes the Nations prove
> The Glories of his Righteousness,
>> And Wonders of his Love.

Watts based the last stanza partly on Psalm 98:9, "with righteousness shall he judge the world, and the people with equity." He begins the strophe by noting that the Savior reigns "with Truth and Grace." This appears to combine the psalm verse with part of the great hymn on the Incarnation that opens the Gospel of John: "And the Word was made flesh, and dwelt among us, (and we beheld his glory, the glory as of the only begotten of the Father,) full of grace and truth" (1:14; see also 1:17). According to Bailey, equity (used in the KJV verse that provides the background for the stanza) "is the Virtue of treating all Persons according to the Rules of Reason and Justice, as we would be treated by them were we in their Circumstances."[5]

The remainder of the stanza emphasizes that because the Lord rules with truth and grace, the nations "prove" his righteousness and love. From Psalm 89:9 Watts took the idea of God's judging in "righteousness" but added that this righteousness is glorious; in typical fashion, he also linked God's righteousness with the "Wonders of his Love," an idea that is not found in the psalm.

Bailey does not give a definition for the word "prove" in either his first or second edition but uses the term in defining a number of verbs, including "to demonstrate," "justify," "try" or "verify"; "demonstrate" or "verify" was probably the sense in which Watts was using it. Thus, the stanza might be understood as "God rules the world and causes the nations to demonstrate the glories of his righteousness and the wonders of his love." The middle lines of the stanza appear to reflect the second half of the psalm's second verse, "his righteousness hath he openly shewed in the sight of the heathen."

At first glance, it appears that the last stanza does not contain a true rhyme. That is certainly the case according to modern pronunciation, but in the early eighteenth century "prove" and "love" had corresponding

---

[5] N. Bailey, *An Universal Etymological English Dictionary*.

vowel sounds.[6]

"Joy to the World," like "Jesus Shall Reign Where'er the Sun," is one of Watts's psalm versions that seems to be more of an "imitation" than a "paraphrase" by capturing the spirit rather than the content or wording of the psalm. Donald Rodgers Fletcher points out that "The 98th psalm (*Cantate Domino*) is an exuberant psalm of praise." Fletcher continues, "Catching this spirit, but interpreting it in a Christian frame, Watts wrote his triumphant hymn, 'Joy to the World; the Lord is come'. The spirit is the same as that of the psalm. Some of the expressions are quite similar; yet the whole has been recast so that the content of the Hebrew psalm is scarcely recognizable as the substance of Watts' Christian song."[7]

"Joy to the World" and Christmas

"Joy to the World" is now linked with the Christmas season. Singing the hymn to celebrate the birth of Jesus is not inappropriate since it observes that "the Lord is come" and, as noted above, there are parallels between the text and several New Testament nativity Scriptures.

However, the association of the lyric with Christmas is indirect at best. There is no mention at all of many of the elements of the Christmas story: Mary, Joseph, baby, Bethlehem, angels, shepherds, manger, star, or wise men; indeed, Jesus himself is not mentioned by name, nor is there any reference to "Immanuel," "Messiah," "Prince of Peace," "Christ," or other names by which Jesus was called.[8] The absence of these topics and names would perhaps be understandable in a psalm version by another author, but as noted several times in this book, Watts commonly transferred New Testament words and concepts into psalm texts in *The Psalms of David Imitated* (see, for example, the chapter on "Jesus Shall Reign Where'er the Sun"). However, it must also be remembered that Watts was a Calvinistic Independent, a group that did not believe in the celebration of Christmas or any other "holy days" except Sunday. Watts frequently wrote about the incarnation but most often in theological

---

[6] Bysshe, "A Dictionary of Rhymes," in *The Art of English Poetry*, 31.

[7] Fletcher, "English Psalmody and Isaac Watts," 120.

[8] Of course, in the New Testament Jesus was called "Lord" but the term was used in the Old Testament exclusively for the Father.

terms rather than about the details of the physical birth.[9]

Thus, Watts did not intend "Joy to the World" to be a specifically Christmas hymn though such usage should not be ruled out. Instead, as observed by Martin A. Wallenstein, the author's "imitation of this psalm preserved the joyous and vigorous flavor of the original while changing the God it celebrated from a Jehovah figure coming to judge the earth to that of a Christ figure, thus making the Hymn based on the psalm celebrate his 'Coming and Kingdom.'"[10] Watts did this in such a way that the text can be understood in a variety of dimensions—God's incarnation as a baby in Bethlehem, Jesus' advent as a spiritual presence in our lives, or Christ's coming as King of Kings and Lord of Lords at the end of time.

The Tune

A few words must be said about the tune ANTIOCH, to which Watts's text is almost universally sung in the English-speaking world. The tune may have first appeared in volume four of Charles Rider's *Psalmodia Britannica*, where it was titled COMFORT and said to be "Partly from J. Leach." None of the volumes of *Psalmodia Britannica* were dated until the fifth, which listed its publication as 1832; thus volume four must have been issued in that year or earlier. A somewhat different version of COMFORT was printed in T. Hawkes's *A Collection of Tunes* in 1833 with the notation "Author [i.e., composer] unknown," and about the same time it appeared in volume three of an undated collection by Thomas Clark, *The Congregational Harmonist* (vol. 1 was published in 1828 and vol. 4 in 1835). Sometime between 1833 and 1835, COMFORT was printed again in W. Holford's *Voci di Melodia*, where it was credited to "Handel" and the melody was arranged in a manner that is very similar to the way ANTIOCH is sung today. In 1836, the American compiler Lowell Mason apparently borrowed the version published by Holford (making a few slight changes), gave it the present title, and set it

---

[9] It is interesting to note, however, that in two of his psalm versions that immediately precede this one Watts makes direct reference to details of the incarnation. See *The Psalms of David Imitated*, Psalm 97 LM, part 2, and Psalm 97 CM.

[10] Wallenstein, "The Rhetoric of Isaac Watts's Hymns, Psalms, and Sermons," 165.

to Watts's text.[11] Mason's setting is the one now universally known and sung.

ANTIOCH appears to be an arrangement of phrases from various movements in George Frederic Handel's oratorio *Messiah*, written in 1741 and first performed in Dublin, Ireland, in 1742. The initial phrase of the tune derives from the opening of the tenor part in Handel's chorus "Glory to God." The chorus begins with two statements of the words "Glory to God" in the rhythm quarter note/dotted eighth note/sixteenth note/quarter note on descending tetrachords (groups of four notes); the first tetrachord uses the pitches D-C#-B-A and the second tetrachord the pitches B-A-G-F#. The opening of ANTIOCH is the same as the first tetrachord but instead of using the second tetrachord the hymn tune continues down the scale to the lower tonic note (D). However, this scalar descent was an alteration made by Mason; in COMFORT (as printed by Holford), the second half of the phrase was given the same pitches as the second tetrachord of "Glory to God," though in a completely different rhythm.[12]

The second phrase of ANTIOCH shows some similarity to Handel's setting of the words "saith your God" in the accompanied recitative "Comfort Ye" (m. 13), while the instrumental introduction to the same movement (mm. 1-2) supplied the fourth phrase of the hymn. The beginning of the tune's third phrase ("Let every heart") bears a slight resemblance to the principal melody in the aria "He Shall Feed His Flock."

There is a certain irony in the fact that Watts's words have been combined with a tune based on themes from Handel's *Messiah*. Like "Joy to the World," *Messiah* has become closely linked with the Christmas season, which is when the majority of performances are programmed. While the first part of *Messiah* has a direct focus on the birth of Christ, the oratorio is much more than that, covering not only the incarnation (though, as in "Joy to the World," mostly indirectly) but also the ministry, crucifixion, death, resurrection, second coming, and eternal reign of the Savior. In fact, the librettist for the oratorio, Charles Jennens, in-

---

[11] For details of these books and arrangements, see Wilson, "The Evolution of the Tune Antioch," 107–14, and "Handel and the Hymn Tune: II, Some Hymn Tune Arrangements," 30–31. Fenner, "Joy to the World."

[12] The opening tetrachord is also the same as the beginning of the first soprano part in the chorus "Lift Up Your Heads."

tended the work to be performed in association with Easter, and its first performance was in April, during Lent. Like "Joy to the World," *Messiah* is also unusual for a "Christmas" work in never once mentioning the name of Jesus.[13]

Regardless of its origin (or not) in *Messiah*, there is little doubt that ANTIOCH makes an excellent match for "Joy to the World." The exuberance of the melody matches well with the hymn's overall theme of joy. The downward movement of the melody in the first phrase aptly illustrates God's descending to earth (implied by the opening line of the text), the octave leap upward on "heaven" vividly portrays this word, and the antiphonal harmonization of the fourth phrase is particularly fitting for the line "Repeat the sounding joy" in stanza 2. Since the early versions of ANTIOCH were not written for "Joy to the World," these bits of "word painting" were not intentional, but they do enhance the message of the text, in each case without adversely affecting the meaning of the other stanzas. It is not often that there is such a satisfying combination of text and tune.

---

[13] It has frequently been pointed out that most of the texts for *Messiah* were drawn from the Old Testament; the New Testament passages that were chosen also did not mention Jesus' name though terms such as "Christ" and "Immanuel" do appear.

15

MY SHEPHERD WILL SUPPLY MY NEED

Psalm 23 was evidently a favorite with Watts—as it has been for many other people before and since his time—for he included three different versions of the entire text in *The Psalms of David Imitated*, one in each of the most common hymnic meters: "My Shepherd Is the Living Lord" (LM), "My Shepherd Will Supply My Need" (CM), and "The Lord My Shepherd Is" (SM). The first of these is labeled "God our Shepherd," but the title obviously refers to all three versions.

"My Shepherd Will Supply My Need" is laid out in six stanzas of iambic meter. This hymn corresponds more directly to the text of the psalm than some of Watts's other paraphrases but though both the psalm and the hymn have six units (six verses of psalm, six stanzas of hymn), the stanzas do not precisely parallel the verses of the psalm. This was common in Watts's paraphrases, in which several verses of Scripture might be shoehorned into a single stanza, or, conversely, the thoughts of one or two verses are expanded over the course of several strophes.

Stanza 1
  My Shepherd will supply my Need,
      Jehovah is his Name;
  In Pastures fresh he makes me feed
      Beside the living Stream.

The hymn's initial stanza paraphrases Psalm 23:1-2:

  ¹The LORD is my shepherd; I shall not want.
  ²He maketh me to lie down in green pastures:
      He leadeth me beside the still waters.

Watts's practice of transferring New Testament concepts into his paraphrases of the psalms is clear from the opening line, for it alludes directly to the first part of Philippians 4:19, "But my God shall supply all your need according to his riches in glory by Christ Jesus."[1] Given changes in meaning since the seventeenth and eighteenth centuries, Watts's "Need" is perhaps a more accurate description for modern singers than the "want" of the King James Version ("I shall not want"), which in context should be understood as "My lack will be supplied" but might be misunderstood as "I will be given what I desire." Modern biblical scholars believe that "Jehovah" is an inaccurate rendering of the Hebrew word that is better transliterated as "Yahweh," but in the King James Version (and in Watts's day) the former was an accepted form of the Tetragrammaton (YHWH), the "unspoken" Hebrew name for God.[2]

Watts makes a couple of changes in the text of the psalm that give it a slightly different emphasis from the original. One is to alter the idea of "lying down" in the green (or "fresh") pastures to "feeding" in them. He also places the "pastures" and "still waters"—which are separated in the psalm—together: now the pastures are "Beside" the "living Stream" (note that the waters are no longer "still"). Perhaps he had in mind here Revelation 7:17a, "For the Lamb which is in the midst of the throne shall feed them, and shall lead them unto living fountains of waters." These modifications do not change the basic message of the stanza but provide a slightly different perspective on God's care for his people.

Stanza 2
    He brings my wand[e]ring Spirit back
        When I forsake his Ways;
    And leads me for his Mercy's sake
        In Paths of Truth and Grace.

Stanza 2 corresponds to the third verse of the psalm, "He restoreth my soul: he leadeth me in the paths of righteousness for his name's sake." The idea of "restoration" is described as the sheep's spirit "wandring" and

---

[1] The author alluded to this verse in another hymn, "In Vain We Lavish Out Our Lives" (3:1: "Our God will ev'ry Want supply").

[2] See chapter 3. Should a substitute for the word be desired, "the Lord God" will fit metrically and is an accurate replacement.

forsaking God's ways but then being brought back into the fold. "Righteousness" is defined as "Truth and Grace" (perhaps an allusion to John 1:14, 17) and the name of God is allegorized as "Mercy."

Stanza 3
> When I walk thro' the shades of Death
> Thy Presence is my stay;
> A Word of thy supporting Breath
> Drives all my Fears away.

The third stanza paraphrases Psalm 23:4, "Yea, though I walk through the valley of the shadow of death, I will fear no evil: for thou art with me; thy rod and thy staff they comfort me." Lines 1 and 2 are a relatively straightforward rendering of "Yea, though I walk through the valley of the shadow of death" and "for thou art with me," while "I will fear no evil" is reserved for the last line ("Drives all my Fears away"). The phrase "thy rod and staff they comfort me" is omitted entirely. In its place, Watts writes that "A Word of thy supporting Breath" is what drives the sheep's fears away.[3] In making this substitution, the implication is that the rod and staff are equivalent to the word of God—which can be understood as either the Bible (the word) or Jesus (the Word), or perhaps both—correcting, guiding, and rescuing the sheep. In the background are echoes of Jesus's words in John 10:27, "My sheep hear my voice, and I know them, and they follow me."

---

[3] This line is similar to one in Watts's version of Psalm 104 ("A Word of thy creating Breath / Repairs the Wast[e]s of Time and Death"), and another in his poem "An Hymn to Christ Jesus, The Eternal Life" ("Where Shall the Tribes of Adam Find")—but with an opposite context—published in *Reliquiæ Juveniles...Written Chiefly in Younger Years* in 1734: "A Word of his Almighty Breath / Dooms the rebellious World to Death." Though printed much later than "My Shepherd Will Supply My Need," the poem may have preceded the psalm paraphrases, as is evident from the subtitle of *Reliquiæ Juveniles*. A portion of "Where Shall the Tribes of Adam Find" (beginning with an alteration of the fourth stanza from "Jesus, our Kinsman, and our God" to "Jesus, our Saviour, and our God") was included in nineteenth-century editions of Watts's Psalms and Hymns.

Stanza 4
> Thy Hand in sight of all my Foes
> Doth still my Table spread;
> My Cup with Blessings overflows,
> Thine Oyl anoints my Head.[4]

Stanza 4 is Watts's version of Psalm 23:5, "Thou preparest a table before me in the presence of mine enemies: thou anointest my head with oil; my cup runneth over," and is probably his most literal rendering of a verse from the psalm. The author provided the following note about this stanza: "St. 4. The Oyl or Ointment that was used of old to anoint and perfume the Head, in the Sense and Language of the New Testament, must signify the Communications of the Holy Spirit, which is call'd the Anointing. I. John 2. 20, 27. as I have explained it in the Long Metre, and Psal. 45. 7. with John 3. 34. approves it."[5] The note refers back to the long meter version of the psalm, the seventh stanza of which reads as follows.

> How I rejoice when on my Head
> Thy Spirit condescends to rest!
> 'Tis a Divine Anointing Shed
> Like Oyl of Gladness at a Feast.

In the long meter setting, Watts links the psalm verse with the New Testament story of the woman who anointed Jesus' head with "ointment" during a dinner in Bethany (Matt 26:7; Mark 14:3), as well as 1 John 2:20 ("But ye have an unction [anointing] from the Holy One") and 27 ("the anointing which ye have received of him abideth in you"). In Christian tradition, anointing the head with oil is often a symbol of the descent of the Holy Spirit on the individual believer, and that was clearly Watts's intent in the long meter paraphrase of the psalm. The common meter version is less direct about this symbolism, which is why the hymn

---

[4] In the second edition of *The Psalms of David Imitated* "Oyl" was changed to "Oil."

[5] Watts, *The Psalms of David Imitated* (1719), 69.

writer appended the note explaining his interpretation of the passage.[6]

It seems likely that the basic framework of this stanza was borrowed from Nahum Tate and Nicholas Brady's setting of the text in *A New Version of the Psalms of David* (1696), the fifth stanza of which reads as follows.

> By him, in sight of all my Foes,
>   My Table's richly spread,
> My Cup o'erflows with gen'rous Wine,
>   With precious Oyls my Head.

Watts's stanza also shows remarkable similarity to the parallel strophe in his short meter version of Psalm 23.

> In spight of all my Foes
>   Thou dost my Table spread,
> My Cup with Blessings overflows,
>   And Joy exalts my Head.[7]

Stanza 5
> The sure Provisions of my God
>   Attend me all my Days;
> O may thy House be mine Abode
>   And all my Work be Praise!

The last two stanzas of Watts's hymn are derived from the final

---

[6] See also chapter 19 ("Sweet Is the Work"). It should be noted that in the LM version of Psalm 23 both this stanza and the following one were marked for possible omission in singing.

[7] The similarity between the short meter stanza and the Tate and Brady version was pointed out by Bishop in "The Poetical Theories of Isaac Watts," 121–22. She did not comment on the relationship of these stanzas to the common meter strophe. Watts both complimented and critiqued the psalm versions of his predecessors John Denham, Luke Milbourne, and Tate and Brady, also observing that he had taken liberty "to borrow a single Line or two from these three Authors" (counting Tate and Brady as a single "Author"), as well as extracts from the psalter by John Patrick (preface to *The Psalms of David Imitated*, xxv).

verse, Psalm 23:6: "Surely goodness and mercy shall follow me all the days of my life: and I will dwell in the house of the Lord for ever." "Goodness and mercy" are now the "sure Provisions of my God." Bailey provides several definitions of "provision," the most relevant of which in this context is "any Thing got or procured which is Necessary for the Subsistance [*sic*] of Life; a providing or taking care of." The implication of Watts's use of this word is that "goodness and mercy" are like food and drink, necessary for the sustenance of (spiritual) life.

It is interesting to note how Watts changed the focus of the two clauses of the psalm verse. The first word in the opening clause of the verse ("Surely") suggests confidence but also hopefulness, saying in essence that "I am sure that goodness and mercy *will* follow me"; in Watts this is changed to a testimony of something that is already happening: "God's provisions *already* attend me." The second clause of the psalm expresses assurance that the singer will "dwell in the house of the Lord"; Watts turns this into a prayer that God's house will be his abode.

Typically for a Watts psalm paraphrase, the author adds an idea not found in the source, in this case, that being in God's house will involve work, the work of praise. This is a subtle allusion to the descriptions of worship found in the book of Revelation; "the house of the Lord" is not an earthly temple or building as it was for King David, but a heavenly one.[8]

Stanza 6
> There would I find a settled Rest,
>> (While others go and come)
> No more a Stranger or a Guest,
>> But like a Child at Home.

Stanza 6 extends and amplifies the thought of stanza 5 about dwell-

---

[8] The last line of this stanza is similar to the concluding verses of several other Watts hymns in both *Hymns and Spiritual Songs* and *The Psalms of David Imitated*. From the former, see "Jesus Invites His Saints" (6:4: "And every Voice be Praise"), "Now Let Our Pains Be All Forgot," (7:4: "And all our Lives be Praise"), and "I Love the Windows of Thy Grace" (2nd ed., 3:3: "And all my Pow'rs be Praise"). From the latter, see "With Earnest Longings of the Mind" (Ps 41, part 1): "And all our Work was Praise."

ing in God's house. While heaven is a place of work (as in stanza 5) it is also a place of repose in the presence of the Lord. Perhaps it is not too far-fetched to compare the ideas of simultaneously working and being at a "settled Rest" with a hen who "settles" into her nest to lay her eggs. Line 2 means essentially that regardless of what others may do, I am going to find my rest in the house of the Lord.

The last two verses of the hymn are among the simplest that Watts ever wrote, but they are also some of the most profound lines in all of Christian hymnody. As he does at the conclusion of "When I Survey the Wondrous Cross," Watts uses climax, a poetic device that creates a memorable and emotional culmination to the hymn: in the house of the Lord, the believer is not going to be a stranger (someone unknown to the occupant), or even a guest (someone known but unrelated to the occupant), but a child (the occupant's own offspring) in the warmth and comfort of his or her own home. The words "No more" suggest that at one time the singer *was* a "Stranger" (someone who did not know God) and a "Guest" (a person who was invited into God's house) but *is now* "a Child at Home" (a son or daughter), thus providing an outline of the believer's progression to faith.

"My Shepherd Will Supply My Need" is a rendering of the "Shepherd's Psalm" that captures well the tender, pastoral nature of the original but expresses it in terms that a Christian who is well versed in the New Testament can immediately apply to his or her own experience of grace. The Twenty-third Psalm is among the most beautiful passages in all of Scripture, and it is difficult to imagine that anyone could begin to match it for the simplicity and sheer charm of its imagery. Watts perhaps came as close as anyone possibly could.

16

OUR GOD, OUR HELP IN AGES PAST

Psalm 90 was either a favorite passage for Watts or else he saw it as one of the most useful Scriptures for the church (or both), for he provided three versions of it in *The Psalms of David Imitated*, one each in long meter, common meter, and short meter. The long meter and short meter arrangements both consisted of a single part, but the common meter rendition was written more expansively in three parts. The opening section of the common meter version is the source of "Our God, Our Help in Ages Past."

Watts wrote the text in nine stanzas of iambic poetic meter. He titled the hymn "Man Frail and God Eternal" and noted that its basis was Psalm 90:1-5 though it appears that the paraphrase extends through v. 6.

It has been supposed that this psalm version was "written in early 1714, just before the death of Queen Anne," and that this was "the origin of that curiously sombre quality in the hymn which has caused it always to be regarded by Englishmen as the indispensable hymn for the day of decision or the day of distress," though it also "rises above local occasions and is...wholly universal."[1] There is no evidence that Watts wrote the paraphrase in these particular circumstances, but the universality of the text is unquestionable.

The first six verses of Psalm 90 deal with the eternal nature of God. However, Watts changed this focus slightly to create an alternating contrast between God's infinitude and the brevity of human existence. The first stanza serves as an introduction to the hymn and repeats as a conclusion. Stanzas 2, 4, 6, and 8 describe the transitory nature of humanity

---

[1] Routley, *Hymns and the Faith*, 34.

while the intervening stanzas (3, 5, and 7) deal explicitly with God's timelessness. In terms of subject matter, the hymn might be diagrammed as ABCBCBCBA.

Stanza 1
    Our God, our Help in Ages past,
        Our Hope for Years to come,
    Our Shelter from the stormy Blast,
        And our eternal Home.

Watts opens the hymn by paraphrasing the first verse of the psalm, "Lord, thou hast been our dwelling place in all generations," which describes the faithfulness of God throughout the ages. Watts gives emphasis to this theme through anaphora ("Our"), consonance (using the same consonant sound with different vowels, "Help" and "Hope"), onomatopoeia ("Blast"), and metaphor ("Shelter," "Home"). Lines 1 and 2 also employ antithesis ("Ages past" / "Years to come").

Perhaps the most important word in this strophe is "our": it appears five times in the stanza, twice in line 1 alone and three times as the first word in a line. This repetition drives home the close identification between God and his people—he is *our* God, *our* help, *our* hope, *our* shelter, and *our* home. Note the progression of the nouns: God is not only our help in the present, he is our hope for the future; the Lord is not only our (temporary) shelter from a storm, he is also our (permanent) place of abode. Watts's use of "help" and "hope" may be a reflection of Psalm 146:5, "Happy is he that hath the God of Jacob for his help, whose hope is in the Lord his God," a passage that was also used in "I'll Praise My Maker with My Breath." While the psalm verse is expressed in past tense ("hast been"), Watts expands the thought to include the future ("Years to come").

In his 1737 *Collection of Psalms and Hymns* (the "Charlestown Collection"), John Wesley, evidently troubled by the number of repetitions of "our," altered the first word of the stanza to "O," a change that became widely adopted. This adjustment, perhaps smoother poetically and less redundant, lessens the immediate identification of God as *our* God, and Watts's original wording seems preferable.

Stanza 2
> Under the Shadow of thy Throne
>> Thy Saints have dwelt secure;
> Sufficient is thine Arm alone,
>> And our Defence is sure.

Though Watts ended the first stanza with a period, it forms only a partial sentence that is not completed until the second stanza. This second stanza shows that the first is a direct address to God, not merely a description of God or his attributes, and it too is based on the first verse of Psalm 90, continuing the sheltering image found in the first stanza.

Watts employs the unusual imagery of the saints having lived in the shadow of God's throne, where they were secure. The implication is that in the shadow of the throne they have been hidden from their enemies. The metaphor also suggests that the saints are close enough to the throne to be in its shadow. The first two lines of the stanza recall several passages in Revelation about the beasts, elders, and redeemed surrounding the throne of God (e.g., Rev 5:11-14), but there the emphasis is primarily on worship and praise (and they are not in the shadow of the throne), not on protection, as in Watts's text. Douglas Bond suggests that Watts might have been looking ahead at a verse in the next psalm, Psalm 91:4, "He will cover you with his pinions, and under his wings you will find refuge" (NRSV); this would be entirely consistent with Watts's manner of working, for he often incorporated ideas from another psalm into the one he was paraphrasing.[2]

In a manner similar to his work in stanza 1, in the next two lines Watts turns from past tense (the saints *have dwelt* secure) to present tense (sufficient *is* thine arm) to show that God's faithfulness continues today. The sufficiency of God's arm to protect his people reflects an idea found in several other psalms, including Psalm 89:13 ("Thou hast a mighty arm") and Psalm 98:1 ("his right hand, and his holy arm, hath gotten him the victory"), as well as Deuteronomy 33:27 ("The eternal God is thy refuge, and underneath are the everlasting arms").

---

[2] See Bond, *The Poetic Wonder of Isaac Watts*, 109. Psalm 91:1-2 could equally well have served as a background for Watts's imagery.

Stanza 3
> Before the Hills in order stood,
>> Or Earth receiv'd her Frame,
> From everlasting Thou art God,
>> To endless Years the same.

Stanza 3 is a close paraphrase of Psalm 90:2, "Before the mountains were brought forth, or ever thou hadst formed the earth and the world, even from everlasting to everlasting, thou art God." Both the psalm verse and the hymn give the reason God's protection can be trusted—he is the great I AM, who is, always has been, and always will be. He was God before there was an earth or humans to call his name, and he will continue to be God long after earth, time, and humanity are gone.

Stanza 4
> Thy Word commands our Flesh to Dust,
>> *Return, ye Sons of Men*:
> All Nations rose from Earth at first,
>> And turn to Earth again.

The fourth stanza—often omitted from hymnals—paraphrases v. 3 of the psalm, "Thou turnest man to destruction; and sayest, Return, ye children of men." Here Watts quotes almost directly the words attributed to God in the psalm, changing "children" to "Sons." He did much the same thing in his long meter version of this psalm, where he gave God's words as "Return, ye Sinners, to your Dust." The psalm and the hymn remind us that we are "but Earth and Dust," as Watts himself expressed it in his version of Psalm 10 (stanza 8), and that our existence is only temporary.

In the last two lines of the stanza, the author introduces an idea not found in Psalm 90 by extending the temporary state of human beings to the temporary nature of nations. Just as the individual is made of dust and will return to dust, nations rise from earth and return to earth again, a fact that Watts emphasizes with mesodiplosis (repeating a word in the middle of successive lines: "Earth"). While this language can be taken metaphorically there is (or can be) a literal meaning as well. In past ages, as one city or civilization has crumbled and gone defunct, another is frequently built on top of it; over time all trace of the original is lost until it is rediscovered by archaeologists. Thus, the city has literally "returned to earth."

Stanza 5

> A thousand Ages in thy Sight
> Are like an Evening gone;
> Short as the Watch that ends the Night
> Before the rising Sun.

As noted above, in the opening stanzas of this hymn Watts made significant use of metaphor. In this stanza he turns to simile, "an explicit comparison of objects" that are "dissimilar in some aspect"[3]; simile differs from metaphor in that the comparison is made using the words "like" or "as": "like an Evening gone," "Short as the Watch."

Verse 4 of the psalm serves as the basis for Watts's fifth stanza: "For a thousand years in thy sight are but as yesterday when it is past, and as a watch in the night," though Watts has made the "years" of the psalm into "Ages." The central idea of the stanza is the same as that of stanza 3, the eternity of God. These stanzas contrast with stanza 4, which emphasizes the transitory nature of humans and human establishments.

Donald Rodgers Fletcher pointed out the effectiveness of Watts's paraphrasing technique in this stanza.

> The psalmist has created two distinct similes, comparing the thousand years in God's sight to yesterday and to a watch in the night. Watts has drawn the two similes closer together, making them both night periods, when also the darkness suggests sleep and the swift, uncertain passage of time. He has further united them by setting one at the beginning of the night and the other at the end, making the 'watch in the night' of the psalmist specifically the morning watch. This also in turn carries to the imagination a suggestion of the eternal Dawn after all time, enforcing the timelessness of God. The whole image is sharp, expressed in the simplest language.[4]

---

[3] Gray, *Hermeneutics of Hymnody*, 183.
[4] Fletcher, "English Psalmody and Isaac Watts," 134.

As Fletcher observes, night is when (most) humans sleep, and during sleep time seems to pass quickly. The suggestion of sleep also links up with the "Dream" of stanza 7.

Stanza 6
    [The busy Tribes of Flesh and Blood
        With all their Lives and Cares
    Are carried downwards by thy Flood,
        And lost in following Years.

Watts bracketed stanzas 6 through 8, indicating that they could be omitted in singing.[5] Stanza 6 is based on the first clause of Psalm 90:5, "Thou carriest them away as with a flood." The "them" of the psalm verse refers back to the "thousand years" in v. 4. In his paraphrase, Watts changes the image to that of "The busy Tribes of Flesh and Blood" being carried away by the flood. Thus, the stanza is not about the eternity of God so much as it is about the fleeting character of human existence (as in stanza 4). The "Tribes" are described as "busy" with "Lives and Cares" that ultimately will count for little in the scope of eternity.

Stanza 7
    Time like an ever-rolling Stream
        Bears all its Sons away;
    They fly forgotten as a Dream
        Dies at the opening Day.

Stanza 7 continues the paraphrase of Psalm 90:5a and adds the second clause of the verse, "they are as a sleep." Here Watts returns to the psalmist's metaphor of time being carried "away as with a flood."

Lines 1 and 3 of the stanza were probably derived from the version of Psalm 90 found in John Patrick's *A Century of Select Psalms, and Portions of the Psalms of David* (London, 1679):

    Death like an over-flowing stream
    Sweeps us away; our Life's a Dream.

---

[5] The bracket at the beginning of stanza 6 is missing in the first edition of *The Psalms of David Imitated*; it has been supplied here from the second edition.

Like Flow'rs i'th' Morning fresh and fair,
Cut down e're Night, and withered are.

In his long meter version of the psalm, Watts quoted portions of Patrick's lines almost verbatim.

Death like an overflowing Stream
Sweeps us away; our Life's a Dream;
An empty Tale; a Morning-flow'r
Cut down and wither'd in an Hour.

Other lines from Patrick were also copied for Watts's long meter version, and because of these borrowings, it seems likely that Watts first wrote the long meter paraphrase, then penned the one in common meter, imitating what both he and Patrick had written earlier.

The word "Sons" in Watts's hymn is somewhat ambiguous. An initial reaction would be that it refers to the "Tribes of Flesh and Blood" from stanza 6 and thus is a reference to humanity. Indeed, Watts's long meter version of v. 5 quoted above seems to have that focus. (Note the similar vocabulary in the LM and CM versions.) This interpretation is also found in recent hymnals that, because of inclusive language concerns, have changed the line to eliminate the masculine term. For example, *Worship and Rejoice* (2001) gives the line as "bears all of us away," while *Celebrating Grace* (2010) has "bears mortals all away."

More likely, however, Watts was using "Sons" not as a reference to humanity but to the "years" of stanzas 5 and 6. While, as noted above, Watts reinterpreted v. 5 of the psalm to refer to humanity in his sixth stanza, here he seems to have returned to a more literal rendering of the Scripture. The subject of the psalm's fourth verse is the "thousand years" that "are but as yesterday." Psalm 90:5 opens with "Thou carriest them away as with a flood," with "them" referring back to the thousand years. In Watts's hymn, the "Sons" of stanza 7 are a component of "Time" ("Time...bears all its Sons away"); the message of the poem is that all the parts of time are borne away. Furthermore, understanding the stanza in this way fits with Watts's plan of alternating stanzas between the eternity of God (including the present strophe) and the transitory nature of humanity. Perhaps, if a change in the text is necessary, it would be better to substitute "years" or "hours" for "Sons."

155

In the latter part of the stanza, the author draws upon the common human experience of dreaming while asleep but not being able to remember the dream upon waking. This compares to a thousand years in the eyes of God—they are just as fleeting as a human dream. Though this is one of the stanzas that Watts marked for possible omission, it is typically included in hymnals and is often sung.

Watts again turns to simile in this and the following stanza: "Time" is "like an ever-rolling Stream," its hours or days "fly forgotten as a Dream," and (in stanza 8) "the Nations stand" "Like flow'ry Fields."

Stanza 8
  Like flow'ry Fields the Nations stand
    Pleas'd with the Morning-light;
  The Flowers beneath the Mower's Hand
    Ly withering e'er 'tis Night.]

Most hymnals have followed Watts's suggestion for omitting stanza 8. As noted above, in this strophe Watts once again alters the focus of the psalm to refer to humans rather than to God's eternal nature, paraphrasing the last clause of v. 5-6:

⁵…in the morning they are like grass which groweth up.
⁶In the morning it flourisheth, and groweth up; in the evening it is cut down, and withereth.

The "they" in the psalm verse refers back to the "thousand years," but the hymn writer applied it to "the Nations." As in stanza 4, the message is that nations may flower for a time in the brightness of the "morning" of their existence; however, they will be cut down by the "Mower's Hand" before nightfall. Thus, the existence of even the most long-lasting nations is but a single (metaphorical) day in the sight of God. Note the alliterative pairing of "flow'ry Fields" in line 1 and the repetition of "Flowers" in line 3.

Stanza 9
  Our God, our Help in Ages past,
    Our Hope for Years to come,

> Be thou our Guard while Troubles last,
>   And our eternal Home.

As he did in "Come Holy Spirit, Heavenly Dove," "I'll Praise My Maker with My Breath," and a few other hymns, Watts concludes "Our God, Our Help in Ages Past" by repeating the first stanza, though with an alteration in the third line to incorporate a prayer for God's continued protection. Watts probably felt that stanza 8 (or stanza 5 if stanzas 6–8 are omitted) did not make a fitting conclusion for the hymn. As previously mentioned, the repetition of the stanza also fits the pattern that Watts set of an introduction followed by alternating stanzas dealing with God's eternal nature and human impermanence, and a conclusion that balances the introduction.

Erik Routley observed that "It is the mystery of Time that is really the subject of the hymn," time that refers to more than just passing moments but also to quality of life. As he summarizes it,

> So when we ruefully reflect on the passing of time, on the resistless flood that carries away the saints and the sinners, the brave and the sly, the beautiful and the dowdy, the young and the old, this hymn makes us able to substitute for the preposterous figure of Father Time the glorious figure of him who is our God, our help, and our Father. For him past and present and future are all one, and they all add up to *life*.[6]

"Our God, Our Help in Ages Past" was not the only hymn about time and the brevity of human existence that Watts wrote. A less well-known text from *Hymns and Spiritual Songs* has the following first two stanzas.

> 1. Time! what an empty Vapour 'tis!
>   And Days how swift they are!
> Swift as an *Indian* Arrow flies,
>   Or like a shooting Star.

---

[6] Routley, *Hymns and the Faith*, 36–37. For another analysis of "Our God, Our Help in Ages Past" see Watson, *The English Hymn*, 157–59.

2. The present Moments just appear,
    And dance away in hast[e],
That we can never say, *They're here*,
    But only say, *They're past*.

The difference between "Time! What an Empty Vapour 'Tis" and "Our God, Our Help in Ages Past" is that the former does not draw a contrast with the eternal nature of God but rather emphasizes that the Lord shares "lasting Favours" and "Bounties" with us in spite of the shortness of our being.

Because of its message of God's being our "Help in Ages past" and our "Hope for Years to come," this hymn is particularly suited—and has often been used—for New Year's services and times of Christian remembrance such as All Saints Day and funerals. In Great Britain, it is typically sung at the annual Remembrance Sunday service at the Cenotaph on Whitehall in commemoration of service men and women and civilians who served in the two World Wars and other conflicts.[7] The hymn is also appropriate for other times and themes.

"Our God, Our Help in Ages Past" is a prayer in which people acknowledge their need for God's protection and guidance. It also serves as a reminder that, though humans are temporal, God is eternal, and they can put their faith and trust in him. As Gracia Grindal put it, "Against death and disaster, only one thing counts, and Isaac Watts wrote of it in this enduring poem which still gives strength and good counsel to anxious hearts today: Your home is in God."[8]

---

[7] On the political ramifications (and misinterpretations) that have been applied to this hymn, see Stackhouse, "Hymnody and Politics," 51–52.

[8] Grindal, "Interpretation: Our God, Our Help in Ages Past," 34.

17

SALVATION! O THE JOYFUL SOUND!

In describing the second book of his *Hymns and Spiritual Songs*, consisting of texts "Composed on Divine Subjects, Conformable to the Word of God," Isaac Watts observed, "If there be Poems in the Book that are capable of giving Delight to Persons of a more refin'd Taste and polite Education, they must be sought for only in this Part," though he also acknowledged that "except they lay aside the humour of Criticism, and enter into a devout Frame, every Ode here already despairs of pleasing." To Watts's way of thinking, the temptation to foster the poetic over the spiritual in this section of the book was sometimes too great for him to resist: "I confess my self to have been too often tempted away from the more Spiritual Designs I propos'd, by some gay and flowry Expressions that gratify'd the Fancy; the bright Images too often prevail'd above the Fire of Divine Affection; and the Light exceeded the Heat." [1]

Nevertheless, the poet expressed the wish that "in many of them the Reader will find that Devotion dictated the Song, and the Head and Hand were nothing but Interpreters and Secretaries to the Heart," and he hoped "to escape the reproof of those who pay a Sacred Reverence to the Holy Bible." [2] In other words, in this part of the book the hymn writer made a special attempt to seek a middle way between poetic quality and fidelity to the Scriptures. "Salvation! O the Joyful Sound" was one of the fruits of that search.

The text appeared as hymn 88 in the second book. Watts titled the hymn simply "Salvation," and wrote it in three stanzas of common meter

---

[1] Watts, preface to *Hymns and Spiritual Songs* (1707), xi.
[2] Ibid., xi–xii.

using his usual iambic pattern and cross rhyme.

> Stanza 1
>> Salvation! O the joyful Sound!
>>> 'Tis Music to our Ears;
>> A Sovereign Balm for every Wound,
>>> A Cordial for our Fears.

The theme of Watts's hymn is expressed not only in its title but also in its very first word, "Salvation," which is further emphasized with an exclamation mark. This is a text about the grace by which humans, delivered from sin, death, and hell, are brought into communion with God. "Salvation" is a beautiful word for the believer, and Watts describes it as a "joyful Sound" that is "Music to our Ears."

In the second edition of *Hymns and Spiritual Songs*, the author altered "Music" to "Pleasure." The "Advertisements concerning the second Edition" published after the preface noted that he had "made various Corrections" in the book, "Having found by Converse with Christians what Words or Lines in the former made them less useful," but the reason for this particular change is not immediately apparent unless it is because "Pleasure" is a more generic word than "Music."

Today the word "sovereign" is generally used either as a synonym for "king/queen" or "ruler," or to describe a self-governing country (a "sovereign state"). However, Watts employed the term in another of its eighteenth-century meanings, defined by Nathan Bailey (under the spelling "Soveraign") as "Absolute, Chief, Supreme; also Excellent in its Kind." Bailey rendered "Balm" as "the Juice of a Tree growing in Palestine and Egypt," but the sense in which Watts used it is probably to be found in Bailey's definition of "Balsam": "the Juice of the Balsam, or Balm-tree.... Also several Medicinal and Chymical Compositions"; that is, a balm is a medicinal herb.[3] Bible students are familiar with this use of the term through Jeremiah 8:22 ("Is there no balm in Gilead; is there no physician there?") and hymn singers through the African American spiritual based on that passage, "There Is a Balm in Gilead." According to Watts, salvation provides the supreme healing for every wound of the human heart.

Another word that needs to be understood in its eighteenth-century

---

[3] N. Bailey, *An Universal Etymological English Dictionary.*

meaning is "Cordial," defined by Bailey as "a Physical Drink to comfort the Heart." Salvation is like a medicine that can be applied to a wound or a drink that comforts the heart of believers by taking away their fears.[4]

It is possible that Watts had in mind Psalm 89:15-18 as he wrote these lines. The stanza certainly reflects a message similar to the one expressed in the scriptural passage.

> [15]Blessed is the people that know the joyful sound: they
>   shall walk, O LORD, in the light of thy countenance.
> [16]In thy name shall they rejoice all the day: and in thy right-
>   eousness shall they be exalted.
> [17]For thou art the glory of their strength: and in thy favour
>   our horn shall be exalted.
> [18]For the LORD is our defence; and the Holy One of Israel
>   is our king.

Stanza 2
>   Bury'd in Sorrow and in Sin,
>   At Hell's dark Door we lay,
>   But we arise by Grace Divine
>   To see a heavenly Day.

Using movie terms, stanza 2 might be called a "prequel" to stanza 1. The first stanza expresses the joys of salvation, whereas the second begins by describing in graphic language the period before salvation was bestowed. This was a time of "Sorrow" and "Sin," the alliterative "s" sounds suggesting the hissing of a snake.[5] The first line is reminiscent of a scene in John Bunyan's *The Pilgrim's Progress*, first published fewer than thirty years before Watts's *Hymns and Spiritual Songs*, when Christian and Pliable, "being heedless, did both fall suddenly into the" Slough of Despond, where "they wallowed for a time, being grieviously [*sic*] bedaubed with the dirt."[6] However, in Watts's text, those in need of rescue did not merely lie or even wallow in their sorrow and sin, they were "Bury'd" in

---

[4] Ibid.

[5] The phrase "Sorrow and Sin" (in various forms) was apparently a favorite with Watts, who employed it several times (see "Joy to the World," stanza 3).

[6] Bunyan, *The Pilgrim's Progress*, 9–10.

REPEAT THE SOUNDING JOY

it, completely covered up by it. Thus, they could not even see to pull themselves out or be detected by any would-be rescuer.

But the situation was even worse than that, for, as observed in the second line, before they received salvation, they lay buried and defenseless at the very door of hell. All Satan had to do was open the door and pull them in. Watts uses alliteration to enhance the vividness of the metaphor ("dark Door").

Then, in a manner reminiscent of antithetical parallelism in a psalm verse, Watts turns things around with the word "but": We were "Bury'd" in "Sorrow" and "Sin" but now "we arise"; we lay at hell's door but now we "see a heavenly Day." And what did believers do to rescue themselves? Nothing; it was all done by "Grace Divine."

It is important to note that Watts did not use future tense in lines 3 and 4 (e.g., "we will arise") but rather placed the rising and seeing in the present. Because of God's salvation, the sinner has already risen, is still rising, and can already see the "heavenly Day." Of course, Christians now see heaven "through a glass, darkly," but the employment of present tense implies that salvation is not only for the future but also for the here and now.

Stanza 3
  Salvation! Let the Eccho [*sic*] fly
    The spacious Earth around,
  While all the Armies of the Sky
    Conspire to raise the Sound.

Watts closes this brief hymn by framing the last stanza with two important words from the first strophe, "Salvation" (which opens both stanzas) and "Sound" (which ends both the first line of stanza 1 and the last line of stanza 3). After the short "prequel" in stanza 2, the final stanza returns to the celebratory mood of the first. The author encourages the readers and singers of the hymn to let "Salvation" resound around the world, perhaps intending this to mean both in celebration of salvation received and witness to those in need of it. The last two lines are a reflection of Revelation 7:9-10:

162

⁹After this I beheld, and lo, a great multitude, which no man could number, of all nations, and kindreds, and people, and tongues, stood before the throne, and before the Lamb, clothed with white robes, and palms in their hands;

¹⁰And cried with a loud voice, saying, Salvation to our God which sitteth upon the throne, and unto the Lamb.

As noted in a previous chapter, the word "conspire" in the last line does not have a negative sense in this context, but simply means "to agree together."

Hymnals published after Watts's death sometimes added a fourth stanza and/or a chorus to Watts's original three.

> Salvation! O thou bleeding Lamb,
>   To thee the praise belongs;
> Salvation shall inspire our hearts,
>   And dwell upon our tongues.

> Chorus:
>   Blessing, honour, praise and power
>   Be unto the Lamb for ever:
>   Jesus Christ is our Redeemer,
>   Hallelujah! Praise the Lord.

These lines were not written by Watts (though the stanza does sound very "Wattsian") but were added in the 1770s.[7]

It is interesting to note lines in later hymns by other authors that, if not direct allusions to Watts's text, at least express some of the same thoughts. A little over thirty years after Watts published *Hymns and Spiritual Songs*, Charles Wesley wrote a hymn of eighteen stanzas beginning "Glory to God, and Praise and Love," from which stanzas were later extracted to form "O for a Thousand Tongues to Sing." One of these stanzas, "Jesus! the name that charms our fears," contains the verse "'Tis Musick in the Sinner's Ears," which is like the original version of the line

---

[7] For a discussion of these additions see Julian, *A Dictionary of Hymnology*, 2:987–88.

"'Tis Music to our Ears" in "Salvation! O the Joyful Sound."[8] In the nineteenth century, American Priscilla J. Owens wrote another hymn about salvation, "We Have Heard the Joyful Sound: Jesus Saves!" the first line of which carries the same basic message as parts of Watts's text.

"Salvation! O the Joyful Sound" is a jubilant expression of joy in salvation. It is perhaps one of the texts E. Paxton Hood had in mind when he said that Watts's "hymns are often raptures and ecstasies."[9] The hymn is not sung as widely as it once was, probably due in part to its brevity but also to the changes in word meaning that have been identified above. Perhaps with some judicious and careful editing the text can again become a useful tool for congregational celebration of the delight that comes from knowing Christ.

---

[8] "Glory to God, and Praise and Love" first appeared in John and Charles Wesley's *Hymns and Sacred Poems* (1740), 120–23.

[9] Hood, *Isaac Watts*, 41.

18

SHOW PITY, LORD, O LORD FORGIVE

Psalm 51 is one of the great confessions of sin and assurances of for-giveness to be found in the Bible. According to its superscription, the psalm was written by King David "when Nathan the prophet came unto him, after he had gone in to Bath-sheba." Whether or not the super-scription reflects the actual circumstance of its writing,[1] the psalm would certainly have been an appropriate expression of grief by the Hebrew king for his triple sin of covetousness, adultery, and murder (breaking three of the Ten Commandments).

The importance of this psalm in the canon is reflected in *The Psalms of David Imitated*, which includes five hymns based on the psalm, a long meter version in three parts and a common meter version in two parts. "Show Pity, Lord, O Lord Forgive" is the first part of the long meter setting. The iambic meter text is arranged in six stanzas with an AABB rhyme scheme. Watts titled the hymn "A Penitent Pleading for Pardon." As is the case with many of the psalm versions, the text is only loosely connected to the scriptural passage, sometimes picking up a single word for elaboration, combining ideas from different verses into a single stan-za, or developing more than one stanza from a single verse.

---

[1] Biblical scholars generally agree that the superscriptions were probably added when the book of Psalms was brought together from previously circulat-ing collections of ancient Hebrew lyric poetry. This is not to say that the super-scriptions are necessarily inauthentic, for they may include material copied from the original collections or reflect common-knowledge oral transmission, but at this point there is no way to be sure.

Stanza 1

> Shew pity, Lord, O Lord forgive,
> Let a repenting Rebel live:
> Are not thy Mercies large and free?
> May not a Sinner trust in Thee?

The first stanza is modeled on v. 1 of the psalm: "Have mercy upon me, O God, according to thy lovingkindness: according unto the multitude of thy tender mercies blot out my transgressions." In the initial lines, Watts substitutes the synonym "pity" for "mercy" and confesses the sin of rebellion against God. It is easy to imagine that Watts here visualized a courtroom scene in which a prisoner has just been condemned to death for his or her crimes; in this case, rebellion, the crime is probably treason. Standing before the judge, the prisoner confesses involvement in the crime, expresses repentance for it, and pleads for the magistrate to "Shew pity." The criminal then reminds the court through a rhetorical question that the judge is known for mercy and asks if this mercy can be extended to the one standing before the bar. Note the parallelisms between lines 1 and 3 ("pity," "Mercies") and two and four ("Rebel," "Sinner").

Stanza 2

> My Crimes are great, but not surpass
> The Power and Glory of thy Grace:
> Great God, thy Nature hath no Bound,
> So let thy pardoning Love be found.

Stanza 2 extends the thoughts of the first verse of the psalm and first strophe of the hymn. The prisoner is still standing before the judge, confessing his or her involvement in "Crimes," which are described as "great." Despite the enormity of the "Crimes," however, the "Grace" of the "Great God" is even larger, having "no Bound." God's grace is described as powerful and glorious. It has to be powerful in order to "surpass" the great crimes committed against the Lord; it is glorious because it brings pardon and is based on "Love."

In this stanza, Watts begins to explore alliterative pairs of words to create a sense of rhythm and rhetorical emphasis: "Glory" / "Grace," "Great God," and "let" / "Love." He maintains this use of alliterative pairs in all the following stanzas.

The first line of stanza 2 is somewhat awkward because its second half lacks a complete verb form. We would normally say something like "My crimes are great, but do not surpass / The Power and Glory of thy Grace" or "My crimes are great, but not surpassing / The Power and Glory of thy Grace." However, these forms would not contain the requisite syllable count. Perhaps for modern usage the word "don't," though somewhat inelegant, can be substituted for "not" to clarify the grammar of the line.

Stanza 3
    O wash my Soul from every Sin,
    And make my guilty Conscience clean;
    Here on my Heart the Burden lies,
    And past Offences pain my Eyes.

After using two stanzas to explicate v. 1 of the psalm, Watts then combines the next two psalm verses to form the third stanza:

    [2]Wash me throughly from mine iniquity,
        and cleanse me from my sin.
    [3]For I acknowledge my transgressions:
        and my sin is ever before me.

While pleading for pardon before the court, the prisoner recognizes that it is not possible to escape without some sort of justice and cleansing, thus the prayer that the crime (sin) be washed away. The plea that the sinner's "guilty Conscience" may be made "clean" is significant. Crimes can be committed and forgiven, but that is not quite the end of the matter: things will never be the same again.

Think, for example, of a robbery. Even if the thief is caught, confesses the crime, returns the goods, and either is forgiven or serves a sentence and is released, he or she will always bear the memory of the event, which will likely either be a source of regret or harden the person into a worse thief. Thus Watts's sinner cries out not only for the sin to be washed away but for the conscience to be cleansed as well so that the crime will be remembered no more, or will at least lose its grip on the offender. The last two lines reveal the extent of the pain caused by the conscience. As noted in the description of stanza 2, pairs of alliterative sounds are prominent in each line of this stanza: "Soul" / "Sin," "make" / "my," "Conscience clean," "Here" / "Heart," and "past" / "pain."

Stanza 4

> My Lips with Shame my Sins confess
> Against thy Law, against thy Grace:
> Lord, should thy Judgment grow severe,
> I am condemn'd, but thou art clear.

In the fourth stanza, Watts continues his exposition of Psalm 51:3 and adds v. 4: "Against thee, thee only, have I sinned, and done this evil in thy sight: that thou mightest be justified when thou speakest, and be clear when thou judgest."

Three things are noteworthy about this stanza. First, the sinner's confession is being made by his "Lips," i.e., publicly. Second, the transgression has not only been made against God's "Law" but also against his "Grace." These two revelations of God are linked by an identical formula introducing each of them ("against thy..."). The sinner accepted neither the discipline of the Law, nor the freedom of Grace, a fact that is acknowledged with "Shame." Third, the punishment administered by God, no matter how severe, is well deserved, and God himself is clear of any blame for it. God made the path to life and faith clear by sending both his Law and his Grace to give the sinner opportunity to repent. There can be no claim that God acted unfairly or unjustly in punishment. Watts drives home his point through the frequent alliteration—"Shame" / "Sins," "should" / "severe," and "condemn'd" / "clear"—in addition to his repetition of "against thy" in line 2. The frequent use of sibilants in the stanza is noteworthy, particularly in the first three lines.

Stanza 5

> Should sudden Vengeance seize my Breath,
> I must pronounce thee just in Death;
> And if my Soul were sent to Hell,
> Thy righteous Law approves it well.

Watts extends the thoughts of Psalm 51:4 into stanza 5. Even if the sentence of the prisoner is "Death," the judge is "just." Note the colorful

168

language used to describe the death throes: the "Vengeance" is "sudden" and the "Breath" is "seized." Watts recognizes the absolute sovereignty of God—should he choose to cast the prisoner into "Hell," the Lord is still blameless. In this stanza, the alliteration is of all sibilant sounds: "Should sudden" / "seize," and "Soul" / "sent," a foretaste of what is to come in the final line of the hymn.

Stanza 6
> Yet save a trembling Sinner, Lord,
> Whose Hope still hovering round thy Word
> Would light on some sweet Promise there,
> Some sure Support against Despair.

In stanza 6, Watts shines a ray of light into the dismal scene painted by the previous stanzas. Returning to the hopefulness for mercy expressed in stanza 1, the author pens a prayer for the "trembling Sinner" who puts his or her trust in God's "Word." The prayer is twofold: for salvation ("save a trembling Sinner") and for assurance ("some sweet Promise"). The stanza seems to have no direct background in Psalm 51 but reflects in general terms the prayer of v. 10, "Create in me a clean heart, O God; and renew a right spirit within me," which is more prominently dealt with in Watts's other paraphrases of the psalm.

The alliterative patterns noted in previous stanzas are also found here and are even enhanced—"save" / "Sinner," "Whose Hope" / "hovering," "some sweet," and "Some sure Support"—and sibilants are again prominent; the last line is particularly remarkable in that each word contains a sibilant sound "Some sure Support against Despair."

Confession of sin is not a popular subject. If nowhere else, this fact can be seen in statistics about the use of hymns of confession, such as this one. The website www.hymnary.org tracks the usage of this lyric in United States hymnals, showing that it was relatively common until about 1860, after which it experienced nearly a century of neglect, appearing in fewer than a quarter of the congregational song books that were published during that period. While the text seems to have rebounded somewhat in the 1970s, it has never been printed in at least half of the hymnals issued since the mid-1800s.

One of the most difficult things for humans to do is to admit wrongdoing, either in secular or religious life. We try to rationalize it, explain it away, deny it, or attack the messenger who calls it to our atten-tion.[2] Often, Christians believe (or at least act as if they believe) that ac-cepting Christ as Savior means that they no longer need to confess their sins, but nothing could be further from the truth. Confession is often seen as bad news—and we want only good news.

The irony is that confession *is* good news! It is the only way to get rid of sin, as noted in 2 Chronicles 7:14 and 1 John 1:9. Without confes-sion, sins pile up higher and higher until they become an unbearable load. To mix metaphors, authentic confession "clears the decks" and al-lows believers to start over with a clean slate.

A good example can be seen in the experience of Isaiah, who, be-holding the holiness of God, was made aware of his own sinful nature and confessed a sin of "unclean lips," after which his mouth was cleansed by burning coals from God's altar. Once his sin had been pardoned, he was then ready to "Go, and tell" (note that his commission was directly related to his confession and expiation).[3] Isaac Watts was well aware of the need for continual repentance and forgiveness, and in his writing of hymns such as "Show Pity, Lord, O Lord Forgive" he provided the church with song material that could be used to express confession in words that are at the same time biblical, heartfelt, and beautiful.

---

[2] Compare these reactions to that of King David: when Nathan the proph-et confronts him with his sin, he immediately confesses it (see 2 Sam 12:7-13).

[3] Isa 6:1-9a.

19

SWEET IS THE WORK, MY GOD, MY KING

As noted in several of the previous chapters, in *The Psalms of David Imitated* Isaac Watts sometimes provided two or three versions of a psalm, usually writing them in different hymnic meters. For Psalm 92, however, he contributed only a single version divided into two parts. "Sweet Is the Work, My God, My King" is the first part of this paraphrase.

In the King James Version of the Bible, this psalm has the superscription "A Psalm or Song for the sabbath day." Following his expressed desire to lead "the Psalmist of Israel into the Church of Christ," Watts titled his hymn "A Psalm for the Lord's-Day."[1] The text is in long meter, follows an iambic metrical pattern, and uses the rhyme scheme AABB. Watts did not indicate which verses of the psalm he was paraphrasing in the first part of the hymn (he noted that the second part was based on "v. 12, &c.") but it is evident from its content that "Sweet Is the Work" drew on selections from the first eleven verses.

Stanza 1
Sweet is the Work, my God, my King,
To praise thy Name, give Thanks and Sing;
To shew thy Love by Morning-light,
And talk of all thy Truth at Night.

Watts opens the hymn by paraphrasing the psalm's first two verses:

---

[1] Watts, *The Psalms of David Imitated*, xxviii.

> ¹It is a good thing to give thanks unto the Lord, and to
> sing praises unto thy name, O Most High:
> ²To shew forth thy lovingkindness in the morning, and
> thy faithfulness every night."

The hymn's first line begins with a choriambus ("**Sweet** is the **Work**"), emphasizing the joy that is expressed in both the psalm and the stanza of singing praise and thanks to God.

Watts reminds the singer that worship is not just pleasurable but is also "Work"; it is "sweet work" but it is work nonetheless. Worship requires intense concentration and sacrifice on the part of the Christian— sacrifice of time, energy, and ego, if nothing else. It is a duty that should be performed with delight, as Watts himself expressed it in another psalm paraphrase: "'Tis good to raise / Our Hearts and Voices in his Praise: / His Nature and his Works invite / To make his Duty our Delight."[2]

J. R. Watson pointed out the significance of Watts employing the parallelism of "my God, my King" in the first line: rather than using "and" ("my God and King"), the author inserts a comma "to make the singer pause and take breath," a feature that is also found in other portions of the hymn. He also noted how often in this text there is a "strong pause after the fourth syllable."[3]

Watts links the second and third lines of stanza 1 through an anaphora on the word "To," implying that this "duty and delight" is especially "Sweet" when it lasts—as the third and fourth lines have it— from "Morning-light" to "Night." The hymn is about more than just the public worship service on the Lord's day, for it emphasizes the fact that we are to "shew" God's love and "talk of" all God's truth throughout the day.

This and the following two stanzas are excellent examples of Watts's "elegant simplicity." They employ common, uncomplicated words (mostly in single syllables) and are characterized by clarity of meaning, with each line expressing a complete thought. At the same time, poetic touch-

---

[2] Ps 147, part one ("Praise Ye the Lord: 'Tis Good to Raise").

[3] Watson, *The English Hymn*, 156–57. See the lines "And bless his Works, and bless his Word" and "How deep thy Counsels! how divine!" in stanza 3 for similar effects.

es such as the use of choriambus and anaphora, and the sureness of rhythm and rhyme elevate the text above mere prosaic sentiment.

Stanza 2
> Sweet is the Day of sacred Rest,
> No mortal Cares shall seize my Breast;
> O may my Heart in Tune be found
> Like *David*'s Harp of solemn Sound!

In the second stanza—which begins with the same word as stanza 1, as well as another choriambus—Watts moves to a different feature of the Lord's day: it is a time of "sacred Rest" when Christians should free themselves at least temporarily from "mortal Cares."[4] From early times, Christian celebration of Sunday as the Lord's day took on some of the features of the Jewish Sabbath, including the idea of rest, reflecting God's commandment that "Six days shalt thou labour, and do all thy work: But the seventh day is the sabbath of the Lord thy God: in it thou shalt not do any work" (Exod 20:9-10). Thus, Sunday is not only a day of worship but also one of rest.

Note, however, that Watts does not mention mere "Rest" but "sacred Rest." There are two ways to understand this phrase: (1) that rest itself is (or can be) a sacred act and (2) that worship is a form of rest ("resting in the Lord"). The word "rest" does not necessarily mean cessation of all activity but doing things that provide rejuvenation of mind, body, and spirit. If nothing else, participation in public worship provides a break in the routine of the week and an opportunity to participate with fellow believers in an exercise of spiritual renewal.

Nearly twenty years after publishing "Sweet Is the Work," Watts issued *The Holiness of Times, Places, and People under the Jewish and Christian Dispensations Consider'd and Compared* (1738). In this book he made several statements that amplify the thoughts behind the hymn.

> There will be some Seasons wherein the animal Nature of Man and Beast require some Rest from their Toil, and that besides the mere Sleep of the Night. Constant and unceasing Toil and Labour, from Morning to Evening, throughout our whole Life,

---

[4] Note the similar thought in the opening line of "Welcome, Sweet Day of Rest" (ch. 23).

would wear out Natures made of Flesh and Blood too fast, and this would not be dealing well with our Bodies, our Servants, or our Cattle. There must be some Seasons also, wherein God our Creator must have Worship paid him by his Creature Man; and as he is a Creature made for Society, he ought to acknowledge God in Societies, and to pay him some publick Worship; and there must be some certain Times appointed for this Purpose....

Let it be observed further, there is some natural Connexion between these two, viz. Rest and Worship; for when Man is at rest from his own Labours, he is more at leisure for Religion, and the Service of God: And when he performs Worship to God, he must rest from his common Labours.[5]

The first two lines of the stanza were freely invented by Watts, continuing the thoughts expressed in vv. 1 and 2 of the psalm. The concluding lines of the stanza are based on v. 3: "Upon an instrument of ten strings, and upon the psaltery; upon the harp with a solemn sound." Watts, a Calvinist whose church did not believe in the use of musical instruments in public worship, is careful not to suggest that the stringed instruments mentioned in the passage were to be played as part of the service.[6] Instead, in a manner that was common among those who objected to instruments, he interpreted them metaphorically, comparing his heart being "in Tune" with "David's Harp of solemn Sound" (note Watts's skillful ending of the stanza with the same two words that conclude the psalm verse). Ironically, Psalm 92 is not one of the psalms directly attributed to David in its superscription though, of course, the whole book became generically known as "the Psalms of David" (as in the title of Watts's collection) since nearly half (seventy-three) of the

---

[5] Watts, *The Holiness of Times*, 3–4. According to the preface, Watts's essay "On the Perpetuity of the Sabbath, and the Observation of the Lord's-Day," from which this extract is taken, originated as a sermon "preached at Berry-street [=Bury Street], in the Year 1733" (iii).

[6] Calvin and his followers believed that the use of musical instruments was part of the "infancy of the church" but that after the coming of Christ such aids were no longer required or even permissible. A good analogy to their way of thinking is that it is natural for babies to play with rattles, but, when they get to be adults, it is expected that they will put rattles behind them.

psalms mention the Hebrew king in their superscriptions.

Stanza 3
> My Heart shall triumph in my Lord,
> And bless his Works, and bless his Word;
> Thy Works of Grace how bright they shine!
> How deep thy Counsels! how divine!

Watts based the first two lines of stanza 3 on v. 4 of the psalm and the last two lines on v. 5:

> [4]For thou, LORD, hast made me glad through thy work: I
>   will triumph in the works of thy hands.
> [5]O LORD, how great are thy works! and thy thoughts are
>   very deep.

However, the poet changed the focus somewhat. Whereas in the psalm it is God's "works" in which the singer will "triumph," in the hymn it is the Lord himself who is the source of triumph for the singer, who then blesses God's "Works" and "Word."

To this point, Watts has remained relatively close to the psalm text, though applying it to the "Lord's-Day" (Sunday) rather than the Sabbath. In line 3 of this stanza, he gives the text a New Testament twist by describing the "works of thy hands" as "Works of Grace." Certainly, the word (and concept of) "grace" is not absent from the Old Testament, but more than 75 percent of its mentions in the Bible come from the New Testament,[7] and it was undoubtedly God's grace as demonstrated through Jesus Christ that Watts had in mind here.

Watts makes use of several rhetorical devices in this stanza. In the second line he employs epizeuxis (immediate repetition of a word or phrase), "and bless his." Mesodiplosis (repeating a word in the middle of successive lines) appears in lines 2 and 3 ("Works"). The last two lines make use of ecphonesis, the employment of exclamation marks to give an emotional element to a phrase. Note the different and much plainer effect of the same words if the exclamation marks are replaced by commas:

---

[7] This figure is derived from the KJV.

175

Thy Works of Grace how bright they shine,
How deep thy Counsels, how divine.

Written in this way, the phrases become merely a list. By using ecphonesis, Watts gives the words a passionate quality, revealing his extraordinary expressivity as a poet.[8]

Stanza 4
Fools never raise their Thoughts so high;
Like Brutes they live, like Brutes they dye;
Like Grass they flourish, till thy Breath
Blast them in everlasting Death.

Like Psalm 92:6-7, Watts's fourth stanza turns from celebration of the day of worship to a description of those who do not put their trust in God:

[6]A brutish man knoweth not; neither doth a fool understand this.
[7]When the wicked spring as the grass and when all the workers of iniquity do flourish; it is that they shall be destroyed for ever."

In contrast to the poetic smoothness of stanzas 1–3, stanza 4 seems rough and incisive—intentionally so. "Fools" is too strong a word not to be stressed. However, if that word is stressed then what is done with "never," which normally is accented on its first syllable? It is possible to see this as another choriambus ("**Fools** nev-er **raise**") but there seems to be no reason in the meaning of the text for such a device. Perhaps Watts designed this as a spondee (a foot consisting of two stressed syllables— "**Fools nev**-er **raise**"); this creates a strident, harsh beginning to the line, which was probably what the author intended. A similar situation occurs in the last line with "Blast them" (an onomatopoeia) which, again, can be either a (somewhat awkward) choriambus or a spondee. The middle lines are characterized by anaphora (as in stanza 1) and the epizeuxis of "like

---

[8] See chapter 1 ("Alas! and Did My Saviour Bleed?") for a similar use of ecphonesis.

Brutes" in line 2.

The roughness of the stanza also results in part from the use of alliterative "b" sounds ("Brutes" [twice], "Breath," "Blast") and the plosive "d" of "Death." The "inelegance" of this stanza is in sharp contrast to the ones that have gone before and aptly emphasizes the brutishness of the "Fools" who do not "raise their Thoughts" to God's "Works of Grace" and "Counsels" (stanza 3).

Stanza 5
> But I shall share a glorious Part
> When Grace hath well refin'd my Heart,
> And fresh Supplies of Joy are shed
> Like holy Oil to chear [*sic*] my Head.

It seems almost with a sigh of relief that Watts turns from describing the unbeliever in stanza 4 to his own response to God's works in stanza 5 (an antithesis), once again writing with the fluidity of the first three strophes. Skipping v. 8 and—for the moment—v. 9, the author draws this stanza from v. 10: "But my horn shalt thou exalt like the horn of an unicorn: I shall be anointed with fresh oil." Watts ignores the bit about the unicorn and concentrates his first two lines on the psalmist's word "exalt," turning it into sharing "a glorious Part." However, this sharing will occur only when the heart has been "refin'd" by "Grace," harking back to the "Works of Grace" in stanza 3.

One of the uses of oil in the Old Testament was to anoint the person who served as the king (2 Kgs 9:6) or high priest (Lev 21:10). For Watts, of course, living in the new dispensation meant that all Christians are "kings and priests unto God" (Rev 1:6), so he uses the oil metaphorically to represent "fresh Supplies of Joy" that will be poured out on his head. Oil was also seen in the New Testament as having healing properties (see Jas 5:14) and anointing with oil became associated in the early church with receiving the Holy Spirit, symbolism that Watts used elsewhere in his hymnody.[9] Significantly, this stanza mentions both the "Heart" and the "Head," both of which are necessary and critical in Christian worship.

---

[9] See chapter 15 ("My Shepherd Will Supply My Need").

Stanza 6
    Sin (my worst Enemy before)
    Shall vex my Eyes and Ears no more;
    My inward Foes shall all be slain
    Nor *Satan* break my Peace again.[10]

Psalm 92:11 served as the source for the first two lines of stanza 6: "Mine eye also shall see my desire on mine enemies, and mine ears shall hear my desire of the wicked that rise up against me." Watts returned to v. 9 for the last two lines: "For, lo, thine enemies, O Lord, for lo, thine enemies shall perish; all the workers of iniquity shall be scattered." At the end of the hymn, Watts appended the following note about this stanza: "Rejoycing in the destruction of our personal Enemies, is not so Evangelical a practice, therefore I have given the 11th v. of this Psalm another Turn," following this with a reference to his note on the third psalm: "In this Psalm I have changed David's personal Enemies into the spiritual Enemies of every Christian, (viz) Sin, Satan, &c. and have mentioned the Serpent, the Tempter, the Guilt of Sin, and the Sting of Death, which are Words well known in the New Testament."[11] In essence, Watts has "spiritualized" the enemies since, as the Apostle Paul put it, "we wrestle not against flesh and blood, but against principalities, against powers, against the rulers of the darkness of this world, against spiritual wickedness in high places" (Eph 6:12).

Watts makes this stanza stand out by employing numerous voiced and unvoiced sibilant sounds; ten of the twenty-six words in the strophe contain a sibilant, an unusually high percentage that cannot be accidental: sin, worst, shall (twice), eyes, ears, foes, slain, Satan, and peace. Added to this are such strong words as "vex" and "break"; the result is a powerful expression of the serpentine satanic guile that Watts wants to put in the past.

---

[10] In the early eighteenth century, "again" was pronounced to rhyme with "slain." See Bysshe, "A Dictionary of Rhymes," in *The Art of English Poetry*, 2.

[11] See also Watts's comment in the preface to the book: "Where the Psalmist uses sharp Invectives against his personal Enemies, I have endeavoured to turn the Edge of them against our spiritual Adversaries, Sin, Satan and Temptation" (xvii).

Stanza 7

> Then shall I see and hear and know
> All I desir'd or wish'd below;
> And every Power find sweet employ
> In that eternal World of Joy.

The seventh stanza is also based loosely on v. 11 of the psalm. The "Eyes and Ears" of stanza 6 are now itemized by what they do ("see and hear"), to which is added "know." Seeing and hearing are one thing but knowing is something altogether different; when a person knows something he or she has internalized it—it has become part of who that person is.

Fittingly, the stanza and hymn end with a reference to praising God "In that eternal World of Joy" (heaven). From ancient times, Sunday was viewed by Christians as the "eighth day of creation," when God continued his creative activity by raising Jesus from the dead. But the "eighth day" is also symbolic of God's final act of creation, the making of a "new heaven and a new earth" at the end of time (Rev 21:1), when the redeemed will "shew [God's] Love" and "talk of all [God's] Truth" not just "by Morning-light" or "at Night," but for all eternity. And the thought of that "sweet employ" leads Watts to end the hymn with one of his favorite words, "Joy."

20

THE HEAVENS DECLARE THY GLORY, LORD

As observed in the chapter on "I Sing th'Almighty Power of God," Isaac Watts seems to have had an affinity for nature as a reflection of the power and love of God. In his writing on this subject his hymns often wax rhapsodic and vividly express a sense of awe and wonder at the created order.

If there is any subject that could possibly surpass the creation in the works of Watts, it would be God's power and love as revealed in the Bible and reflected in his son Jesus. Paraphrasing Psalm 19 gave Watts an opportunity to deal with both the general and the specific revelations in a single hymn.

"The Heavens Declare Thy Glory, Lord" is Watts's long meter version of the psalm from *The Psalms of David Imitated* (1719). It was preceded in the book by a short meter paraphrase that was divided into two parts and followed by one "To the Tune of the 113. Ps." (888888).

The author titled this text "The Books of Nature and of Scripture compar'd; or, The Glory and Success of the Gospel." The hymn was written in six stanzas of iambic meter with an ABAB rhyme scheme. The following note was appended to the hymn:

Tho' the plain design of the Psalmist is to shew the Excellency of the Book of Scripture above the Book of Nature, in order to convert and save a Sinner, yet the Apostle Paul in Rom. 10. 18. applies or accommodates the 4th v. to the spreading of the Gospel over the

Roman Empire, which is called the whole World in the New Testament; and in this Version I have endeavoured to imitate him.[1]

Paul's quotation from Psalm 19 follows a familiar passage in which he asks a series of linked questions: how shall people call on the Lord in whom they have not believed, how shall they believe if they have not heard, how shall they hear without a preacher, and how shall they preach if they are not sent? The Apostle observes that "faith cometh by hearing, and hearing by the word of God," then cites Psalm 19:4: "But I say, Have they not heard? Yes verily, their sound went into all the earth, and their words unto the ends of the world" (Rom 10:18). Watts used this passage as a springboard for writing about the gospel being spread throughout the world of his own day.

Stanza 1
> The Heavens declare thy Glory, Lord,
> In every Star thy Wisdom shines:
> But when our Eyes behold thy Word,
> We read thy Name in fairer Lines.

Stanza 1 sets a pattern for the following two stanzas in which the opening lines are drawn from the psalmodic description of the "heavens" (the general revelation) and the next ones show the superiority of the Scriptures (the specific revelation) to the "book of nature." The beginning of the first stanza paraphrases Psalm 19:1: "The heavens declare the glory of God; and the firmament sheweth his handywork." By scanning the heavens, humans can see both the "Glory" and the "Wisdom" of God. This is enough to prove that there is a God, an eternal Creator. But, as the next two lines of the hymn make clear, to know the Creator's "Name" requires the Word of God. The "Heavens" are beautiful, but God's word is even "fairer" because it shows not just that there is a Creator, but how to have a relationship with that Creator. As Watts put it in one of his other versions of this psalm, "We are not left to Nature's Voice, / To bid us know the Lord."[2] Similar ideas are also expressed in the opening stanza of the poem "Great God, with Wonder, and with

---

[1] Watts, *The Psalms of David Imitated* (1719), 57.

[2] "Behold the Lofty Sky," *The Psalms of David Imitated* (Ps 19, SM, part 1, stanza 4).

Praise" from *Horæ Lyricæ* (see ch. 10).

Stanza 2
> The rolling Sun, the changing Light,
> And Nights and Days thy Power confess:
> But the blest Volume thou hast writ
> Reveals thy Justice and thy Grace.

The opening of stanza 2 parallels v. 2 of the psalm: "Day unto day uttereth speech, and night unto night sheweth knowledge." The stanza is constructed in precisely the same way as the first stanza, with the word "But" beginning the third line to show the antithesis between the revelation provided by astronomical phenomena and that of the Bible. In addition to God's "Glory" and "Wisdom," the created order "confesses" God's "Power." However, it shows nothing of God's "Justice and...Grace," which are revealed only through the "Volume thou hast writ." The sun is described as "rolling," a word that Watts often uses to suggest motion.

The word "writ," which was common in Watts's day as a form of "written," is no longer used in everyday English speech. Perhaps, if the archaisms in the stanza are retained, the line could be changed to "But the blest Volume thou didst write," which also provides a truer rhyme with the first verse. If the archaisms are expunged, a possible change could be "But your blest Volume, shining bright."

Stanza 3
> Sun, Moon and Stars convey thy Praise
> Round the whole Earth, and never stand:
> So when thy Truth begun its Race,
> It touch'd and glanc'd on every Land.

As noted above, stanza 3 follows the pattern set by stanzas 1 and 2, with one slight difference: the word "But" is not found at the beginning of the third line, and instead of setting up an antithesis Watts uses complementary parallelism, with the last two lines extending the thought of the first two. Here the "Truth" of God is compared to the heavenly bodies in that both "convey thy Praise / Round the whole Earth."

This is a remarkable statement, especially considering that the modern English missionary movement would not begin for another seventy years or so. Perhaps this was what Watts was referring to in his appended note: in the hymn writer's view, Paul suggested that the Word had gone throughout the entire known world (the Roman Empire), and in Watts's day the Word was also being spread throughout the whole world; to this point, however, it had only "touch'd and glanc'd on every Land" through the work of European explorers and traders. Only later would there be an intentional and sustained effort to evangelize the world.[3]

The first two lines essentially repeat the ideas of vv. 1 and 2 of the psalm that were covered in the initial stanzas, adding v. 3 and the first part of v. 4:

> [3]There is no speech nor language, where their voice is not
> heard.
> [4]Their line is gone out through all the earth, and their
> words to the end of the world.

Watts also alludes to the last part of v. 5, which says that the sun "rejoiceth as a strong man to run a race," and he allegorizes this to "Truth [having] begun its Race."

Stanza 4
    Nor shall thy spreading Gospel rest
    Till thro' the World thy Truth has run;
    Till *Christ* has all the Nations blest
    That see the Light, or feel the Sun.

Watts continues to dwell on the third and fourth verses of the psalm as the background for stanza 4 but essentially this one is freely written. Now he anticipates that the gospel will continue to spread throughout the world until all nations have been blessed with the knowledge of Christ. This is a reflection of Matthew 24:14: "And this gospel of the

---

[3] In a hymn added to the second edition of *Hymns and Spiritual Songs* (1709), "Let Everlasting Glories Crown," Watts tried to describe "The Excellency of the Christian Religion" (hymn title), the second stanza of which reads "What if we trace the Globe around, / And search from Britain to Japan, / There shall be no Religion found / So Just to God, so safe for Man."

kingdom shall be preached in all the world for a witness unto all nations; and then shall the end come." The anaphora in the middle lines gives special emphasis to the idea that Christ will bless all the nations with the truth of God.

Stanza 5
>Great Sun of Righteousness, arise,
>Bless the dark World with heavenly Light;
>Thy Gospel makes the Simple Wise;
>Thy Laws are pure, thy Judgments right.

Watts's metaphorical use of the sun continues in stanza 5. He begins by referencing Malachi 4:2, "But unto you that fear my name shall the Sun of righteousness arise with healing in his wings," turning the quotation into a prayer that the "Sun" will shed its "heavenly Light" on the "dark World." He then returns to Psalm 19 to paraphrase the last clause of v. 7 and all of v. 8, but in place of the "testimony of the Lord" substitutes the New Testament word "Gospel":

>[7]...the testimony of the Lord is sure, making wise
> the simple.
>[8]The statutes of the Lord are right, rejoicing the heart:
> the commandment of the Lord is pure,
>   enlightening the eyes.

He next skips to the second half of v. 9 to pick up the idea of God's "Judgments" being "right" ("the judgments of the Lord are true and righteous altogether"). Watts retains the "wise-simple" antithesis of the psalm and adds another pair, "dark World-heavenly Light."

Stanza 6
>The noblest Wonders here we view
>In Souls renew'd and Sins forgiven:
>Lord, cleanse my sins, my Soul renew,
>And make thy Word my Guide to Heav'n.

As spectacular as are the heavenly bodies and the vast reaches of space, Watts claims that "The noblest Wonders" are "Souls renew'd and

185

Sins forgiven." The ability of humans to have a relationship with the Divine far outweighs in significance all the natural phenomena that God created.

Lines 1 and 2 of the stanza might be characterized as descriptive, while lines 3 and 4—based on the second half of v. 12, "cleanse thou me from secret faults"—form a prayer, a request for both forgiveness and guidance, the latter to be provided by the Word of God. The description and the prayer are linked by a chiasmus, "Souls" / "Sins" and "sins" / "Soul." The large number of sibilant sounds in these lines is also noteworthy.

"The Heavens Declare Thy Glory, Lord" is a remarkable hymn for its directness, rhythmic stability, and formal structure. The hymn gives full recognition to the wonders and greatness of God's physical creation but claims the superiority of the "new creation" as seen in the pages of the Bible and in "Souls renew'd and Sins forgiven." Psalm 19 provided a perfect vehicle for the expression of these thoughts.[4]

The hymn is also striking because of its missionary emphasis. "Jesus Shall Reign Where'er the Sun" has sometimes been labeled as the first (English) missionary hymn but "The Heavens Declare Thy Glory, Lord" could just as easily hold that designation. Stanzas 3, 4, and 5 are particularly pointed in their view of the universality of the gospel message. Isaac Watts doubtless would have denied having prophetic powers, but in this instance he seems to have anticipated the beginning of the modern mission movement in the 1790s. As demonstrated in many of his psalm versions, Watts had a particular concern for the spiritual health of his native country. However, his vision was much larger than just Britain and, indeed, encompassed "all the Nations... / That see the Light, or feel the Sun." Perhaps it was partly through singing hymns such as those by

---

[4] A similar approach is found in several other texts by Watts. See, for example, "Now Let a Spacious World Arise" (*Hymns and Spiritual Songs*, 1709): "Lord, while the Frame of Nature stands, / Thy Praise shall fill my Tongue; / But the new World of Grace demands / A more exalted Song" (st. 11).

Watts that William Carey and others caught the vision to share the gospel around the world.[5]

---

[5] In fact, Carey requested that two lines from a Watts hymn, "How Sad Our State by Nature Is," be engraved on his tombstone; see Houghton, *Isaac Watts*, 34–35. Note also the following first stanzas of Watts texts from *Hymns and Spiritual Songs*: "'Twas the Commission of our Lord, / 'Go teach the Nations, and Baptize,['] / The Nations have receiv'd the Word / Since he ascended to the Skies" (1707) and "'Go preach my Gospel, saith the Lord; / 'Bid the whole Earth my Grace receive; / 'He shall be sav'd that trusts my Word, / 'He shall be damn'd that won't believe[']" (1709).

21

THERE IS A LAND OF PURE DELIGHT

"There Is a Land of Pure Delight" appeared in the second book of Watts's *Hymns and Spiritual Songs* (hymn no. 66). The author labeled the text "A Prospect of Heaven makes Death easy" and wrote it in six stanzas of common meter using iambic poetic meter and cross rhyme.

An article in the August 1857 issue of the Edinburgh *North British Review* suggested that portions of this hymn and "When I Can Read My Title Clear" were inspired by the local scenery of Southampton, where Watts grew up and to which he returned after completion of his formal schooling. Later writers repeat this supposition but indicate that "There Is a Land of Pure Delight" was probably not written until a visit to Southampton in 1706. No contemporary documentary evidence for any of these claims has been discovered.[1]

"There Is a Land of Pure Delight" is one of several hymns in Book II that specifically deal with heaven, including the text that appears immediately before this one, "When I Can Read My Title Clear" (see chapter 24). According to Frederic Palmer, "The incomparable joys of heaven, eagerness to reach it, and the consequent insignificance of death, are [Watts's] favorite subjects."[2] Because of the vivid imagery it uses to describe the joys of paradise, the present text has been called "a work of pure imagination," "The most beautiful of Watts's hymns," the author's "nearest approach to romantic poetry in hymnody," and "perhaps the

---

[1] "Art. II.—1. *Horæ Lyricæ*," 28–29; Wright, *Isaac Watts and Contemporary Hymn-Writers*, 69–71; Benson, *Studies of Familiar Hymns*, 23. Perhaps the most extreme example of trying to link specific hymns by Watts to the Southampton area is in the fourth chapter of Joshua E. Wills's *Dr. Isaac Watts, "The Bard of the Sanctuary"*; there is not a shred of proof for any of the assertions made there.

[2] Palmer, "Isaac Watts," 383.

richest of all his hymns in many-faceted imagery."[3]

However, as implied by its title in *Hymns and Spiritual Songs*, the main purpose of the text is not so much description as it is comfort and encouragement for believers as they face the prospect of death. As Madeleine Forell Marshall and Janet Todd put it, the text follows "the demands of the hymn genre to begin with common feeling or perception, to entertain, and to teach."[4]

Stanza 1
> There is a Land of pure Delight
>> Where Saints Immortal reign,
> Infinite Day excludes the Night,
>> And Pleasures banish Pain.

"There Is a Land of Pure Delight" demonstrates Watts's almost uncanny ability to write an opening stanza in which the words fairly roll off the tongue. In part, this derives from the simple beauty of the sounds created by specific words, words such as "pure," "delight," "immortal," "infinite," and "pleasures." The effect is heightened by the true rhymes and the use of alliteration in the last line, as well as the antitheses between day and night, pleasures and pain (note also the alliteration between the last pair). Every word somehow seems just right, both for the sense it makes and for its sound.

As might be expected in a hymn about heaven, Watts draws upon the book of Revelation for much of the background of the first stanza. The "Land of pure Delight" is described in detail in Revelation 21, but the author also employs verses from Revelation 20 and 22. From Revelation 20:6 he derives the idea of the immortal reign of the saints ("Blessed and holy is he that hath part in the first resurrection: on such the second death hath no power, but they shall be priests of God and of Christ, and shall reign with him a thousand years"), and from chapters 21 and 22 the "exclusion" of night: "for there shall be no night there" (21:25); "And

---

[3] See, respectively, A. E. Bailey, *The Gospel in Hymns*, 50; Watson, "The Hymns of Isaac Watts and the Tradition of Dissent," 56; and Routley, *Hymns Today and Tomorrow*, 40.

[4] Marshall and Todd, *English Congregational Hymns in the Eighteenth Century*, 42.

190

there shall be no night there; and they need no candle, neither light of the sun; for the Lord God giveth them light" (22:5). The banishing of pain also reflects Revelation 21:4: "And God shall wipe away all tears from their eyes; and there shall be no more death, neither sorrow, nor crying, neither shall there be any more pain." Note that in Watts's text it is not simply that night or pain are absent; instead they are excluded or banished because of the presence of "Day" and "Pleasures." Heaven is not a place of nothingness—"suspended animation," if you will—but of all that is good and pleasurable.

The beginning of line 3 is a bit troublesome to sing because it begins with a dactylic foot ("In-fi-nite"). Perhaps Watts intended this as a choriambus to show the joy of heaven, but when sung to an iambic tune an awkward stress is created on the second syllable "In-fi-nite." It is possible that the word was pronounced this way in the eighteenth century (note that the opposite of "infinite" is pronounced with the stress on "fi"—"fi-nite"). At any rate, it might be better when singing this hymn in some circumstances to substitute a synonym that better fits the meter, such as "eternal."

Stanza 2
    There everlasting Spring abides,
        And never-withering Flowers:
    Death like a narrow Sea divides
        This Heav'nly Land from ours.

In stanza 2, Watts departs from the apocalyptic description of paradise to let his imagination run freely in describing the realm of the blessed. In heaven, it is always springtime and the flowers never fade. These ideas may have been prompted by Song of Solomon 2:11-12a: "For, lo, the winter is past, the rain is over and gone; The flowers appear on the earth."

Believers cannot reach this ideal land now since they are separated from it by the sea of death. However, the sea is a "narrow" one. This adjective can be interpreted as meaning that because the sea is narrow (1) we will pass through it quickly, (2) we can already get a glimpse of what is on the other side, or (3) both. Any of these possibilities goes to the very heart of Watts's heading the hymn "A Prospect of Heaven makes Death easy."

Stanza 3
  Sweet Fields beyond the swelling Flood,
    Stand drest in living Green:
  So to the *Jews* Old *Canaan* stood,
    While *Jordan* roll'd between.

In the second edition of *Hymns and Spiritual Songs*, Watts bracketed stanzas 3 and 4, indicating that they could be omitted. In the first two lines of the third strophe he continues his metaphorical comparison of death to a sea (though now it is a "swelling Flood") and the land beyond to pleasant "Fields" at a delightful time of the year, which recalls Psalm 23:2: "He maketh me to lie down in green pastures." It is interesting to compare the similar imagery of "heavenly" flowers and greenery found in this and the previous stanza with another Watts hymn, "Lord! What a Wretched Land Is This" (stanza 10).

  There on the green and flowry Mount
    Our weary Souls shall sit,
  And with transporting Joys recount
    The Labours of our Feet.

The last two lines of stanza 3 in the present hymn make an apt connection with the experience of the Israelites when they came to the Jordan River. Just as they could see "Old Canaan" on the other side of the "rolling" Jordan River, so the believer can already see the "living Green" on the other side of death.

Stanza 4
  But timorous Mortals start and shrink
    To cross this narrow Sea,
  And linger shivering on the Brink,
    And fear to la[u]nch away.

Watts will return to the analogy with the ancient Israelites, but first he interjects a note about human fear of crossing the sea of death. "Mortals" (note the contrast with the "Saints Immortal" of the first stanza) are "timorous" ("fearful"), "start" ("give a sudden Leap...begin to run"), and "shrink" ("contract or lessen in Length or Breadth"—i.e., try to hide) in the face of death.[5] The natural tendency of humans is to avoid unpleasantness, and death is the ultimate unpleasantness. As Watts puts it, we stand shivering on the shore, afraid to "launch away" and cross "this narrow Sea." Plosive "t" and "k" consonants, alliterative "s" sounds, the onomatopoetic "shivering," and the tripartite repetitions of "and" (including an anaphora) give this stanza a stark quality that well characterizes the fear implicit in the contemplation of death.

Watts's description of this fear is reminiscent of one of the last scenes in John Bunyan's *The Pilgrim's Progress.*

> Now I further saw that betwixt them and the Gate was a River, but there was no Bridge to go over, the River was very deep; at the sight therefore of this River, the Pilgrims were much stunned, but the men that went with them said, You must go through, or you cannot come at the Gate.
>
> The Pilgrims then, began to enquire if there was no other way to the Gate; to which they answered, Yes, but there hath not any, save two, to wit, *Enoch* and *Elijah*, been permitted to tread that path, since the foundation of the World, nor shall, untill [*sic*] the last Trumpet shall sound. The Pilgrims then, especially *Christian*, began to dispond [*sic*] in his mind, and looked this way and that, but no way could be found by them, by which they might escape the River.[6]

Eventually, of course, Christian and his companion (Hope) plunge into the river, cross it successfully, and enter the heavenly city. But they were typical human beings (even if metaphorically so in this instance) in

---

[5] The definitions are all from N. Bailey, *An Universal Etymological English Dictionary.*

[6] Bunyan, *The Pilgrim's Progress,* 222–23.

experiencing the dread of death described by Watts.[7]

Stanza 5
> O could we make our Doubts remove,
>> These gloomy Doubts that rise,
> And see the *Canaan* that we love,
>> With unbeclouded Eyes.

One reason humans are afraid of death is simply fear of the unknown. As Watts himself put it in a later sermon, "to be at once convey'd into a new strange World, a strange and unknown State both of Being and Action, has something in it so surprizing [*sic*], that 'tis a little frightful to the Nature of Man, even when he is sanctified and fitted for Heaven."[8] People of faith know that the God who created the heavens and the earth, the same God who raised Jesus from the dead, will take them to himself. However, even Christians will experience "Doubts," a characteristic that Watts emphasizes by the use of mesodiplosis (using the same word in the middle of successive lines). These doubts often rise unwillingly, and all the believer can do is to pray that they will be removed.

One thing that will help remove doubts, according to Watts, is to catch a clear glimpse of our destination, "the Canaan that we love." Here, Watts returns to the metaphor of the ancient Hebrews and the Promised Land from stanza 3.

"Unbeclouded" is an unusually long word for Watts—four syllables; he seldom goes beyond two. It is also an uncommon word; we would normally say simply "clear." However, its very singularity makes it stand out and be particularly memorable.

Stanza 6
> Could we but climb where *Moses* stood,
>> And view the Landskip o're [*sic*],

---

[7] In his discussion of this text in *Hymns Today and Tomorrow*, Erik Routley points out that the use of water symbolism for death is not restricted to Jewish and Christian usage, noting "the myth in classical Greek and Roman religions of the river Styx across which souls are ferried to Hades by the boatman Charon" (41).

[8] Watts, *Death and Heaven*, 9–10.

Not *Jordan*'s Stream, nor Death's cold Flood
Should fright us from the Shore.

Stanza 6 continues the comparison between the promised lands of
Canaan and heaven by recalling the experience of Moses. Because the
leader of the Exodus "trespassed against [God] among the children of
Israel at the waters of Meribah" (Deut 32:61), he was not allowed to enter Canaan. However, God did permit him to see the promised land to
which he had led the people: "And Moses went up from the plains of
Moab unto the mountain of Nebo, to the top of Pisgah, that is over
against Jericho. And the Lord shewed him all the land" (Deut 34:1). In
Watts's view, if we could only have the perspective of Moses in seeing
the promised land, nothing—not even "Death's cold Flood"—could prevent us from striking out for its "Shore." A "Landskip" is "a Description
of the Land, by Hills, Vallies, Cities, Woods, Rivers, &c. in a mixt Picture or Drawing" (Bailey)—in other words, what today is called a "land-
scape."[9]

Another lyric in *Hymns and Spiritual Songs*, "Death Cannot Make
Our Souls Afraid," which Watts titled "Moses dying in the Embrace of
God" contains some lines that are similar to the opening of this stanza.

3. Might I but climb to *Pisgah*'s Top,
    And view the promis'd Land,
My Flesh it self should long to drop,
    And pray for the Command.

While the analogy between Moses's seeing the Promised Land and
the Christian believer's desire to see beyond death into heaven is effective, it should not be carried too far. Moses was allowed to see the ultimate goal, but he was prevented from going there. Christians, on the
other hand, are not allowed to see the final goal (at least literally) but are
assured of a place in the "Land of pure Delight."

This hymn has received criticism because it "contains no recognition
of, or praise to, the Redeemer," and, indeed, not once does it mention
Jesus, or even God the Father.[10] While this critique is certainly justified,

---

[9] N. Bailey, *An Universal Etymological English Dictionary.*
[10] Hood, *Isaac Watts*, 93.

it should also be noted that Christian belief and theology do not rise or fall on a single hymn (or sermon or Scripture verse). Watts's purpose in this hymn was to write a description of the realm of the blessed to encourage believers as they face the trial of death. For recognition of and praise to the Redeemer, one need only point to "AlasI and Did My Savior Bleed," "When I Survey the Wondrous Cross," or any of a host of other texts by Watts.

"There Is a Land of Pure Delight" is remarkably similar in its central message and some of its wording to a hymn that appeared earlier in Book II (no. 31), "Why Should We Start and Fear to Die?" which Watts labeled with a title that is comparable to this one, "Christ's Presence makes Death easy."

1. Why should we start and fear to die?
   What timorous Worms we Mortals are!
   Death is the Gate of Endless Joy,
   And yet we dread to enter there.
2. The Pains, the Groans, and dying Strife
   Fright our approaching Souls away;
   Still we shrink back again to Life,
   Fond of our Prison and our Clay.
3. O, if my Lord would come and meet,
   My Soul should stretch her Wings in hast[e],
   Fly fearless thro' Death's Iron Gate,
   Nor feel the Terrors as she past [sic].
4. *Jesus* can make a dying Bed
   Feel soft as downy Pillows are,
   While on his Breast I lean my Head,
   And breath[e] my Life out sweetly there.

In both texts, Watts describes the terrors of death that are common to humans but emphasizes that the presence of Christ or a view of heaven can ease the passage for the Christian. These hymns are an encouragement for Christians to recognize that the ultimate trial of life—death—is but a preparation for an eternity that they cannot see directly, but that can be discerned well enough to know the bliss that waits for them there. These are not "pie-in-the-sky-by-and-by" lyrics but an assurance that believers can break the power of the fear of death if they keep in mind the presence of Christ and the "Prospect of Heaven." Watts sees death as a passageway rather than an obstacle. And his texts are powerful reminders that the faithful will see "a new heaven and a new earth," where there will be "no more sea" to be crossed (Rev 21:1).[11]

---

[11] A comparison of "There Is a Land of Pure Delight" with one of his other hymns ("Joy to the World") can be found in Stephenson, "The Heroic Hymn of Isaac Watts," 196–200. See also chapter 14.

22

THIS IS THE DAY THE LORD HATH MADE

Psalm 118 is the last of the Egyptian Hallel Psalms (Psalms 113–118), which were recited or sung by the Israelites during the Passover meal and on other festival occasions. It is thought by some scholars that the last part of the Hallel was the "hymn" sung by Jesus and his disciples at the end of the Last Supper (Matt 26:30; Mark 14:26).

Be that as it may, Psalm 118 certainly contains some of the most beloved passages in all Scripture. It was a favorite with the German reformer Martin Luther, who called it "my beloved psalm." He commented that "When emperors and kings, the wise and the learned, and even saints could not aid me, this psalm proved a friend and helped me out of many great troubles" and used v. 17 ("I shall not die, but live, and declare the works of the Lord") as his personal motto.[1] The twenty-nine verses of the psalm include several others that have been important in the theology and liturgy of the Christian church: "The Lord is my strength and song, and is become my salvation" (v. 14); "Open to me the gates of righteousness: I will go into them, and I will praise the Lord" (v. 19); "The stone which the builders refused is become the head stone of the corner" (v. 22).

Perhaps few sections of the psalm have been more important or widely used than vv. 24-26a. In the medieval church, v. 24 ("This is the day which the Lord hath made; we will rejoice and be glad in it") became

---

[1] Martin Luther, "Dedication of Commentary on Psalm 118 to Abbot Fredrick of Nuremberg," trans. George Beto, in Pelikan, ed., *Luther's Works*, 14:45. Luther himself apparently wrote a brief four-part Latin motet setting of v. 17 based on the Gregorian *cantus firmus*; see *Luther's Works*, 53:337–41.

the introit (entrance song) for Easter Sunday (*Haec dies quam fecit Dominus*), while vv. 25-26a have been the source of some of the principal Scriptures for Palm Sunday: "Save now, I beseech thee, O Lord: O Lord, I beseech thee, send now prosperity. Blessed be he that cometh in the name of the Lord." The link with Palm Sunday derives from the quotation of these verses by the people at the Triumphal Entry of Jesus into Jerusalem (Matt 21:9; Mark 11:9-10; John 12:13). The word "Hosanna" found in these New Testament passages is a transliteration of the Greek words (themselves transliterations from Hebrew) for "save" and "pray" or "beseech" ("Save now, I beseech" in KJV). Thus, a term that was originally a prayer for salvation became an acclamation of joy.

The importance of this psalm in the Christian tradition is also reflected in the fact that Isaac Watts provided three versions of it in *The Psalms of David Imitated*, one each in common meter, short meter, and long meter. Both the short meter and long meter paraphrases consisted of a single hymn based on vv. 22-27, but the common meter version was divided into four parts, a total of nineteen stanzas, covering most of the psalm. "This Is the Day the Lord Hath Made" is part four of the common meter paraphrase.

The hymn is laid out in five stanzas of iambic meter using cross rhyme. Watts noted its source as vv. 24-26 of the psalm and titled it "Hosanna; the Lord's Day: or, Christ's Resurrection, and our Salvation." Thus, he relates the psalm to the Resurrection rather than to the Triumphal Entry. "This Is the Day the Lord Hath Made" maintains a close relationship with its source, at the same time bringing other Scriptures and nonscriptural thoughts into play.

Stanza 1
>This is the Day the Lord hath made,
>>He calls the Hours his own;
>Let Heaven rejoice, let Earth be glad,
>>And Praise surround the Throne.

At the conclusion of the hymn, Watts included some notes about this text, one of which referred to the opening stanza: "This is the Day wherein Christ fulfill'd his Sufferings, and rose from the Dead, and has honoured it with his own Name. Rev. I. 10. The Lord's Day." In Revelation 1:10, the author of the Apocalypse wrote, "I was in the Spirit on the

Lord's day," presumably meaning Sunday; at least that is the way Watts understood the reference.

The book of Genesis implies that God began the creation on Sunday, since he "rested" on the seventh day (Saturday). Of course, there were no "days" until God created them, but early in Christian tradition the idea of Sunday as the beginning, not only of the creation but also of a new creation (because of the resurrection) took firm root. Though in one sense every day is alike (they all have a sunrise and sunset, twenty-four hours, etc.), the first day of the week was set apart early in Christianity as a special day of worship.[2]

The hymn writer's first line is a direct quotation of the initial clause of v. 24 in the KJV, omitting the word "which." In the second line, he reinforces the idea of the "Lord's day" by observing that each hour of it belongs to God. The Lord's day is a time for the church to meet corporately, but even when the church is not together the whole day is God's.

As he sometimes did in other paraphrases, Watts then turns to a different psalm for line 3: "Let the heavens rejoice and let the earth be glad," which is taken from Psalm 96:11, and which he also used in "Joy to the World" (see chapter 14). The last line suggests Revelation 5:11-12.

> [11]And I beheld, and I heard the voice of many angels round about the throne and the beasts and the elders: and the number of them was ten thousand times ten thousand, and thousands of thousands;
> [12]Saying with a loud voice, Worthy is the Lamb that was slain to receive power, and riches, and wisdom, and strength, and honour, and glory, and blessing.

Stanza 2

> To day he rose and left the Dead,
> And *Satan's* Empire fell;

---

[2] For fuller discussions by Watts of the Sabbath and the Lord's day, see his sermons on "The Perpetuity of a Sabbath, and the Observation of the Lord's-Day" in *The Holiness of Times*, 1–82, and "The Lord's Day, or Christian Sabbath" in *The Works of the Late Reverend and Learned Isaac Watts*, 1:806–14.

> To day the Saints his Triumph spread,
> And all his Wonders tell.

Despite the note that Watts made regarding stanza 1, there is nothing in the actual wording of that strophe that refers directly to Jesus or his work, so the author makes his emphasis plain in the first line of the second stanza by specifically mentioning the resurrection, which occurred "To day" (i.e., Sunday). The resurrection is the ultimate act of Jesus, for by it "Satan's Empire fell."

Lines 3 and 4 parallel lines 1 and 2 by starting with the same words, "To day" and "And." Sunday is a day when Christians witness to the resurrection by spreading Christ's "Triumph" and telling of "all his Wonders." Watts does not suggest that Sunday is the *only* day to proclaim this message, but that by the very observance of the first day of the week as the time of public worship Christians acknowledge the resurrection of the Lord.

Stanza 3

> *Hosanna* to th'anointed King,
> To *David's* holy Son:
> Help us, O Lord; descend and bring
> Salvation from the Throne.

Stanza 3 is based on Psalm 118:25: "Save now, I beseech thee, O Lord: O Lord, I beseech thee, send now prosperity." Watts's note at the end of the hymn clarifies that "This Verse is explained Matth. 21. 9. Hosanna to the Son of David. Blessed is he that cometh in the Name of the Lord: Hosanna in the Highest. The Word Hosanna signifies, save, we beseech." At the end of the long meter version of the psalm, Watts made another reference to the word "Hosanna": "It seems to mean properly, An Acclammation [*sic*] to Christ, as King; as we say in our Language; God save the King, or God bless the King, tho' in the Common Metre I have turn'd it as a short Prayer for our own Salvation in the Sense in which 'tis often understood."[3] Watts thus constructs the last two lines of the stanza with a return to the original meaning of "Hosanna" as a plea for salvation. As pointed out by Donald Rodgers Fletcher, in this stanza

---

[3] Watts, *The Psalms of David Imitated*, 310.

"Hosanna is interpreted both ways, as praise and prayer for salvation."[4]

> Stanza 4
>> Blest be the Lord who comes to Men
>>> With Messages of Grace;
>> Who comes in God his Father's Name
>>> To save our sinfull [*sic*] Race.

Stanza 4 paraphrases the first part of Psalm 118:26, "Blessed be he that cometh in the name of the Lord." The half-verse is split into two parts to form lines 1 and 3. Lines 2 and 4 are freely written, explaining how and why Jesus came to earth: "With Messages of Grace...To save our sinfull Race." Note the use of "comes" in both lines 1 and 3 as well as the use of "save" in line 4, paralleling the "Salvation" of the same line in stanza 3. The rhyming of "Men" and "Name" in lines 1 and 3 is unusually loose, even for Watts.

> Stanza 5
>> *Hosanna* in the highest Strains
>>> The Church on Earth can raise;
>> The highest Heavens in which he reigns
>>> Shall give him nobler Praise.

In the last strophe, Watts departs from the psalm text to write a freely conceived stanza. He calls upon "The Church on Earth" to raise its own hosannas to Jesus and as it does so even "nobler Praise" will be declared from "The highest Heavens." As he did in stanza 4, Watts makes lines 1 and 3 parallel by repeating a word, in this case, "highest," which he derived from either Matthew 21:9 or Mark 11:10 (or both).

Congregationalists (Puritans) of the seventeenth and eighteenth centuries generally did not observe the Christian year; holidays such as Christmas, Palm Sunday, and Easter were not celebrated because they found no biblical command to do so. Their belief was also a reaction against what they saw as the too slavish adherence to special days and seasons by the Anglican and Roman Catholic communions.

However, Sunday, as the day of the Lord's resurrection, was a dif-

---

[4] Fletcher, "English Psalmody and Isaac Watts," 149–59.

ferent matter. Except for an occasional feast or fast day, it was the only day wholly set apart for religious services, and it was to be dedicated completely to God.

Watts demonstrated the importance he attached to the Lord's day by providing hymns specific to it in both *Hymns and Spiritual Songs* and *The Psalms of David Imitated*.[5] "This Is the Day the Lord Hath Made" gives "The Church on Earth" a means by which to sing "Hosanna in the highest Strains" to the One whose resurrection made the day special.

---

[5] In addition to "This Is the Day the Lord Hath Made," see "Blest Morning, Whose Young Dawning Rays" and "Welcome, Sweet Day of Rest" (ch. 23) from *Hymns and Spiritual Songs*; "Lord, In the Morning Thou Shalt Hear" (Ps 5), "Early, My God, Without Delay" (Ps 63), and "Sweet Is the Work, My God, My King" (Ps 92, discussed in ch. 18) from *The Psalms of David Imitated*.

23

WELCOME, SWEET DAY OF REST

"Welcome, Sweet Day of Rest" was published as hymn number fourteen in Book II of *Hymns and Spiritual Songs*. A short meter text in iambic poetic meter, the hymn employs cross rhyme. Like "This Is the Day the Lord Hath Made" (ch. 22), this lyric has the first day of the week as its subject. Watts titled the hymn "The Lord's Day; or, Delight in Ordinances."

Some five years after first publishing this hymn, Watts was stricken with a severe illness that kept him from attending upon worship with his congregation. In a poem written in 1712 or 1713, titled "The Wearisome Weeks of Sickness," Watts poured out his anguish at not being able to function properly on the Lord's day in images that would be familiar to anyone who has experienced sleepless nights because of physical pain.

> Thus pass my Days away. The chearful Sun
> Rolls round and gilds the World with lightsome Beams,
> Alas, in vain to me; cut off alike
> From the blest Labours, and the Joys of Life;
> While my sad Minutes in their tiresome Train
> Serve but to number out my heavy Sorrows.
> By Night I count the Clock; perhaps Eleven,
> Or Twelve, or one; then with a wishful Sigh
> Call on the lingring Hours, *Come Two; come Five*:
> *When will the Day-light come?* Make haste, ye Mornings,
> Ye Evening-shadows haste; wear out these Days,
> These tedious Rounds of Sickness, and conclude
> The Weary Week for ever—

Then, in words reminiscent of the first line of "Welcome, Sweet Day of Rest," Watts notes the coming of Sunday. It is obvious that Watts was anticipating this day, and it is almost with a sigh of relief that he notes its appearance.

Then the sweet Day of sacred Rest returns,
Sweet Day of Rest, devote to God and Heaven,
And heavenly Business, Purposes divine,
Angelick Work...

One wonders if his looking forward to the day of worship caused him to recall and echo the hymn he had published half a dozen years earlier.

Unfortunately, Watts found little relief for his suffering for several more years. Indeed, the poem goes on to note that even the much-anticipated Lord's day brought him little relief.

...but not to me returns
Rest with the Day: Ten Thousand hurrying Thoughts
Bear me away tumultuous far from Heaven
And heavenly Work. In vain I heave and toil,
And wrestle with my inward Foes in vain,
O're-power'd [sic] and vanquish'd still: They drag me down
From Things cœlestial, and confine my Sense
To present Maladies. Unhappy State,
Where the poor Spirit is subdu'd t'endure
Unholy Idleness, a painful Absence
From God, and Heaven, and Angels blessed Work,
And bound to bear the Agonies and Woes
That sickly Flesh and shatter'd Nerves impose.
How long, O Lord, how long?[1]

---

[1] Watts, *Reliquiæ Juveniles*, 180–81. Portions of this poem are remarkably similar to the third and fourth stanzas from Watts's common meter version of Psalm 6, titled "Complaint in Sickness; or, Diseases healed" in *The Psalms of David Imitated*: "Sorrow and Pain wear out my Days; / I waste the Night with Cries, / Counting the Minutes as they pass, / Till the slow Morning rise. / Shall I be still tormented more? / Mine Eye consum'd with Grief? / How long, my

Despite this lack of hoped-for relief, the poet's love for the day of corporate worship and the "blessed Work" of "God, and Heaven, and Angels" is evident in both the poem and the hymn he had written several years before.

Stanza 1
>Welcome sweet Day of Rest
>That saw the Lord arise;
>Welcome to this reviving Bre[a]st,[2]
>And these rejoycing Eyes!

Watts opens the hymn by using the poetic device apostrophe, addressing an inanimate object as though it can hear and understand. In this case, the object is the "Day of Rest" (Sunday). As noted in the chapter on "Sweet Is the Work, My God, My King," Christians have often transferred the concept of rest from the Sabbath day (Saturday) to the Lord's day (Sunday). Thus the first two lines of this stanza cover the two main aspects of Sunday for many Christians—it is a day of rest and commemoration of the Lord's resurrection.

The last two lines parallel the first two, a format that is set up by the repetition of "Welcome" at the beginning of line 3; as a day of rest Sunday helps revive the body, and as the day of the resurrection it leads to "rejoycing." The parallel is enhanced by the word "Eyes" in the last line, which corresponds with "saw" in line 2.

Note that the repetition of "Welcome" at the beginning of lines 1 and 3 cause them both to begin with a choriambus, creating a dance-like quality to these verses that expresses well the sense of "rejoycing." The jubilant mood is further promoted by the exclamation mark that closes the stanza, giving it a festive flair.

God, how long before / Thine Hand afford Relief?" Watts's *Reliquiæ Juveniles* poem was probably written in imitation of a passage from John Milton's *Paradise Lost* (III, 41); see Hoyles, *The Waning of the Renaissance 1640–1740*, 205–206.

[2] In the first edition, the last word in the line was spelled "Brest"; this was corrected to "Breast" in the second edition (1709).

Stanza 2

> The King himself comes near,
> And feasts his Saints to Day,
> Here we may sit, and see him here,
> And love and praise and pray.

For the second stanza Watts changes the line of communication from "human to inanimate object" to "human to human." The initial lines are likely a reference to Revelation 19:9, "Blessed are they which are called unto the marriage supper of the Lamb," but are also reminiscent of Matthew 21:5 ("Tell ye the daughter of Sion, Behold, thy King cometh unto thee"—quoted from Zechariah 9:9—along with parallel verses in the other Synoptic gospels) and John 21:12 ("Jesus saith unto them, Come and dine"). Perhaps significantly, the first of these passages has an eschatological dimension, the second is from the account of the Triumphal Entry (on Palm Sunday), and the third is from one of Jesus' post-resurrection appearances, emphasizing several important aspects of Sunday for the Christian.

Line 3 uses epanadiplosis, in which a verse begins and ends with the same word. Presumably, by "here" Watts means the place of worship where believers can sit down, see the "King," be feasted, "And love, and praise and pray." The picture that is imaginatively drawn is that of a banquet hall where the sovereign is in full view of all, there is good food to eat, and the people can adore their beloved King. Though idealized, this description fits well with the Christian view of worship: God is present through his word, he dines with his people in communion, and his praise is proclaimed.

Stanza 3

> One Day amidst the Place,
> Where my dear God hath been
> Is sweeter than ten thousand days
> Of pleasurable Sin.

Stanza 3 alludes to Psalm 84:10, "For a day in thy courts is better than a thousand. I had rather be a doorkeeper in the house of my God, than to dwell in the tents of wickedness," though Watts has increased the number of days "Of pleasurable Sin" tenfold. It is interesting to note that in line 2 the hymn writer does not say "Where my dear God is" but "Where my dear God hath been." In other words, even if God is not present at a particular place, it is enough that he was once there to make that place "sweeter than ten thousand days / Of pleasurable Sin."

Of course, Watts and other Christians believe that God is omnipresent, so the metaphor should not be stretched too far, but it does provide a vivid and memorable reminder of the lasting effects of God's presence. Perhaps a good analogy is the anointing by Mary of Jesus' feet with spikenard, when "the house was filled with the odour of the ointment" (John 12:3); the smell of the spikenard was not restricted to the physical location of the bottle.

Stanza 4

>My willing Soul would stay
>In such a Frame as this,
>To sit and sing her self away
>To Everlasting Bliss.

In the final stanza of this brief hymn, Watts repeats the "sit" motif from stanza 2 and translates the "praise" from that stanza into "sing." Observe the large number of sibilant sounds in the current strophe: "Soul," "stay," "such," "this," "sit," "sing," "self," "Everlasting," and "Bliss." These sibilants help give a rhythmic flow to the stanza, and particularly to the third line, where every other word begins with an "s."

Watts expresses his preference to stay in the present "Frame," perhaps meaning the place of worship or—more likely—the frame of mind and spirit he has experienced on the Lord's day. This is reminiscent of Peter's outburst at the transfiguration, "Master, it is good for us to be here: and let us make three tabernacles; one for thee, and one for Moses, and one for Elias" (Mark 9:5; see also Matt 17:4). Many Christians have undoubtedly felt the same way after a particularly moving experience of worship. Peter wanted to stay on the mountaintop of a spiritual high, not realizing that there was ministry to be done in the valley below (see Mark 9:14-27). It is always a temptation to want to linger in the enjoyable presence of God rather than to descend to the nitty-gritty of doing his work in the world.

That said, Watts has made an important point: in order to have the cleansing, vision, and power to do God's work, Christians must regularly spend time in his presence. While one could choose from among many possible biblical texts to illustrate this truth, the well-known passage in Isaiah 6:1-9 provides a clear example. Isaiah was given a directive by the Lord to "Go, and tell this people" the message that God wanted to communicate to them. Before that could occur, however, Isaiah had to be cleansed of his own sin, obtain a vision of the needs of the people around him, and receive the power that comes from having a vision of God.[3] Sunday is a day that is set apart from the rest of the week when Christians can specially receive this cleansing, vision, and empowerment through worship.

It is difficult to overemphasize the importance of Sunday for Independents such as Isaac Watts. As noted in chapter 22, Independents in general did not celebrate special days or seasons such as those found in the Christian year, believing that such observance was not warranted either by command or example in the New Testament. The one exception was the magnification of Sunday, which, because of the resurrection and several mentions of Sunday gatherings in the New Testament, was set apart as the only special time for corporate worship. Thus this one day became Christmas, Easter, Pentecost—essentially the entire Christian year—wrapped up in a single day. By writing hymns such as "Welcome, Sweet Day of Rest," Isaac Watts provided his fellow Independents—and Christians of many other denominations and persuasions—with appropriate material to celebrate this special time.

---

[3] See Music, "Worship: Prelude to Evangelism," 19–21.

24

WHEN I CAN READ MY TITLE CLEAR

"When I Can Read My Title Clear" was published in the second book of *Hymns and Spiritual Songs* (no. 65), where it immediately preceded another hymn on a similar topic, "There Is a Land of Pure Delight" (see chapter 21). Watts headed the text "The Hope of Heaven our Support under Trials on Earth." As was frequent in his hymns, he wrote the text in iambic meter and used cross rhyme. The hymn also employs common meter.

Like "There Is a Land of Pure Delight," "When I Can Read My Title Clear" describes the joys that await the redeemed in heaven as an encouragement in the present life.[1] However, whereas "There Is a Land of Pure Delight" centers on conquering the terrors of death, "When I Can Read My Title Clear" emphasizes overcoming the trials the Christian faces in everyday life. In both hymns, the key concept is "hope" though that word is not used in either lyric: the hope of heaven enables believers to bear adversity in the present and face future death with certainty.

Stanza 1
> When I can read my Title clear
>> To Mansions in the Skies,
> I bid farewel[l] to every Fear,
>> And wipe my weeping Eyes.

---

[1] See chapter 21 for a discussion of claims that this hymn and "There Is a Land of Pure Delight" were possibly inspired by the scenery of Southampton, England.

Watts begins the hymn with a bit of legal jargon about reading his "Title," which, as Bailey puts it, is "a Right, a Claim; a just Cause for Possessing or Enjoying of any Thing; also Writings or Records to prove one's Right." Thus Watts likens his place in heaven to having a title or claim to possession or ownership of it. Bailey defines "When" as "at what time." The word can have either a sense of future action ("when I come to town I will do thus and so") or of continuing action ("when I come to town I always do thus and so").

The context of this hymn suggests that Watts took the word in the second sense: "whenever" he reads his "Title" he bids "farewell to every Fear": his reading of the title is not a one-time thing but something to which he often returns. Note that his title is "clear"; there are no liens or other obstacles to his possession of it. The reference to "Mansions" in the second line is an allusion to John 14:2, where Jesus tells his disciples, "In my Father's house are many mansions: if it were not so, I would have told you. I go to prepare a place for you."

It is in the third line of the hymn that Watts's use of the word "When" as an ongoing rather than a future activity becomes evident, for he states simply "I bid farewell to every Fear." He appears to be saying that "Every time I read my title clear I bid farewell to every fear." Perhaps confused by the word "can" in the first line, compilers of subsequent hymnals have sometimes interpreted "When" in that same line in the first (future) sense noted above and changed the initial word of line 3 to "I'll." This makes the stanza mean something like "At some (future) time I will be able to read my title clear and then I will bid farewell to every fear." By using "can," Watts probably meant to suggest that he often sees his "Title clear" but that sometimes he is not able to read it so clearly ("Those times when I can read my title clear"). The difference between using "I" and "I'll" in the third line is not theologically serious, but it is significant. Watts says he can read his title *now* and almost any time he wants to; the revision suggests that the believer cannot yet read the title. Watts simply likes to remind himself of his possession of the title; the singer of the revision does not yet even have one.

Reading his "Title" (i.e., remembering his ownership of a place in heaven) not only causes Watts to lose his fear but also to say "farewell" to it; the fear will be seen no more, as though it were dead or on a long journey. Bidding farewell to fear also relieves the tears of sorrow that accompany it; now the singer can wipe the tears away from his or her eyes, no more will be shed, and the person will have clear vision to see the title once again.

The effectiveness of lines 3 and 4 is enhanced by alliteration: "farewel[l]" / "Fear" and "wipe" / "weeping." This rhetorical device is also characteristic of two of the three following stanzas.

Stanza 2
> Should Earth against my Soul engage,
>> And Hellish Darts be hurl'd,
> Then I can smile at *Satan*'s Rage,
>> And face a frowning World.

Whereas stanza 1 begins with legal language, the second stanza opens with that of warfare. One of Bailey's definitions of "engage" is "to encounter or fight," and that seems to be the sense in which Watts uses the term here, particularly when linked with the "Hellish Darts" of the second line.[2] "Hellish" has sometimes been altered to "fiery" in later hymnals, which actually aligns it more directly with a scriptural passage, Ephesians 6:16, "Above all, taking the shield of faith, wherewith ye shall be able to quench all the fiery darts of the wicked."[3] Bidding "farewell to every Fear" and wiping one's "weeping Eyes" does not mean that there will be no more challenges in the present life. Indeed, there are powerful adversaries to be faced: "Earth," which seeks to fight with the believer; "Hellish Darts"; "Satan's Rage"; and a "frowning World." Though believers are not delivered from these foes (at least in this life), their clear title to "Mansions in the Skies" means that they can "smile" at Satan and have courage in the face of a world that looks upon them with disdain or even hatred. Note the antithesis between "smile" and "frowning" in lines 3 and 4. Once again, alliteration figures prominently ("smile" / "Satan's" and "face" / "frowning").

---

[2] N. Bailey, *An Universal Etymological English Dictionary.*

[3] See the similar use of "darts" in a hymn added to the second edition of *Hymns and Spiritual Songs* (1709), "With Joy We Meditate the Grace": "But spotless, innocent and pure / The Great Redeemer stood, / While Satan's fiery Darts he bore, / And did resist to Blood."

Stanza 3
> Let Cares like a wild Deluge come,
>> And Storms of Sorrow fall,
> May I but safely reach my Home,
>> My God, my Heaven, my All.

Like the opening stanzas, Watts employs alliteration in two verses of the third strophe, but this time it appears in the initial lines: "Cares" / "come" and "Storms" / "Sorrow." He also changes from metaphor to simile, here comparing earthly troubles to floods and storms. The vividness of Watts's language adds to the impact of the simile—"Cares" are not merely a "Deluge" but a "wild Deluge"; the sorrows are "Storms of Sorrow." The use of "Let" to open the stanza almost sounds like a challenge: "Come on, deluge and storms, I have nothing to fear from you." At the very least, the singers can have confidence if they can merely reach "Home," which Watts defines in the last line as "My God, my Heaven, my All"; note the use of "my" as every other word in the line, emphasizing the personal nature of the hymn.

In a text about the afterlife, it is not surprising to find heaven called the singer's home, but this hymn also calls God "Home": heaven is where God is, so for the believer home is also where God is. Furthermore, God and heaven are "All" that are needed. Note the use of climax in a manner similar to the last line of "When I Survey the Wondrous Cross" (see chapter 25).

Stanza 4
> There shall I bath[e] my weary Soul
>> In Seas of heavenly Rest;
> Nor dares a Wave of Trouble roll
>> Across my peaceful Breast.

Watts links stanzas 3 and 4 by the word "There" (which refers back to "Home" in 3:3) to begin the fourth strophe. He also ties them together by continuing to employ water imagery in stanza 4, but now instead of a deluge and storms that assail the Christian, the believer is bathing in "Seas of heavenly Rest." Note the difference between the sea in this hymn and "There Is a Land of Pure Delight": in one, the sea represents death, a barrier that must be passed before getting into paradise; in this lyric it symbolizes the water of (eternal) life after one has arrived. Just as bathers immerse themselves in water, so the redeemed souls will immerse themselves in the peace of heaven. Watts indulges in a bit of irony in line 3: while the "Seas" are now composed of "heavenly Rest" there are still waves of "Trouble," which, fortunately, will not "roll / Across my peaceful Breast." In the second edition of *Hymns and Spiritual Songs* Watts altered line 3 to "And not a Wave of Trouble roll."

In a sermon preached in the same year that *Hymns and Spiritual Songs* was published, Watts reflected on heaven in a similar manner to the thoughts he expressed in "When I Can Read My Title Clear."

> What a blessed state are we travelling to, where we shall be possessed of life without any danger or fear of dying; where we shall be vested with immortality and life in perfection: where we shall live a life of strength, without weakness; of health, without sickness; of safety, without danger; of peace, without disturbance; of holiness, without sin or temptation; and unknown joy, without fear or sorrow, for ever.[4]

"When I Can Read My Title Clear" is remarkable for its use of metaphors and similes from the legal profession, warfare, and water. Despite the starkness of some of its imagery ("weeping Eyes," "Hellish Darts," "frowning World," "wild Deluge," "Storms of Sorrow"), the overall mood is one of joy and triumph.[5] The singer anticipates leaving behind the cares and sorrow of this world for an eternity of peace with God in heaven—and that is reason for singing indeed.

---

[4] *The Posthumous Works of the Late Learned and Reverend Isaac Watts, D.D.*, 2:306. On the dating of this sermon, see p. [242] of *The Posthumous Works*.

[5] In Benson's discussion of "The Hymn of the Church Triumphant" in *The Hymnody of the Christian Church*, he described this hymn as "complacent selfishness" without specifying what makes it either complacent or selfish (170). The present writer would characterize it more as "confident assurance."

25

WHEN I SURVEY THE WONDROUS CROSS

It is coincidental but providential that "When I Survey the Wondrous Cross" is the last hymn to be discussed in this book, because this text on the crucifixion has long been recognized as one of the greatest hymns in the English language.[1] It has become part of the standard repertory of congregational song in England and America—and, indeed, around the world—and no English-language hymnal would be considered complete without it.[2]

"When I Survey" was published in *Hymns and Spiritual Songs* (1707) under the heading "Crucifixion to the World by the Cross of Christ" and with the Scripture reference Galatians 6:14. The text appeared as number seven in the third part of the book, which contained hymns for "Celebration of the Lord's Supper."[3] Two years later (1709), the second edition of the book included a slightly revised version of the hymn, and this form of the text eventually found its way into many other collections of congregational song. Nearly every word Watts chose for "When I Survey" is pregnant with meaning, and the structure of the text reveals a remarkable

---

[1] This chapter first appeared as "'When I Survey the Wondrous Cross': A Commentary" in *The Hymn* 65/2 (Spring 2014): 7–13. The article has been extensively revised for the present book. I am grateful to Jan Kraybill, former executive director of the Hymn Society in the United States and Canada, for permission to reprint this revision of the article.

[2] Benson, *Studies of Familiar Hymns*, 131. Benson also calls it "the best of all Watts's hymns" (131) and notes a comment by British poet Matthew Arnold (1822–1888), who though not particularly fond of hymns, called "When I Survey" the greatest hymn in the language (135). See also the references to the hymn in the introduction to this book.

[3] Watts, *Hymns and Spiritual Songs* (1707), xii.

sense of both form and theological and spiritual insight.[4] Thus this chapter will take an approach that differs somewhat from the previous ones in that each line—indeed, almost every word—will receive detailed attention.

"When I Survey" was initially laid out in five stanzas. When Watts reprinted the text in 1709, he marked the original stanza 4 for possible omission, a suggestion that has been followed by most subsequent hymnal editors, though (as will be seen below) this omission spoils one of the most distinctive structural features of the hymn. The hymn is in long meter and iambic poetic meter, which gives a sense of forward momentum; several lines begin with a choriambus.[5] These temporary modulations mark important words and ideas in the text and keep the meter from falling into a jog trot.

Watts cast "When I Survey" in an ABAB rhyme scheme (cross rhyme). Cross rhyme is difficult to write since a correspondence must be found for each line of the text. Like the use of iambic poetic meter, cross rhyme creates a sense of forward motion as one anticipates the next rhyming word.[6] Watts's skill as a poet is seen in the fact that nine of the ten combinations he used are true rhymes, with only the "God"/"blood" pair in stanza 2 employing a false rhyme.

Watts's practical bent is evident not only from his use of a hymnic

---

[4] Commenting on this hymn, Breed, in *The History and Use of Hymns and Hymn-Tunes*, suggested that "there is no temptation to analyze it, to dissect its lines, and point out its particular beauties" (103); however, the present writer has succumbed to that very temptation. Particular attention should be drawn to the excellent and penetrating analyses of "When I Survey" in Davie, *The Eighteenth-Century Hymn in England*, 39–47; Watson, *The English Hymn*, 160–70; and Meszaros, "Isaac Watts: A Universal Hymn Writer," 391–95. A shorter but still valuable study is in A. E. Bailey, *The Gospel in Hymns*, 49–50. That the present commentary differs from these writings in several respects demonstrates the richness of meaning to be found in Watts's hymn.

[5] "Save in the Death," "All the vain things," "See from his Head," "Sorrow and Love," etc. As noted in previous chapters, Watts often employs a choriambus to express joy, but that does not seem to be his purpose in "When I Survey."

[6] Lovelace, *The Anatomy of Hymnody*, 25. Since Watts made frequent use of cross rhyme in hymns on various subjects, not too much should be made of its use in this text on the "cross." However, it *is* interesting that this great hymn on the cross employs that rhyme scheme!

meter that could be sung to an already familiar tune but also by the character of the words he used. As published in 1709, "When I Survey" contained 139 words. One hundred twenty of these (more than 86 percent) consisted of a single syllable, seventeen (12.23 percent) used two syllables ("survey," "wondrous," etc.), and only two (1.44 percent) contained three syllables ("sacrifice," "amazing"). The use of so many short words fit well with the author's objective of trying "to make the Sense [of the hymns] plain and obvious."[7] Erik Routley observed that "this is the most penetrating of all hymns, the most demanding, the most imaginative...precisely because its style is so simple. It is drawn throughout in strong, clear, simple lines and colours."[8]

Stanza 1
When I survey the wondrous Cross
Where the young Prince of Glory dy'd,
My richest Gain I count but Loss,
And pour Contempt on all my Pride.

When I survey the wondrous Cross. Watts opens his hymn with the adverb "When." In using this word, Watts seems to mean "As often as" or "Every time I...." The implication is clear: Watts is not relating a one-time experience; rather, his vision of the cross is something to which he returns again and again. It is as though, having caught a glimpse of the cross, he has difficulty looking away and must often come back for another look. The singular pronoun "I" personalizes the text: this is the singer's own experience, and it is the singer who keeps returning to the vision.

Bailey explains "survey" as meaning "to view or look about on all sides," "to oversee," or "to measure land," thus to examine thoroughly, to look at every aspect of the subject, or to measure carefully.[9] The mental image that is conjured up is of a person on his or her hands and knees with a ruler measuring every facet of the cross. The cross does not receive a cursory glance or a quick look from Watts but a careful and sustained

---

[7] Watts, preface to *Hymns and Spiritual Songs* (1707), viii.
[8] Routley, *Hymns and the Faith*, 112.
[9] N. Bailey, *An Universal Etymological English Dictionary*.

examination.[10] In modern parlance, "survey" is also employed to mean a brief overview of an entire subject area, as in a "survey of music history" or "a survey of English literature." Thus "survey" could indeed connote a "cursory glance or a quick look" over the whole object, though the definitions given by Bailey do not seem to point in that direction. Watts might have used any of a variety of two-syllable synonyms at this point— "observe," "look at," or "review," for example—but none of these convey the richness of "survey," which at the same time suggests both an overall picture and a detailed examination of the object.

The systematic precision suggested by the term "survey" is quickly dispelled by the word "wondrous," which Bailey identifies as "wonderful," "surprising," or "marvellous."[11] The experience of surveying the cross is not one of mere scientific objectivity—the cross is something magical; it can be analyzed and measured up to a certain point but will always remain wrapped in wonder, surprise, and marvel. One could make an analogy with our knowledge of the universe: the more we observe it, learn about it, and measure it, the more mysterious it becomes.

The last word of the first line makes plain that the focus of Watts's contemplation is the cross. Taken as a whole, the line creates a vivid image of measuring every aspect of a cross, but this is not an ordinary cross—it is an extraordinary one.

Where the young Prince of Glory dy'd. In the second edition of *Hymns and Spiritual Songs* (1709), Watts revised this line to read "On which the Prince of Glory dy'd," a change that was almost universally adopted in later hymnals. Lionel Adey points out that the original line might have been a bit of "self-projection [by the author], since at the time of writing Watts was about the same age" as Jesus when he was crucified.[12]

A number of commentators have maintained that the original line is superior to Watts's revision. For example, Percy Dearmer called the first

---

[10] In her article "The Dramatic Art of Hymnody," Marshall sees Watts's use of "survey" in this hymn in a different light, calling it "almost mathematically cold" (17).

[11] N. Bailey, *An Universal Etymological English Dictionary.*

[12] Adey, *Hymns and the Christian "Myth,"* 120. The traditionally accepted age at which Jesus was crucified was approximately thirty-three. Watts, who was born in 1674, turned thirty-three in 1707, the year his *Hymns and Spiritual Songs* first appeared.

version a "finer and more original line" and commented that "We can only suppose that...some one who had no feeling for poetry persuaded the young author to change it," while the English poet laureate John Betjeman lamented the revision as being "more pedantic" and claimed that it was not "*really* an improvement."[13] On the other hand, J. R. Watson observed that the use of the word "young" to refer to the "Prince" was superfluous, and perhaps it was for this reason—as well as because of the metrical awkwardness of the original—that Watts altered the line.[14] The revision seems much stronger than the original, especially when sung, though the 1707 wording does call more direct attention to the young age at which Jesus was crucified.[15]

Continuing the thought of the first line, v. 2 tells us why the cross is "wondrous": it is where the "Prince of Glory dy'd." "Prince of Glory" is a curious construction. This phrase does not appear in the KJV but seems to be a conflation of two familiar messianic Old Testament passages—Isaiah 9:6 and Psalm 24:7 (with a parallel in verse 10), in which Christ is referred to respectively as the "Prince of Peace" and the "King of glory."[16] "Prince of Peace" would not fit the line metrically, but why did Watts not simply use "King of glory," which would fit both metrically and logically?

A possible explanation may be in the traditional Christian usage of the two passages. Isaiah 9:6 has generally been associated with the incarnation of the Messiah, while Psalm 24:7 is usually linked with two events in the life of Christ: the triumphal entry and—more to the present point—the ascension. Thus, Watts may have created this combination as a veiled abbreviation for the entire scope of Jesus' life and ministry on earth. And, of course, using "King of glory" would not suggest Jesus' relative youth at the time of the crucifixion, whereas "Prince of Glory"

---

[13] Dearmer, *Songs of Praise Discussed*, 87; Betjeman, *Sweet Songs of Zion*, 27.

[14] Watson, *The English Hymn*, 166.

[15] As originally written, the line does not sing well with either of the tunes to which "When I Survey" is usually sung, HAMBURG or ROCKINGHAM, nor with O WALY, WALY, with which it has sometimes been linked.

[16] Isa 9:6: "For unto us a child is born, unto us a son is given: and the government shall be upon his shoulder: and his name shall be called Wonderful, Counsellor, The mighty God, The everlasting Father, The Prince of Peace"; Ps 24:7: "Lift up your heads, O ye gates; and be ye lift up, ye everlasting doors; and the King of glory shall come in."

does.[17]

The last word of the line reminds us that the cross may be "wondrous" but also that it is an instrument of death. Jesus did not merely pass out to be revived later—he suffered actual physical death through an instrument of torture.

My richest Gain I count but Loss. Line 3 is a close paraphrase of Philippians 3:7, "What things were gain to me, those I counted loss for Christ." Watts may also have had in mind Jesus' words in Matthew 16:26, "What is a man profited, if he shall gain the whole world, and lose his own soul?" "My" reinforces the personal perspective of the text, reminding us again that this is the singer's own story. Bailey defines "rich" as "that has great incomes," "plentiful," or "very precious," and "gain" as "profit" or "lucre."[18] Thus Watts's "richest Gain" might be understood as "plentiful profit" or "very precious lucre." While this phrase may signify worldly goods (such as money), the language is nebulous enough to refer to any sort of human striving for things of lesser ultimate worth, such as fame, self-fulfillment, or power.

"Count" parallels "survey" in the first line in its suggestion of measurement and calculation but this time the implication is of a person totaling up coins. The inference is that the person has spent a lifetime seeking "richest Gain," but upon catching a glimpse of the cross realizes that this represents not gain but loss if it means separation from Christ. Watts is careful to preserve the paradox between "Gain" and "Loss" that is found in the Scripture on which the line is based—the singer's gain is counted as a loss.[19]

And pour Contempt on all my Pride. Bailey defines "contempt" as "despite," "disdain," or "scorn."[20] In Watts's view, the sinner who surveys the cross does not merely dislike his or her pride but has contempt for it. "Pour" conjures up the image of a person drowning his or her pride by

---

[17] It should be noted that Watts used the phrase "Prince of Glory" in at least one other hymn from *Hymns and Spiritual Songs*, "When the First Parents of Our Race" (3:1-2: "Aside the Prince of Glory threw / His most divine Ar[r]ay").

[18] N. Bailey, *An Universal Etymological English Dictionary.*

[19] A paradox is a combination of contradictory statements into a single truth.

[20] N. Bailey, *An Universal Etymological English Dictionary.*

inundating it with a bucket full of "contempt." As in the previous line, Watts employs a paradox by combining "Contempt" with "Pride." "Contempt" and "Pride" also form a syntactical chiasmus with "Gain" and "Loss" in the previous line; people normally express "Pride" in "richest Gain" and "Contempt" for "Loss," but in this case everything is reversed.

> My **richest gain** I count but *loss*,
> And pour *contempt* on all my **pride**.

Watts himself must have been fond of the ideas found in this stanza, for as Harry Escott pointed out, some of the same basic concepts—and even some of the same wording—are used in a different hymn from the second edition of *Hymns and Spiritual Songs*.

> Now for the Love I bear his Name
> What was my Gain I count my Loss,
> My former Pride I call my Shame,
> And nail my Glory to his Cross.

However, as noted by Escott, the ideas of the stanza "appeared in a more perfect form" in "When I Survey," an opinion with which few would disagree.[21]

Stanza 2
Forbid it, Lord, that I should boast
Save in the Death of Christ my God;
All the vain things that charm me most,
I sacrifice them to his Blood.

Forbid it, Lord, that I should boast / Save in the Death of Christ my God. The opening lines of the second stanza are a close paraphrase of the

---

[21] "No More, My God, I Boast No More" (Book II, hymn 109); Escott, *Isaac Watts, Hymnographer*, 190. Escott's wording makes it seem like he is saying that the stanza in "No More, My God, I Boast No More" preceded "When I Survey"; that was undoubtedly not his intent—since "When I Survey" was published before "No More, My God"—but rather to note that the similar ideas were worked out better in "When I Survey."

basic scriptural reference for the hymn, Galatians 6:14a, "But God forbid that I should glory, save in the cross of our Lord Jesus Christ." The author does make several significant changes to the Scripture text, the most important of which is its alteration in form from Paul's bold declaration to a humble prayer. The substitution of "boast" for "glory" was perhaps made for reasons of rhyme and meter but such an explanation does not suffice for the change from "Cross" to "Death." It is interesting to note that after the first line of the hymn, the word "Cross" does not appear again in the text: Watts's use of "Death" instead of "Cross" here marks a subtle shift in emphasis—the focus is now more specifically on the death of Jesus himself, rather than on the instrument of that death.[22]

Another meaningful change Watts made to the scriptural reference is his addition of the words "my God" after "Christ." Because of some of his later theological writings, Watts has occasionally been accused of unorthodox views on the Trinity. "When I Survey" shows that at least during this period his views on the deity of Jesus were thoroughly orthodox.

All the vain things that charm me most. Bailey defines "vain" as "empty," "frivolous," "useless," or "foolish," and "charm" as "to bewitch," "to please," or "to delight extremely."[23] The "things" in which humans delight are mostly void of any lasting significance ("vain"). Today "charm" is normally used in the second and third senses given by Bailey but it is meaningful to consider the "bewitch" definition: we follow vain things because we are under their spell—we are mesmerized or beguiled by them. The use of a word associated with magic recalls Watts's description of the cross in stanza 1 as "wondrous." It takes a powerful antidote to break the spell of "vain things," but that antidote is readily available: "the Death of Christ my God." "Most" suggests that "the things that charm me" are the ones that the singer really loves and dotes upon.

I sacrifice them to his Blood. The last line of the stanza contains one of the two three-syllable words in the hymn, "sacrifice." This is a critical word, because it says, in essence, "I am not merely going to give up the 'vain things'—I am going to sacrifice them." The word implies a deliberate act of the will, and likely the destruction of the vain things, just as the life of a sacrificed animal was snuffed out and the body consumed by fire

---

[22] To be sure, the original stanza 4 does contain a reference to "tree" as a synonym for "cross."

[23] N. Bailey, *An Universal Etymological English Dictionary.*

in the Old Testament. This is more than simply doing without something—it is consigning it to oblivion as an offering to God, never to be seen or thought of again.

The preposition "to" in this line is of interest. Normally, Christians think of Jesus' blood as *being* the sacrifice—and, of course, that is true—but in this case it is the blood that is the *object* of sacrifice. In other words, the sacrifice is made in response to the blood Jesus shed on the cross. The parallel between the last two lines of this stanza and the corresponding verses of the first stanza should be noted: richest gain is loss and vain things are sacrificed.

Stanza 3
See from his Head, his Hands, his Feet,
Sorrow and Love flow mingled down;
Did e're such Love and Sorrow meet?[24]
Or Thorns compose so rich a Crown?

Stanza 3 is the heart of the hymn, both in terms of its form and its content: the lines constitute the middle stanza of the original five-stanza text, and it is here that the intensity of Watts's meditation on the crucifixion reaches its climax. Scotty Gray has noted this stanza as an example of hypotyposis, "the use of a vivid description to bring a scene to mind."[25] A critical part of the stanza's dramatic impact is the shift in focus from the actions of the singer ("*I* survey," "*I* count," "*I* should boast," "*I* sacrifice") to straightforward contemplation of Christ on the cross: note that the pronouns "I," "me," "my," and "mine"—all of which figure prominently in the other stanzas—are completely missing here; the focus is entirely on the Savior.

See from his Head, his Hands, his Feet. The imperative verb with which the stanza opens ("See") implies that a visual image is about to be painted. It is as though Watts is saying "Behold! Pay attention! Some-

---

[24] In both the first and second editions of *Hymns and Spiritual Songs*, Watts used the spelling "e're."

[25] Gray, *Hermeneutics of Hymnody*, 192. He further gives the first line of the stanza as an example of diaeresis, "in which parts or attributes of something are enumerated rather than repeated" (192). See also the analysis of this hymn by Arnold in *Trinity of Discord*, 55–56.

thing important is happening." The order of the words "Head," "Hands," and "Feet" is meaningful, for it suggests a person slowly "surveying" Christ's body on the cross, following the flow of the blood downward from the head to the hands and ultimately to the feet (note the word "down" at the end of the next line).[26] In a sense, this might be seen as a "reverse climax"—moving downward instead of upward. Though not specifically mentioned, the crown of thorns and the nails with which Jesus was pierced hover in the background.

Sorrow and Love flow mingled down. Watts probably had three Scripture passages in mind as he wrote this line. Albert Edward Bailey suggested a link with John 19:34 ("But one of the soldiers with a spear pierced his side, and forthwith came there out blood and water"), observing that "Watts takes from that [verse] the idea of 'mingled,' and then by the alchemy of his imagination changes the revolting physical details into their spiritual equivalents, 'sorrow and love.'"[27] The words "flow" and "down" confirm that Watts was using "sorrow" and "love" as metaphors for Jesus' blood (and perhaps the water, as suggested by Bailey); recall that the last two words of the previous stanza were "his blood." The flow of "sorrow" and "love" are "mingled": that is, they are so intertwined that they cannot be separated from each another.

The other two relevant Scripture passages are Lamentations 1:12 ("Behold, and see if there be any sorrow like unto my sorrow") and John 15:13 ("Greater love hath no man than this, that a man lay down his life for his friends"), which are probably the sources for the words "Sorrow" and "Love"; both are widely used Passion texts. Note that the verse from Lamentations also calls on the hearer to "see," the word that opens this stanza. "Sorrow" does not imply that Jesus was sorrowful about his own death but that he had pity for humans because of the sins that separate them from God (see also his lamentation over Jerusalem, Matt 23:37).

That Jesus felt both sorrow and love for humanity is important because we can feel sorry for someone without loving them. For example, when people in another state or country lose their homes in a natural disaster we may feel sorrow for them, knowing that they will have a difficult

---

[26] While "feet" needed to be placed at the end of the line for rhyming purposes, Watts could just as well have written "See from his hands, his head, his feet." However, this would have lessened the vividness of the imagery.

[27] A. E. Bailey, *The Gospel in Hymns*, 50.

time recovering from such a loss; we may even seek to help them through donations or personal relief efforts. However, since we do not have personal knowledge of them, we can hardly be said to love them in the same sense we would love our parent, spouse, child, or best friend.

Did e're such Love and Sorrow meet. In line 3 Watts repeats the words "Sorrow" and "Love" but this time reverses them to create a chiasmus with the second verse of the stanza.

> **Sorrow** and *Love* flow mingled down;
> Did e're such *Love* and **Sorrow** meet?

While chiasmus is a common device in English poetry and hymnody, its usage at this point in "When I Survey" carries considerable symbolic significance. The Greek letter *chi* (X), from which the device gets its name, is the first letter of "Christ" and has long been an accepted abbreviation of that title. The shape of the letter also suggests a cross, and from early Christian times it was used with this meaning. Chiasmus is thus symbolic of both Christ and the cross, the central theme of Watts's hymn.

Watts's use of the device at this point is particularly striking, for it appears in the very center of the hymn. As noted above, in its original form "When I Survey" contained five stanzas, making this third stanza the center one. Furthermore, the chiasmus occurs in the two inner lines of the stanza.

1. When I survey the wond'rous Cross...
2. Forbid it, Lord, that I should boast...
3. See from his Head, his Hands, his Feet,
> **Sorrow** and *Love* flow mingled down;
> Did e'er such *Love* and **Sorrow** meet,
Or Thorns compose so rich a Crown?
4. His dying Crimson, like a Robe...
5. Were the whole Realm of Nature mine...

The meaning of this placement is clear: Watts has placed an early Christian symbol of both Christ and his cross at the very heart of the text. Jesus and the instrument of his death are not only the subjects of the hymn—they are literally at the center of it. Unfortunately, this symbolic gesture is lost when the original fourth stanza is omitted.

The word "meet" at the end of line 3 corresponds to "mingled" in the second: sorrow and love meet together in the blood of Jesus. In addition to the chiasmus, the two lines represent a type of synonymous parallelism that is found in many verses of the psalms.

Or Thorns compose so rich a Crown. Line 4 rounds out the stanza by using "Thorns" and "Crown" in parallel with the "Head" of the first line. Bailey defines "compose" as "to put together for the making up of one body." Donald Davie notes that "compose" can have a double meaning: the one given it by Bailey and the idea of comforting or "composure," thus either "making beauty out of what is most brutal and squalid" or valuing "these atrocious occasions for the challenge they pose...to our understanding."[28] It is difficult for us to imagine a crown made of thorns as being "rich," but Watts perhaps had in mind here his use of "richest Gain" in the first stanza; whereas he has counted his "richest Gain" as loss, these lost riches have been more than compensated for by the richness of the crown of thorns.

Stanza 4
His dying Crimson like a Robe
Spreads o'er his Body on the Tree,
Then am I dead to all the Globe,
And all the Globe is dead to me.

As noted previously, in the second edition of *Hymns and Spiritual Songs* Watts enclosed this stanza with brackets, indicating that it "may be left out in Singing without disturbing the Sense."[29] Subsequent hymnal editors have generally followed his lead.[30] Nevertheless, in addition to its

---

[28] Davie, *The Eighteenth-Century Hymn in England*, 42. N. Bailey does not give a definition of "compose" that corresponds with the idea of comfort or composure.

[29] *Hymns and Spiritual Songs* (1709), xiv. In his explanation of the "Crotchets," Watts goes on to say that sometimes they have been used when the stanzas "contain Words too Poetical for meaner Understandings, or too particular for whole Congregations to sing," but that does not seem to be the case for this specific hymn.

[30] Julian, in *A Dictionary of Hymnology*, credits George Whitefield's 1757 supplement to *A Collection of Hymns for Social Worship* (originally published in

presence making the chiasmus in the middle of stanza 3 the center of the hymn, the fourth stanza includes some interesting features, including its return to a focus on the singer's actions rather than the simple contemplation of the crucifixion as found in the third stanza. Furthermore, this is the part of the hymn that reflects the closing portion of Galatians 6:14, "by whom the world is crucified unto me, and I unto the world." Perhaps hymnal committees and worship leaders should consider reinstating this stanza, both for the message it contains and to maintain the exceptional structure of the text as a whole.[31]

His dying Crimson like a Robe / Spreads o'er his Body on the Tree. In these lines Watts uses a simile to paint a word picture of Jesus' blood completely covering his body "like a Robe." John M. Hull has pointed out that the "dying" (of "dying Crimson") can have a double meaning—death and the practice of dying something a different color—and that crimson dye "was a particularly costly one, which only the wealthy could afford."[32] The author may have been indulging in a bit of irony here, since Matthew's Gospel says that when the soldiers mocked Jesus just before the crucifixion they "put on him a scarlet robe." John calls it a

---

1753) as "the first to popularize the four-stanza form of the hymn" (1270). The present author did not find the text in any edition or supplement of Whitefield's book until the 1767 (14th) edition, where it appeared as hymn sixty-two (174) in the main body of the book (Julian's "1757" might have been a typographical error for "1767," but this would not explain the statement about the supplement). The 1767 printing does indeed use the four-stanza version, together with some significant alterations in the text, particularly in changing the viewpoint from first-person singular ("When I survey") to third-person plural ("When saints survey"), a change that Whitefield commonly made to the hymns in his book. The four-stanza version (but using Watts's original wording) also appeared in 1767 in Conyers's *A Collection of Psalms and Hymns from Various Authors* as hymn 137 (157).

[31] True, Harry Escott pointed out that "By omitting verse 4, the hymn becomes an architectural gem of alternating recital and response; verse 1, Recital; verse 2, Response; verse 3, Recital; verse 5, Response in the form of a burst of almost seraphic praise" (*Isaac Watts, Hymnographer*, 246). However, as seen above, deleting the stanza obscures an even more fascinating and meaningful architectural feature of the text.

[32] Hull, "From Experiential Educator to Nationalist Theologian," 271. He also points out that Watts's father was in the cloth trade (272).

"purple robe," and Luke was noncommittal, it being merely a "gorgeous robe."[33] Perhaps Watts also had in mind the gambling of the soldiers for Jesus' garments, which were replaced by his flowing blood.[34]

In either case, the point is that his physical apparel has been removed and now, according to the hymn, he is being clothed in blood. The fact that the blood is "spreading" creates an image of the blood slowly enveloping Christ's body rather than gushing forth, in contrast to the "pouring" of contempt mentioned in stanza 1. Madeleine Forell Marshall aptly (if anachronistically) compares Watts's vision to "a filmmaker…soaking the scene in red light, deeper and darker red, to the point of absolute black-out."[35]

Then am I dead to all the Globe, / And all the Globe is dead to me. However, it is not only Jesus who is dying—the singer is also experiencing death, death to the world. The word "Then," which Bailey defines as "at that time," suggests that this "death" of the singer occurs simultaneously with the shedding/spreading of Jesus' blood.[36] Drawing from the Scripture reference, Watts again uses a chiasmus, this time between "dead" and "Globe," to emphasize that as far as the world is concerned the singer is already dead (that is, the world has rejected the singer), and that for the singer the world is also dead (it holds no more attraction or allure).

Stanza 5
Were the whole Realm of Nature mine,
That were a Present far too small;
Love so amazing, so divine
Demands my Soul, my Life, my All.

In the last stanza, the emotional intensity of Watts's meditation on the crucifixion gives way to a doxological outburst of praise and com-

---

[33] Matt 27:28; John 19:2; Luke 23:11.

[34] Matt 27:35; Mark 15:24; Luke 23:34; John 19:24. The background may also include the word picture in Rev 19:13 of the conquering Christ wearing a "vesture dipped in blood."

[35] Marshall, "The Dramatic Art of Hymnody," 17.

[36] Davie, *The Eighteenth-Century Hymn in England*, 42, links Watts's use of "then" with the opening word of the hymn, "when," the implication being that the singer becomes "dead to all the globe" as he or she "surveys" the cross.

mitment. An act of sacrifice like the one made by Christ calls for two fitting responses: "dying to the world" and praise.

Were the whole Realm of Nature mine, / That were a Present far too small. Watts lived during a period of significant advancement in science. Telescopes were increasingly being trained on the night sky and microscopes on terrestrial objects. The "Realm of Nature"—or at least its understanding by humans—was rapidly expanding: Saturn's moon Titan was discovered by Christiaan Huygens in 1655 (only fifty-two years before the publication of Watt's hymn); cells were first observed by Robert Hooke ten years later (1665), and Isaac Newton's "Law of Universal Gravitation" had been published even more recently (1687). The careful measurement suggested by Watts's use of the word "survey" in the first stanza was being applied to all areas of the natural world.

In the hyperbolic opening line of the fourth stanza, the author claims that even if he owned all these and other wonders of nature (much less the "vain things" of the second stanza), this would not suffice to repay the sacrificial gift Jesus made on the cross, for Christ is bigger than and far beyond the universe. Since Watts's time, discoveries have been made that dwarf the early eighteenth-century understanding of the universe, but the principle is still the same: Jesus willingly gave up lordship of everything to die on a cross for one simple reason…

Love. "Love" is the key word in the hymn. Everything to this juncture can be seen as leading to its use in this stanza. Certainly, Watts had used the word previously in the picture of the crucifixion painted in stanza 3 and the "Sorrow" / "Love" *chiasmus.* But now "Sorrow" is gone and only "Love" remains, love that is…

[S]o amazing, so divine. Bailey describes the verb "to amaze" as "to astonish," "to daunt," "to surprize" [*sic*]. Christ's love is astonishing because of its sacrificial nature, daunting because of its demands on both Jesus and humanity, and surprising because of its lavishing on undeserving humans. But Christ's love is not only amazing, it is divine: it is that of a God. Here again Watts states an orthodox understanding of the Trinity in which Jesus is fully God.

In describing the differences between the hymns of Watts and Charles Wesley, Bernard Lord Manning noted an aspect of Watts that is particularly relevant to this hymn.

231

Charles Wesley in his hymns concerns himself mainly (I had almost written exclusively) with God and the soul of man: their manifold relations, their estrangement, their reconciliation, their union. Watts, too, concerns himself with this drama; but he gives it a cosmic background. Not less than Wesley, he finds the Cross the centre of his thought: all things look forward or backward to the Incarnation and the Passion. But Watts sees the Cross, as Milton had seen it, planted on a globe hung in space, surrounded by the vast distances of the universe. There is a sense of the spaciousness of nature, of the vastness of time, of the dreadfulness of eternity, in Watts which is missing or less felt in Wesley.... You constantly find Watts "surveying" the whole realm of Nature and finding at the centre of it its crucified and dying Creator.

And, for Manning, there is "no thought, no expression [that] is more characteristic of Watts" than the line "Were the whole realm of nature mine."[37]

Demands my Soul, my Life, my All. "Demand" is defined by Bailey as "to ask," "to require," "to lay claim to." The love of Jesus does not call for some half-hearted commitment on our part: it is so amazing, so divine that it *requires* something from us. Using climax, Watts proceeds to enumerate three areas of human existence to which this love lays claim: the soul, the life, the all.

According to Bailey, the soul is "the principle of life; also the immortal part of mankind, capable of enjoying or suffering after the separation from the body." This is the inner, eternal part of humans through which they interact with God, and that will last after death. This internal being manifests itself during our earthly existence through the spirit, mind, and emotions.

"Life" is "the union of the soul with the body, manner of living; also sprightliness, spirit, mettle." Bailey's definition makes it clear that it is the soul and body joined together that make up life (at least in humans), but without a body life in earthly terms is impossible. What Watts probably had in mind in his use of "life" is the outer being, the physical nature through which we interact with nature and other people.

Thus, Christ's love demands both the inner and outer selves, or, as

---

[37] Manning, *The Hymns of Wesley and Watts*, 83.

Watts sums it up in the last word of the hymn, the "All," everything humans have to offer. The words of the last line almost seem to tumble over one another in a breathtaking rush of dedication to the God-Man whose self-sacrifice is the basis for humanity's relationship with the divine.[38]

In this simple, yet profound hymn Watts explores both the depth of Christ's suffering and its meaning for the singer. The text is "a chaste, reflective, meditative work, rich with the decorum of its grave and simple lines," yet it is also one that is laden with emotional content.[39] Each word is thoughtfully chosen, scriptural references are carefully used, and the structure of the hymn demonstrates remarkable creativity and insight. Writers of Christian song in all styles and genres would do well to study Watts's hymn for its economy of means, faithfulness to the biblical revelation, and sophistication of expression.

While the text demonstrates artistry of the highest caliber, the author's craft is not employed for its own sake; instead, Watts brings his considerable skill to bear in fashioning a means of witness to the cross, and to the suffering and glory of the Savior who died on that cross. The language and devices employed do not call attention to themselves when the hymn is sung as an act of worship. Rather, the singer is drawn to a realization of the enormity of Jesus' sacrifice and its meaning for humanity. This is ultimately the goal of all Christian song: to praise God for his power, mercy, and grace, and to make a difference in the lives of people for whom Jesus died, an act by which he demonstrated his amazing, divine love.

---

[38] Watts used similar language for a line from his hymn "From Heav'n the Sinning Angels Fell": "To thee, to thee Almighty Love, / Our souls, our Selves, our All we pay" (3:1-2).

[39] Watson, *An Annotated Anthology of Hymns*, 136.

BIBLIOGRAPHY

Adey, Lionel. *Class and Idol in the English Hymn*. Vancouver: University of British Columbia Press, 1988.

———. *Hymns and the Christian "Myth."* Vancouver: University of British Columbia Press, 1986.

Anonymous. *The Christian's Duty*. 2nd ed. 1801.

Argent, Alan. *Isaac Watts, Poet, Thinker, Pastor*. London: Congregational Memorial Hall Trust, 1999.

Arnold, Richard. *The English Hymn: Studies in a Genre*. New York: Peter Lang, 1995.

———. *English Hymns of the Eighteenth Century: An Anthology*. New York: Peter Lang, 1991.

———. *Trinity of Discord: The Hymnal and Poetic Innovations of Isaac Watts, Charles Wesley, and William Cowper*. New York: Peter Lang, 2012.

"Art. II.—1. *Horæ Lyricæ*" North British Review 27/53 (August 1845): 23–44.

Ashworth, Caleb. *Reflections on the Fall of a Great Man: A Sermon Preached to a Congregation of Protestant Dissenters at Daventry in Northamptonshire, on Occasion of the Death of the Late Reverend Isaac Watts, D. D.* London: J. Waugh, et al., 1749.

Bailey, Adrienne Thompson. "The Hymnal Preface and the Clergyman: The Importance of Isaac Watts and John Newton, as Clergymen, to the Development of Western Hymnody." DMus dissertation, Indiana University, 2006.

Bailey, Albert Edward. *The Gospel in Hymns: Backgrounds and Interpretations*. New York: Charles Scribner's Sons, 1950.

Bailey, N. *An Universal Etymological English Dictionary*. London: For E. Ball et al., 1721; 2nd ed., London, 1724.

The Beauties of the Late Reverend Dr. Isaac Watts. Elizabeth-Town, NJ: Shepard Kollock, 1796. Newburyport, MA: Edmund M. Blunt for Mathew Carey, 1797.

[Belknap, Jeremy]. *Memoirs of the Lives, Characters and Writings of Those Two Eminently Pious and Useful Ministers of Jesus Christ, Dr. Isaac Watts and Dr. Philip Doddridge*. Boston: Peter Edes and David West, 1793.

Belles, Jonathan. "5 Things Hurricanes Can Do That Are Actually Good." Weather.com, 10 March 2017. https://weather.com/storms/hurricane/news/hurricane-landfall-benefits-2016 (accessed 5 December 2017).

Benson, Louis F. "The Early Editions of Watts's Hymns." *Journal of the Presbyterian*

Historical Society 1/4 (June 1902): 265–79.

———. *The English Hymn: Its Development and Use in Worship*. N.p.: George H. Doran Company, 1915; reprinted, Richmond, VA: John Knox Press, 1962.

———. "The Evolution of a Great Hymn." *Journal of the Presbyterian Historical Society* 1/5 (September 1902): 237–340.

———. *The Hymnody of the Christian Church*. New York: George H. Doran, 1927; reprinted, Richmond, VA: John Knox Press, 1956.

———. *Studies of Familiar Hymns*. First Series, new edition. Philadelphia: Westminster Press, 1926.

———. *Studies of Familiar Hymns*. Second Series. Philadelphia: Westminster Press, 1923.

Betjeman, John. *Sweet Songs of Zion: Selected Radio Talks*. Edited by Stephen Games. London: Hodder & Stoughton, 2007.

Beynon, Graham. *Isaac Watts: Reason, Passion and the Revival of Religion*. London: Bloomsbury T&T Clark, 2016.

Bishop, Selma L. *Isaac Watts. Hymns and Spiritual Songs, 1707–1748: A Study in Early Eighteenth Century Language Changes*. London: Faith Press, 1962.

———. *Isaac Watts's Hymns and Spiritual Songs (1707): A Publishing History and a Bibliography*. Ann Arbor, MI: Pierian Press, 1974.

———. "The Poetical Theories of Isaac Watts." PhD dissertation, University of Colorado, 1956.

Bond, Douglas. *The Poetic Wonder of Isaac Watts*. Sanford, FL: Reformation Trust, 2013.

Bowman, Clarice M. "Isaac Watts in Dialogue with Contemporary Christian Education." *Religious Education* 58/3 (May–June 1963): 262–68.

Brawley, Benjamin. *History of the English Hymn*. New York: Abingdon Press, 1932.

Breed, David R. *The History and Use of Hymns and Hymn-Tunes*. Chicago: Fleming H. Revell, 1903.

Bridges, Robert. *The Yattendon Hymnal*. Oxford: Oxford University Press, 1899.

Bunyan, John. *The Pilgrim's Progress from This World to That Which Is to Come: Delivered Under the Similitude of a Dream*. London: For Nath. Ponder, 1678.

Bysshe, Edward. *The Art of English Poetry*. London: For R. Knaplock, 1702.

The Canterbury Dictionary of Hymnology. Edited by J. R. Watson and Emma Hornby. https://hymnology.hymnsam.co.uk/.

Conder, Josiah. *The Poet of the Sanctuary. A Centenary Commemoration of the Labours and Services Literary and Devotional of the Rev. Isaac Watts, D. D.* London: John Snow, 1851.

Conyers, Richard. *A Collection of Psalms and Hymns from Various Authors*. London: T and J. W. Pasham, 1767.

Cook, Paul E. G. "Isaac Watts: Father of English Hymnody." In *'Living the Christian Life': being Papers Read at the 1974 Conference*, 29–44. Warboys, England: Westminster Conference, 1974.

Cornick, David. "Looking Back: A Historical Overview of Reformed Worship." *Reforming Worship: English Reformed Principles and Practice*, edited by Julian

Templeton and Keith Riglin, 22–42. Eugene, OR: Wipf & Stock, 2012.

Cousland, Kenneth Harrington. "The Significance of Isaac Watts in the Development of Hymnody." *Church History* 17/4 (December 1948): 287–98.

Davie, Donald. *The Eighteenth-Century Hymn in England.* Cambridge: Cambridge University Press, 1993.

Davies, Horton. *From Watts and Wesley to Maurice, 1690–1850.* Vol. 2 (part 3) of *Worship and Theology in England.* Princeton: University Press, 1996 (originally published 1961).

Davis, Arthur Paul. *Isaac Watts: His Life and Works.* New York: Dryden Press, 1943.

de Sola Pinto, V. "Isaac Watts and the Adventurous Muse." In *Essays and Studies by Members of the English Association. Vol. XX,* 86–107. Oxford: Clarendon Press, 1935.

Dearmer, Percy. *Songs of Praise Discussed.* London: Oxford University Press, 1933.

Dickinson, Clarence, ed. *The Hymnal.* Presbyterian Church of the U.S.A. Philadelphia: Presbyterian Board of Christian Education, 1950.

Edwards, Jonathan. *A Faithful Narrative of the Surprizing [sic] Work of God in the Conversion of Many Hundred Souls in Northampton, and the Neighbouring Towns and Villages of New-Hampshire in New-England. In a Letter to the Revd. Dr. Benjamin Colman of Boston. Written by the Revd. Mr. Edwards, Minister of Northampton, on Nov. 6, 1736. And Published, with a Large Preface, by Dr. Watts and Dr. Guyse.* London: For John Oswald, 1737.

Escott, Harry. *Isaac Watts, Hymnographer: A Study of the Beginnings, Development, and Philosophy of the English Hymn.* London: Independent Press, 1962.

"An Ever-Rolling Stream?" Hymn Society of Great Britain and Ireland *Bulletin* (167) 11/6 (April 1986): 139.

Fenner, Chris. "Joy to the world." *Hymnology Archive.* 13 December 2018; revised 20 February 2020. https://www.hymnologyarchive.com/joy-to-the-world (accessed September 5, 2019).

Figures, D. J. "Isaac Watts and His Position in the Eighteenth Century." *The Congregational Quarterly* 35/4 (October 1957): 341–56.

Fletcher, Donald Rodgers. "English Psalmody and Isaac Watts." PhD dissertation, Princeton University, 1945.

Fountain, David G. *Isaac Watts Remembered.* Worthing, England: Henry E. Walter, 1974.

Gibbons, Thomas. *Memoirs of the Rev. Isaac Watts, D. D.* London: For James Buckland, 1780.

Glass, Henry Alexander. *The Story of the Psalters: A History of the Metrical Versions of Great Britain and America.* London: Kegan Paul, Trench & Co., 1888.

Gray, Scotty. *Hermeneutics of Hymnody: A Comprehensive and Integrated Approach to Understanding Hymns.* Macon, GA: Smyth & Helwys Publishing, 2015.

Grindal, Gracia. "Interpretation: Our God, Our Help in Ages Past." *The Hymn* 40/2 (April 1989): 33–34.

Harsha, D. A. *The Life and Choice Works of Isaac Watts, D. D.* New York: Derby & Jackson, 1857.

Hastings, Thomas, and William Patton. *The Christian Psalmist*. New York: Ezra Collier, 1836.

Holland, John. *The Psalmists of Britain. Records, Biographical and Literary of Upwards of One Hundred and Fifty Authors, Who have Rendered the Whole or Parts of the Book of Psalms, into English Verse*. 2 vols. London: R. Groomsbridge, 1843.

Hood, E. Paxton. *Isaac Watts: His Life and Writings, His Homes and Friends*. London: Religious Tract Society, 1875.

Hope, Norman Victor. *Isaac Watts and His Contribution to English Hymnody*. The Papers of the Hymn Society 13. Fort Worth: Hymn Society of America, 1947.

Horder, W. Garrett, *The Hymn-Lover. An Account of the Rise and Growth of English Hymnody*. London: J. Curwen & Sons [1889].

Houghton, S. M. *Isaac Watts: A Lecture Delivered on the 16th July, 1974 in Commemoration of the 300th Anniversary of Watts' Birth*. London: Evangelical Library, 1975.

Hoyles, John. *The Waning of the Renaissance 1640–1740: Studies in the Thought and Poetry of Henry More, John Norris and Isaac Watts*. The Hague: Martinus Nijhoff, 1971.

Hull, John M. "From Experiential Educator to Nationalist Theologian: The Hymns of Isaac Watts." Hymn Society of Great Britain and Ireland *Bulletin* (264) 19/9 (July 2010): 260–77.

Idle, Christopher. "The Hymns of Isaac Watts: A Study in Space and Time." Hymn Society of Great Britain and Ireland *Bulletin* (223) 16/2 (April 2000): 38–45.

Jackson, Thomas. *Christian Biography. The Life of Isaac Watts, D. D. The Life of Thomas Haliburton*. New York: Carlton & Phillips, 1853.

Johnson, Samuel. *The Life of the Rev. Isaac Watts, D. D.* London: For J. F. and C. Rivington, and J. Buckland, 1785.

———. *The Works of the English Poets. With Prefaces, Biographical and Critical*. Vol. 5. London: John Nichols, 1790.

Julian, John. *A Dictionary of Hymnology*. 2nd ed. 2 vols. London: John Murray, 1907; reprint ed., New York: Dover Publications, 1957.

Kolodziej, Benjamin A. "Isaac Watts, the Wesleys, and the Evolution of 18th-Century English Congregational Song." *Methodist History* 42/4 (July 2004): 236–48.

Leaver, Robin A. "Isaac Watts's Hermeneutical Principles and the Decline of English Metrical Psalmody." *Churchman* 92/1 (1978): 56–60.

Lovelace, Austin C. *The Anatomy of Hymnody*. New York: Abingdon Press, 1965.

Lund, Roger. "Making an Almost Joyful Noise: Augustan Imitation and the Psalms of David." *Journal for Eighteenth-Century Studies* 39/1 (March 2016): 121–39.

Magnusson, Sally. *Glorious Things: My Hymns for Life*. London: Continuum, 2004.

Manning, Bernard Lord. *The Hymns of Wesley and Watts: Five Informal Papers*. London: Epworth Press, 1942.

Marlow, Isaac. *A Discourse Concerning Singing in the Publick Worship of God in the Gospel-Church*. London: For the author, 1690.

Marshall, Madeleine Forell. "The Dramatic Art of Hymnody." *The Hymn* 42/4 (October 1991): 14–19.

————, and Janet Todd. *English Congregational Hymns in the Eighteenth Century.* Lexington, KY: University Press of Kentucky, 1982.

Memoirs of the Life and Writings of Isaac Watts, D. D.: with Extracts from His Correspondence. [London]: Albion Press, 1806.

Meszaros, Andrew. "Isaac Watts: A Universal Hymn Writer." Hymn Society of Great Britain and Ireland *Bulletin* (256) 18/11 (2008): 391–95.

Milner, Thomas. *The Life, Times, and Correspondence of the Rev. Isaac Watts, D.D.* London: Simpkin and Marshall, 1834.

Montgomery, David J. "Isaac Watts and Artistic Kenosis: The Rationale Behind the Work of Britain's Pioneer Hymnwriter." *Scottish Bulletin of Evangelical Theology* 5/2 (1987): 174–84.

Music, David W. *Hymnology: A Collection of Source Readings.* Lanham, MD: Scarecrow Press, 1996.

————. "War and Peace in Christian Hymnody." *Criswell Theological Review* 4/2 (Spring 2007): 97–110.

————. "Was 'Behold the Glories of the Lamb' Isaac Watts's First Hymn?" Hymn Society of Great Britain and Ireland *Bulletin* (298) 22/5 (Winter 2019): 186–92.

————. "Worship: Prelude to Evangelism." *The Church Musician* 44/1 (October 1992): 19–21.

Orchard, Stephen. "The Hymns of Isaac Watts." *Journal of the United Reformed Church History Society* 6/3 (1998): 155–67.

Palmer, Frederic. "Isaac Watts." *Harvard Theological Review* 12/4 (October 1919): 371–403.

Pelikan, Jaroslav, ed. *Luther's Works.* 55 vols. Saint Louis, MO: Concordia Publishing House, 1958.

Phillips, Christopher N. *The Hymnal: A Reading History.* Baltimore: Johns Hopkins University Press, 2018.

Plett, James Wendall. "The Poetic Language of Isaac Watts's Hymns." PhD dissertation, University of California, Riverside, 1986.

The Poetical Works of Isaac Watts and Henry Kirke White: With a Memoir of Each. Boston: Houghton, Mifflin and Company, 1881.

The Posthumous Works of the Late Learned and Reverend Isaac Watts, D.D. In Two Volumes. Compiled from Papers in Possession of His Immediate Successors: Adjusted and Published by a Gentleman of the University of Cambridge. London: For T. Becket and J. Bew, 1779.

Rivers, Isabel, and David L. Wykes, eds. *Dissenting Praise: Religious Dissent and the Hymn in England and Wales.* Oxford: Oxford University Press, 2011.

Roth, Herbert J. "A Literary Study of the Calvinistic and Deistic Implications in the Hymns of Isaac Watts, Charles Wesley, and William Cowper." PhD dissertation, Texas Christian University, 1978.

Routley, Erik. *Hymns and the Faith.* London: John Murray, 1955.

————. *Hymns Today and Tomorrow.* New York: Abingdon Press, 1964.

———. *I'll Praise My Maker*. London: Independent Press, 1951.

———. *Isaac Watts (1674–1748)*. London: Independent Press, 1961.

———. "The Eucharistic Hymns of Isaac Watts." *Worship* 48/9 (November 1974): 526–35.

Rupp, Gordon. *Six Makers of English Religion 1500–1700*. New York: Harper & Brothers, 1957.

Rust, Cyprian T. *Break of Day in the Eighteenth Century: A History and a Specimen of Its First Book of English Sacred Song, 300 Hymns of Dr. Watts*. London: William Hunt and Company, 1880.

Smith, Ruth. *Handel's Oratorios and Eighteenth-Century Thought*. Cambridge: Cambridge University Press, 1995.

Spell, Lota M. *Music in Texas: A Survey of One Aspect of Cultural Progress*. Austin, TX: N.p., 1936.

Stackhouse, Rochelle A. "Hymnody and Politics: Isaac Watts's 'Our God, Our Help in Ages Past' and Timothy Dwight's 'I Love Thy Kingdom, Lord.'" In *Wonderful Words of Life: Hymns in American Protestant History and Theology*, edited by Richard J. Mouw and Mark A. Noll, 42–66. Grand Rapids, MI: William B. Eerdmans Publishing Company, 2004.

Stephenson, William Eaton. "The Heroic Hymn of Isaac Watts." PhD dissertation, University of California, 1963.

Stevenson, Robert M. "Dr. Watts's 'Flights of Fancy.'" In *Patterns of Protestant Church Music*, 93–111. Durham, NC: Duke University Press, 1953.

Stone, Wilbur Macy. *The Divine and Moral Songs of Isaac Watts*. New York: for *The Triptych*, 1918.

Tajchman, Ronald. "Isaac Watts's Communion Hymns: An Application of Classical Rhetoric." *The Hymn* 46/1 (January 1995): 18–22.

Trimmer, Sarah. *A Comment on Dr. Watts's Divine Songs for Children*. London: For J. Buckland, et al., 1789.

Uvin, Tielke. *A Descriptive Bibliography of British and Irish Editions of Isaac Watts's Divine Songs (1715–ca. 1830)*. https://biblio.ugent.be/publication/8633724 (accessed February 9, 2020).

Wallenstein, Martin A. "The Rhetoric of Isaac Watts's Hymns, Psalms, and Sermons." PhD dissertation, Indiana University, 1978.

Watson, J. R. *An Annotated Anthology of Hymns*. Oxford: Oxford University Press, 2002.

———. *The English Hymn: A Critical and Historical Study*. Oxford: Clarendon Press, 1997.

———. "The Hymns of Isaac Watts and the Tradition of Dissent," in Rivers and Wykes, eds., *Dissenting Praise: Religious Dissent and the Hymn in England and Wales*, 33–67.

Watts, Isaac. *Death and Heaven: Or the Last Enemy Conquer'd and Separate Spirits Made Perfect…Attempted in Two Funeral Discourses in Memory of Sir John Hartopp Bar. and His Lady Deceased*. London: For John Clark, et al., 1722.

———. *Divine Songs Attempted in Easy Language for the Use of Children*. London:

For M. Lawrence, 1715.

⸻. *Divine Songs Attempted in Easy Language for the Use of Children. Facsimile reproductions of the first edition of 1715 and an illustrated edition of* circa *1840, with an introduction and bibliography by J. H. P. Pafford.* London: Oxford University Press, 1971.

⸻. *The Glory of Christ as God-Man Display'd in Three Discourses.* London: For J. Oswald and J. Buckland, 1746.

⸻. *A Guide to Prayer. Or, a Free and Rational Account of the Gift, Grace and Spirit of Prayer.* London: For Emanuel Matthews and Sarah Cliff, 1715.

⸻. *The Holiness of Times, Places, and People under the Jewish and Christian Dispensations Consider'd and Compared.* London: For R. Hett and J. Brackstone, 1738.

⸻. *Horæ Lyricæ: Poems Chiefly of the Lyric Kind.* London: S. and D. Bridge, 1706.

⸻. *Hymns and Spiritual Songs.* London: J. Humphreys, 1707; 2nd ed., London, 1709.

⸻. *The Knowledge of the Heavens and the Earth Made Easy.* London: For J. Clark, et al., 1726.

⸻. *The Psalms of David Imitated in the Language of the New Testament.* London: For J. Clark, et al., 1719; 2nd ed., London, 1719.

⸻. *Reliquiæ Juveniles: Miscellaneous Thoughts in Prose and Verse on Natural, Moral, and Divine Subjects; Written Chiefly in Younger Years.* London: For Richard Ford and Richard Hett, 1734.

⸻. *Sermons on Various Subjects.* London: For John Clark, et al., 1721; vol. 2, London, 1723; vol. 3, London, 1729.

Wendeln, Ronald A. "Isaac Watts's *Horae Lyricae* as Dissenting Conversion Literature." PhD thesis, Boston College, 1978.

Wesley, John, and Charles Wesley. *Hymns and Sacred Poems.* London: W. Strahan, 1740.

Wills, Joshua E. *Dr. Isaac Watts, "The Bard of the Sanctuary." His Birthplace and Personality; His Literary and Philosophical Contributions; His Life and Times; Hymnology and Bible.* N.p.: n.p., 1914.

Wilson, John. "The Evolution of the Tune Antioch." Hymn Society of Great Britain and Ireland *Bulletin* (166) 11/5 (January 1986): 107–114.

⸻. "Handel and the Hymn Tune: II, Some Hymn Tune Arrangements." *The Hymn* 37/1 (January 1986): 25–31.

Witty, Robert G. "Isaac Watts and the Rhetoric of Dissent." Ph.D. dissertation, University of Florida, 1959.

The Works of the Late Reverend and Learned Isaac Watts, D. D. Published by Himself, and Now Collected into Six Volumes. Edited by D. Jennings and P. Doddridge. London: T. and T. Longman, et al., 1753.

The Works of the Reverend and Learned Isaac Watts, D. D....Selected from His Manuscripts by the Rev. Dr. [David] Jennings, and the Rev. Dr. [Philip] Doddridge, in 1753: to Which are Added, Memoirs of the Life of the Author, Compiled by the Rev.

George Burder. 6 vols. London: J. Barfield, 1810–1811.

The Works of the Rev. Isaac Watts, D. D. in Nine Volumes. Leeds: For William Baynes, et al., 1812–1813.

The Works of the Rev. Isaac Watts, D. D. in Seven Volumes. Edited by Edward Parsons. Leeds: Edward Baines for the Editor, [1800].

Wright, Clifford J. "Isaac Watts—the Man, His Mind and Message." *Modern Churchman* 38/4 (December 1948): 348–56.

Wright, Thomas. *Isaac Watts and Contemporary Hymn-Writers*. Vol. 3 of The Lives of the British Hymn-Writers. London: C. J. Farncombe & Sons, 1914.

Wykes, David L. "From David's Psalms to Watts's Hymns: The Development of Hymnody among Dissenters Following the Toleration Act." In *Continuity and Change in Christian Worship: Papers Read at the 1997 Summer Meeting and the 1998 Winter Meeting of the Ecclesiastical History Society*, edited by R. N. Swanson, 227–39. Woodbridge, UK: Boydell Press, 1999.

INDEX

Hymn and poem texts are all by Watts unless otherwise noted.

Aberdeen University, 2
Abney, Elizabeth, 91
Abney, Mary, 91
Abney, Lady Mary, 1
Abney, Sarah, 91
Abney, Sir Thomas, 1, 91
Adey, Lionel, 59, 220, 235
"Alas! and Did My Savio[u]r
    Bleed?" 10, 18, 23-29, 35,
    176, 196
"Am I a Soldier of the Cross?" 10,
    24, 31-40, 59, 97, 115
"And Now the Scales Have Left
    Mine Eyes," 27
Anglicans, 12, 203
Anglo-Genevan psalter, 4
Anne, Queen, 149
ANTIOCH, 21, 137-39, 241
Arians, 3, 27
Arnold, Matthew, 217
Arnold, Richard, 16, 225, 235
Art of Reading and Writing English
    (Watts), 2
Ashworth, Caleb, 4, 235
"At the Cross" (Hudson), 29
AVON, 29
Bailey, Albert Edward, 120, 190,
    218, 226, 235
Bailey, Nathan, 18, 19, 24, 36, 37,
    38, 45, 51, 52, 53, 58, 70, 74,
    77, 98, 122, 127, 135, 146,
    160, 161, 193, 195, 212, 213,
    219, 220, 222, 224, 228, 230,
    231, 232, 235
Baptists, 31, 71-72
Bath-sheba, 165
Bay Psalm Book, 17
"Before Jehovah's Awful Throne,"
    18, 41-48
"Behold the Glories of the Lamb,"
    55, 113, 239
"Behold the Lofty Sky," 183
Benedictus, 4
Benson, Louis F., 7, 16, 42, 189,
    215, 217, 235-36
Betjeman, Sir John, 14-15, 221,
    236
Beto, George, 199
Beynon, Graham, 17, 29, 236
Bishop, Selma L., 8, 16, 145, 236
"Blest Be the Wisdom and the
    Pow'r," 92
"Blest Is the Man Whose Cautious
    Feet," 6
"Blest Morning, Whose Young
    Dawning Rays," 204
Bond, Douglas, 17, 134, 151, 236
Bradbury, Thomas, 3
Brady, Nicholas, 5, 145
Breach Repaired in God's Worship
    (Keach), 72
Breed, David R., 218, 236
Bridges, Robert, 14, 236
Bunyan, John, 161, 193, 236

Bury Street Church (Congregational), 1, 2, 174
Bysshe, Edward, 35, 136, 178, 236
Calvin, John, 4, 106, 174
Calvinist(s), 10, 25, 36, 62, 129, 130, 134, 136, 174, 239
Cambridge University, 3
Cameron, W., 14
Canterbury Dictionary of Hymnology, 31, 110, 163, 236
Carey, William, 187
Century of Select Psalms (Patrick), 42, 154
Charlestown Collection (*Collection of Psalms and Hymns*, Wesley), 42-43, 45, 110, 150
Chauncey, Isaac, 1
"Christ Hath a Garden Wall'd Around," 14
Christian Doctrine of the Trinity (Watts), 2
Christian Psalmist (Hastings & Patton), 100, 102, 238
Christian's Duty (anon., 1801), 75
Cinquante Pseaumes (Marot & Calvin), 4
Clark, Thomas, 137
Clay, Eleazar, 75
Collection of Hymns for Social Worship (Whitefield), 228-29
Collection of Psalms and Hymns (Wesley; see Charlestown Collection)
Collection of Psalms and Hymns (Conyers), 229, 236
Collection of Tunes (Hawkes), 137
Colman, Benjamin, 63, 237
"Come Holy Spirit, Heavenly Dove," 49-54, 152
"Come Let Us Join Our Cheerful Songs," 10, 14, 55-59

"Come Sound His Praise Abroad," 17, 61-68
"Come, We That Love the Lord," 69-78
COMFORT, 137-38
Comment on Dr. Watts's Divine Songs (Trimmer), 102-103 240
Conder, Josiah, 16, 236
Congregational Harmonist (Clark), 137
Congregationalists, 72, 203
Conyers, Richard, 229, 236
Cook, James, 122
Cook, Paul E. G., 9, 18, 236
Cornick, David, 13, 236
Cowper, William, 17, 73, 235, 239
Dampier, William, 122
David, King, 3, 4, 71, 81, 124, 130, 146, 165, 170, 173, 174, 178, 202, 238, 242
Davie, Donald, 16, 218, 228, 230, 237
Davies, Horton, 4, 10, 13, 237
Davis, Arthur Paul, 11, 12, 15, 16, 237
Day of Doom (Wigglesworth), 93
Dearmer, Percy, 220-221, 237
Death and Heaven (Watts), 2, 98, 194, 240
"Death Cannot Make Our Souls Afraid," 195
Deists, 33, 37, 102
Denham, John, 145
Dickinson, Clarence, 100, 237
Dictionary of Hymnology (Julian), 163, 228, 238
Dictionary of North American Hymnology, 17
Discourse Concerning Singing (Marlow), 71-72, 238
Dissenters (see Independents)

Dissertations Relating to the Christian Doctrine of the Trinity (Watts), 2

Divine Songs Attempted in Easy Language (Watts), 8, 18, 91-92, 94, 102-103, 240-241

"Do I Believe What Jesus Saith?" 31

Dryden, John, 7

"Early, My God, Without Delay," 204

Edinburgh University, 2

Edwards, Jonathan, 62-63, 237

ELLACOMBE, 102

Es wolle Gott uns gnädig sein (Luther), 128

Escott, Harry, 5, 16, 41, 43, 114, 128, 223, 229, 237

Evans, John, 32

Faithful Narrative of the Surprizing Work of God (Edwards), 62, 237

Fenner, Chris, 138, 237

"Firm and Unmov'd Are They," 6

Fletcher, Donald Rodgers, 14, 19, 124-125, 136, 153-54, 202-203, 237

Frederick of Nuremberg, 199

FOREST GREEN, 102

"From All That Dwell Below the Skies," 14, 22, 58, 79-83, 121

"From Heav'n the Sinning Angels Fell," 233

Gaunt, Alan, 110

Geneva Bible, 19

Genevan Psalter (Calvin), 106

Gibbons, Thomas, 2, 16, 237

"Give to Our God Immortal Praise," 82, 94

Glory of Christ as God-Man Display'd (Watts), 2, 3, 241

"Glory to God, and Praise and Love" (Wesley), 163

"Go Preach My Gospel, Saith the Lord," 187

"God Moves In a Mysterious Way" (Cowper), 73

Gray, Scotty, 21, 102, 118, 153, 225, 237

Great Awakening, 62

"Great God, Whose Universal Sway," 119

"Great God, with Wonder, and with Praise," 93, 183

Greiter, Matthäus, 106

Grindal, Gracia, 158, 237

Guide to Prayer (Watts), 2, 26, 35, 241

Guyse, John, 63, 237

Hallel psalms, 79, 199

Handel, George Frederick, 43, 137-38, 240, 241

"Happy the Man Whose Cautious Feet," 6

Harsha, D. A., 16, 237

Hartopp, Sir John, 1, 240

Harvard University, 3

Hastings, Thomas, 100, 102, 238

Hawkes, T., 137

Holford, W., 137-38

Holiness of Times, Places, and People (Watts), 173-174, 201, 241

Hood, E. Paxton, 5, 16, 114, 164, 195, 238

Hooke, Robert, 231

Hopkins, John, 4-5, 106

Horæ Lyricæ (Watts), 5, 41, 113, 114, 183, 189, 235, 241

Houghton, S. M., 187, 238

"How Are Thy Glories Here Display'd," 77

"How Beauteous Are Their Feet," 85-89

"How Bright These Glorious Spirits Shine," 14
"How Honourable Is the Place," 76
"How Sad Our State by Nature Is," 187
Hoyles, John, 207, 238
Hudson, Ralph E., 29
Hull, John M., 229, 238
Humble Attempt Toward the Revival of Practical Religion (Watts), 2
Hymnal (1950, Presbyterian), 100, 237
Hymns and Sacred Poems (Wesleys), 164, 241
Hymns and Spiritual Songs (Clay), 75
Hymns and Spiritual Songs (Watts), 5, 6, 7, 8, 9, 10, 11, 12, 16, 18, 23, 25, 27, 28, 41, 49, 52, 55, 57, 69, 70, 72, 75, 76, 77, 78, 85, 89, 92, 113, 114, 146, 157, 159, 160, 161, 163, 184, 186, 187, 189, 190, 192, 195, 204, 205, 211, 213, 215, 217, 219, 220, 222, 223, 225, 228, 236, 241
Huygens, Christiaan, 231
"I Love the Lord: He Heard My Cries," 107
"I Love the Windows of Thy Grace," 146
"I Sing th'Almighty Power of God," 8, 10, 17, 69, 91-103, 181
"I'll Praise My Maker with My Breath," 17, 21, 105-11, 126, 150, 157
"I'm Not Ashamed to Own My Lord," 113-118
Improvement of the Mind (Watts), 2
"In God's Own House Pronounce His Praise," 107

"In Judah God of Old Was Known," 76
"In Vain the Wealthy Mortals Toyl," 6
"In Vain We Lavish Out Our Lives," 142
Independents, 1, 4, 12, 136, 210,
"Is There Ambition In My Heart?" 6
Israel in Egypt (Handel), 43
"Jesus Invites His Saints," 146
"Jesus Shall Reign," 7, 20, 79, 82, 119-128, 136, 186
"Joy to the World," 15, 20, 21, 69, 72, 129-39, 161, 197, 201, 237
Judas Maccabeus, 43
Julian, John, 163, 228-29, 238
Keach, Benjamin, 72
Kethe, William, 106
Knowledge of the Heavens and the Earth (Watts), 2, 121, 241
Kolodziej, Benjamin, 44, 238
Kraybill, Jan, 217
Leland, John, 75
"Let All the Earth Their Voices Raise," 94
"Let Everlasting Glories Crown," 184
"Let Them Neglect Thy Glory, Lord," 72
Lining out, 13, 52
"Lo, What an Entertaining Sight," 6
Logick (Watts), 2-3
"Look, Gracious God, How Numerous They," 6
"Lord, In the Morning Thou Shalt Hear," 204
"Lord, What a Feeble Piece," 6
"Lord, What a Thoughtless Wretch Was" I, 6

"Lord! What a Wretched Land Is This," 192

"Loud Hallelujahs to the Lord," 6

Lovelace, Austin C., 21, 79, 218, 238

Lowry, Robert, 78

Magnificat, 4

Magnusson, Sally, 15, 238

Manning, Bernard Lord, 16, 231-32, 238

MARCHING TO ZION, 78

Mark Lane Church (Congregational), 1

Marlow, Isaac, 71-72, 238

Marshall, Madeleine Forell, 16, 190, 220, 230, 238-39

MARTYRDOM, 29

Mason, Lowell, 137-38

"May God Bestow On Us His Grace (Luther)," 128

Messiah (Handel), 138-139

Meszaros, Andrew, 218, 239

Milbourne, Luke, 145

military imagery, 39-40, 77

Milner, Thomas, 2, 16, 239

Milton, John, 207, 232

Moses/Mosaic, 4, 124, 194-95, 209

Music, David W., 4, 40, 113, 210, 239

musical instruments, 129-130, 138, 174,

"My God, How Many Are My Fears," 6

"My Shepherd Is the Living Lord" (Sternhold), 13-14

"My Shepherd Is the Living Lord" (Watts), 14, 141

"My Shepherd Will Supply My Need," 10, 119, 141-47, 177

"My Soul, How Lovely Is the Place," 6

Nathan (prophet), 166, 170

New Version of the Psalms (Tate & Brady), 5, 145

New Voyage Round the World (Dampier), 122

Newton, Isaac, 98, 231

Newton, John, 73, 235

"No More, My God, I Boast No More," 223

Nonconformists (see Independents)

"Now Let a Spacious World Arise," 186

"Now Let Our Pains Be All Forgot," 146

Nunc dimittis, 4

"O For a Thousand Tongues to Sing" (Wesley), 163

"O God, Our Help in Ages Past" (see "Our God, Our Help in Ages Past")

"O 'Tis a Lovely Thing for Youth," 92

"O When Shall I See Jesus" (attr. Leland), 75

OLD 113TH, 94, 105, 106, 107, 181

Old Version (Sternhold & Hopkins), 4-5, 106

Olney Hymns (Newton & Cowper), 73

Orchard, Stephen, 66, 239

"Our God, Our Help in Ages Past," 10, 11, 14, 18, 48, 149-58, 237, 240

Owens, Priscilla J., 164

Ovid, 7

Oxford University, 3

Pafford, J. H. P., 91, 241

Palmer, Frederic, 189, 239

Paradise Lost (Milton), 207

Patrick, John, 42, 145, 154-55

Patton, William, 100, 102, 238

Paul, St., 7, 39, 66, 81, 178, 182, 184, 224

Pelikan, Jaroslav, 200, 239

Phillips, Christopher N., 12, 239

Philosophical Essays on Various Subjects (Watts), 2

Pilgrim's Progress (Bunyan), 161, 193, 236

Pinhorne, John, 1

Pinner's Hall Church (Congregational), 1

Plett, James Wendall, 9, 10, 11, 25, 55, 239

Practical Discourses (Evans), 32

"Praise Ye the Lord: 'Tis Good to Raise," 172

Price, Samuel, 1-2

Psalmodia Britannica (Rider), 137

Psalms of David Imitated (Watts), 5, 6, 7, 8, 9, 12, 18, 31, 41, 42, 46, 47, 61, 62, 66, 76, 79, 81, 92, 94, 95, 101, 105, 106, 108, 119, 121, 129, 130, 136, 137, 141, 144, 145, 146, 149, 154, 165, 171, 181, 182, 183, 200, 202, 204, 206, 241

Reeves, Jesse, 16

Reflections on the Fall of a Great Man (Ashworth), 4, 235

Reliquiæ Juveniles (Watts), 20, 48, 96, 143, 206, 207, 241

Rider, Charles, 137

Rippon, John, 31

Rivers, Isabel, 16, 239, 240

Roman Catholics, 10, 203

Roth, Herbert J., 102, 239

Routley, Erik, 16, 128, 149, 157, 190, 194, 219, 239-240

Rowe, Thomas, 1

Rupp, Gordon, 15, 240

Rust, Cyprian T., 8, 10, 240

"Salvation! O the Joyful Sound!" 87, 159-64,

Samson, 43

Selection of Hymns from the Best Authors (Rippon), 31

Sermons on Various Subjects (Watts), 23, 31-32, 35, 37, 49, 55, 71, 115, 116, 241

"Shall Atheists Dare Insult the Cross?" 116

"Shepherds Rejoice, Lift Up Your Eyes," 5

"Shew Pity, Lord, O Lord Forgive" (see "Show Pity, Lord")

"Shine, Mighty God, on Britain Shine," 6, 43

Short View of the Whole Scripture History (Watts), 2

"Shout to the Lord, and Let Our Joys," 113

"Show Pity, Lord, O Lord Forgive," 165-170

"Sing to the Lord with Joyful Voice," 6, 41, 42

Smith, Ruth, 43, 240

Spell, Lota M., 29, 240

Stackhouse, Rochelle, 158, 240

Stephenson, William Eaton, 9, 10, 12, 20-21, 34, 134, 197, 240

Sternhold, Thomas, 4-5, 13-14, 106

Stone, Wilbur Macy, 91, 240,

Strength and Weakness of Human Reason (Watts), 2

"Sweet Is the Work, My God, My King," 26, 145, 171-79, 204, 207

"Take Me Home to the Place" (anon.), 29

Tate, Nahum, 5, 145

"The Heavens Declare Thy Glory, Lord," 17, 128, 181-87

"The Lord My Shepherd Is," 141

"There Is a Balm in Gilead" (spiritual), 160

"There Is a Land of Pure Delight," 69, 134, 189-97, 211, 214

"There's No Ambition Swells My Heart," 6

"This Is the Day the Lord Hath Made," 199-204, 205

Three Dissertations Relating to the Christian Doctrine of the Trinity (Watts), 2

"Thus Pass My Days Away," 205-207

"Time! What an Empty Vapour 'Tis!" 157-58

"'Tis by Thy Strength the Mountains Stand," 95, 99

"To Our Almighty Maker God," 129-30

Todd, Janet, 16, 190, 239

Tomlin, Chris, 16

Trimmer, Sarah, 102-103, 240

"'Twas the Commission of the Lord," 187

Universal Etymological English Dictionary (Bailey), 18, 24, 36, 37, 51, 70, 98, 127, 160, 193, 195, 213, 219, 220, 222, 224, 235

"Unshaken As the Sacred Hill," 6

Uvin, Tielke, 91, 240

Voci di Melodia (Holford), 137

Voyage to New Holland (Dampier), 122

Wallenstein, Martin A., 137, 240

Walt, J. D., 16

Watson, J. R., 16, 31, 77, 98, 157, 172, 190, 218, 221, 233, 236, 240

Watts, Enoch, 113

Watts's Compleat Spelling-Book (Watts), 2

"We Have Heard the Joyful Sound" (Owens), 164

"Welcome, Sweet Day of Rest," 17, 173, 204, 205-10

"We're Marching to Zion" (Lowry), 78

Wesley, Charles, 1, 42, 163-64, 231-32, 241

Wesley, John, 42-45, 110-11, 150, 164, 241

"When I Can Read My Title Clear," 189, 211-15

"When I Survey the Wondrous Cross," 10, 14, 15, 16, 23, 69, 79, 97, 147, 196, 214, 217-33

"When Saints Survey the Wondrous Cross" (alt. Whitefield), 229

"When the First Parents of Our Race," 222

"Where Shall the Tribes of Adam Find," 143

Whitefield, George, 228-29

Whole Book of Psalms (Sternhold & Hopkins) see Old Version

"Why Did the Jews Proclaim Their Rage?" 6

"Why Do the Proud Insult the Poor?" 6

"Why Should We Start and Fear to Die?" 196

Wigglesworth, Michael, 93

Wills, Joshua E., 189, 241

Wilson, John, 138, 241

"With Earnest Longings of the Mind," 146

"With Joy We Meditate the Grace," 213

World to Come (Watts), 2

Wright, Thomas, 16, 31, 189, 241

Wykes, David, 16, 239, 240, 242
Yale University, 3
Yattendon Hymnal (Bridges), 14,
    236
"Ye Children Which Do Serve the
    Lord" (Kethe), 106
"Ye Saints, How Lovely Is the
    Place," 6
"Ye Servants of th'Almighty King,"
    82
"Ye That Obey th'Immortal King,"
    6
Zwingli, Ulrich, 72